Urban Drama

Urban Drama

The Metropolis in Contemporary North American Plays

J. Chris Westgate

palgrave
macmillan

First published in 2011 by
PALGRAVE MACMILLAN®
in the United States—a division of St. Martin's Press LLC,
175 Fifth Avenue, New York, NY 10010.

Where this book is distributed in the UK, Europe and the rest of the World,
this is by Palgrave Macmillan, a division of Macmillan Publishers Limited,
registered in England, company number 785998, of Houndmills,
Basingstoke, Hampshire RG21 6XS.

Palgrave Macmillan is the global academic imprint of the above
companies and has companies and representatives throughout the world.

Palgrave® and Macmillan® are registered trademarks in the United
States, the United Kingdom, Europe and other countries.

ISBN: 978–0–230–11453–1

Library of Congress Cataloging-in-Publication Data

Westgate, J. Chris.
   Urban drama : the metropolis in contemporary North American
plays / J. Chris Westgate.
      p.   cm.
   ISBN 978–0–230–11453–1 (hardback)
   1. American drama—20th century—History and criticism.   2. City and
town life in literature.   3. Space and time in literature.
   4. Theater—United States—History—20th century.   I. Title.
PS352.W47 2011
812′.5409—dc22   2011000534

A catalogue record of the book is available from the British Library

Design by Integra Software Services

First edition: June 2011

10 9 8 7 6 5 4 3 2 1

Printed in the United States of America.

For my wife, Sarah, and our beautiful son, Will

Contents

Preface

In the title of this book is a double subject. On the one hand "urban drama" refers to the crises of urbanism—homelessness, rioting, gentrification, et cetera—that were unfolding in cities during the 1980s and 1990s. Of course, such crises had occurred in previous decades, especially the 1930s and 1940s, and the 1960s and 1970s. What was different about the period considered in this book is that 1980 was the year that Ted Turner launched Cable News Network (CNN), a business venture that not only changed the landscape of network and cable news but additionally changed the way that news covered the urban landscape of cities. Homelessness has been a problem in various decades, but the media's coverage of homelessness made a profound leap forward with the advent of 24 hour news, probably as big a leap as the introduction of photography into newspapers that facilitated the work of Jacob Riis a century earlier. A better example, though, may be the rioting that took place in Los Angeles in 1992 after the acquittal of the four police officers who were caught on tape assaulting Rodney King. As the rioting played out in the streets of Los Angeles, it simultaneously played out in the living rooms of people all across the country. The relationship, epistemologically, of viewer to riot and of viewer to city was changed radically and, no doubt, irrevocably by images of the rioting playing out live.

With this new access to dramatic conflicts of urbanism came, critical geographers have argued, new understanding of the roles played by spatiality, here, the roles of urban spatiality. That is, changes to the media precipitated changes in epistemology that would inform most, if not all, of U.S. culture. Interestingly, a number of playwrights seemed to be at the forefront of this change, as many plays responded not just to the crises of urbanism of these decades but to the implications of those crises. This leads to the second way of reading "urban drama": as the ways that dramatists writing during these decades made these concerns—political, cultural, and epistemological—part of their dramaturgy. In many cases, the link between dramatic event and dramatic representation was direct, such as Anna Deavere Smith's *Twilight Los*

Angeles, 1992, which she composed and performed in response to the aforementioned rioting in Los Angeles, or José Rivera's *Marisol,* which was written, largely, in response to Mayor Ed Koch's campaign against the homeless of New York City in the 1980s. In other cases, the link is less direct but still evident, as with Tony Kushner's *Angels in America,* which addresses a number of themes about America, homosexuality, and history but which is deeply concerned with the ideological mapping of urban spaces by conservatism, or with Cherrie Moraga's *Giving Up the Ghost,* which addresses various concerns about immigration, nationalism, and sexuality but which locates those concerns in the ethnical and racialized fault lines of Los Angeles in the 1980s.

The purpose of this book is to investigate this convergence of subjects, with particular emphasis on how the dramas written in response to urban crises experimented with aspects of form in order to advance the epistemological change described by critical geographers. That is, to consider how the plays deliberately spatialize concerns of identity politics and social justice that have been debated for decades and what this spatialization adds to these debates. Obviously, this study builds on the "spatial turn" of theater and drama criticism that began with the work of Marvin Carlson, Stanton Garner Jr., and Una Chaudhuri. While I could not have developed this argument without standing on these considerable shoulders, I also offer refinements of this "spatial turn" through rigorous investigation of contextualization and through case studies, along the lines of Michael McKinnie's *City Stages.* The hope is that this book will amend some of the limitations of earlier theorizing of theater, drama, and spatiality and, therefore, open up new lines of discussion for drama and theater, now and in the future.

Acknowledgments

Behind this book were a number of people who gave their feedback and encouragement at different stages. First, I want to thank Scott Shershow, my dissertation advisor, who originally helped me develop the ideas behind this study and, maybe more importantly, remained steadfast in his support as I submitted this project for publication. Additionally, I want to thank Lynette Hunter and W. B. Worthen, who also were instrumental in the early versions of this study, which began with my doctoral work. Thanks, too, to Stephanie Tucker, who helped inspire my interest in contemporary drama with the fabulous material in her class, "The Absurdist Vision in Modern Drama," and her unwavering enthusiasm. Thanks to the Whiteley Center at Friday Harbor Labs who supported revisions of this project in 2005–2006. I want to thank the editors of *Theatre Journal,* who not only published a portion of Chapter 1 in 2007 but gave excellent suggestions about how to revise the submitted material that eventually led to this argument. Finally, I want to thank my colleague, Lana Dalley, who offered a discerning eye on portions of this manuscript during its final stages. This book would not have been possible without these contributions.

Introduction: A Rhetoric of Sociospatial Drama

The subject of this book is old and new. It is old in that the synergy of drama, theater, and urbanism, which this book considers during the contemporary period, reflects a shared genealogy in western literature. Marvin Carlson has defined something of this genealogy in *Places of Performance: The Semiotics of Theatre Architecture*,[1] an invaluable work about the interrelationship of the theater and the city. But here I examine the corollary to his work: what is written for the theater, regardless of where or how it will be staged, is often intricately linked with conditions of urbanism. While this link may be true during any period, it emerges most prominently during times of transition and transformation: when the ways that towns, cities, or metropolises are organized, legislated, and inhabited undergo profound changes. Finding examples of this corollary is easy enough: during the Great Depression in the United States, plays addressed the shift from city to metropolis by dramatizing the stratification of classes (Elmer Rice's *Street Scene* 1929, Sidney Kingsley's *Dead End* 1935, Arthur Miller's *Death of a Salesman* 1949); as a response to the emergence of the merchant class in sixteenth-century London, City Comedies[2] mirrored the increasing tensions among classes (Ben Jonson's *Every Man in his Humour* 1598, Thomas Dekker's *The Shoemaker's Holiday* 1599, Thomas Middleton's *A Chaste Maid in Cheapside* 1613); going all the way back to ancient Greece, plays were part of civic festivals that helped define the city-state (Sophocles' *Oedipus Rex* 429 B.C.E. and *Antigone* 442 B.C.E.). What accounts for this link is beyond the scope of my argument, though it surely has much to do with the fact that dramas are public and therefore mirror society. Regardless of why, it is obvious that drama and urbanism have nourished each other from the beginning.

Nevertheless, the subject of this book is new in that it considers an original branching of this genealogy during the 1980s and 1990s. What is original about this period, first of all, is the diversity of the backgrounds of those writing about urbanism in North America: José Rivera originally from Puerto Rico, Cherríe Moraga from Mexico, Eduardo Machado from

Cuba; Djanet Sears and Sally Clark from Canada; Tony Kushner and Sam Shepard, Anna Deavere Smith, David Henry Hwang, and Richard Greenberg from the United States. Writing from different backgrounds or perspectives, they have brought a diversity of voices to the conversation about urbanism. This is true biographically: the immigrant has a distinctly different experience in the metropolis than the native citizen; the minority, likewise, has a different—more tragic—understanding of the metropolis than the white citizen; the female, different from the male; the homosexual, different from the heterosexual. This is also true politically: the playwrights discussed here often self-consciously employ the voice of the outsider—along the lines of bell hooks's argument about writing from the margin[3]—to critique both the dichotomy of insider/outsider and the social structures (of class, race, gender) that sustain this dichotomy. Among the things that feminism has established during the last two decades is the recognition that the personal *is* political, something reaffirmed in this multiethnic playwriting. Never before in the genealogy of drama and urbanism has there been such a polyphony of perspectives about urbanism, with the necessary infrastructure to get those voices heard, than today.[4]

Beyond diversity, this branching is new in terms of how contemporary playwrights represent urbanism in their dramaturgy. However differently they may experience the city, they nevertheless share one commonality that brings them together here. Their plays have become increasingly *about* urbanism: both the built environment (housing, community planning, commercial development—anything part of the physical character of the city) and the social ordering of that environment (zoning laws, gentrification campaigns, the privatization of public space—anything part of the legislative or ideological governance of the city). Before the 1980s and 1990s, drama generally represented the city as the setting for concerns: it was *where* characters struggled with disrupted lines in class definition or the shift toward commodity capitalism or the loss of the American dream. Importantly, the city was not *why* characters did so. The urban environment was treated as the context for social transitions or transformations that were key to debates of the time instead of being complicit in them. During the 1980s and 1990s, by contrast, more plays began to represent social conflicts as unfolding *in* and *because* of the ways that the urban environment was organized, legislated, and inhabited. Questions of identity politics and social justice became increasingly spatial in contemporary drama. Urban space is now recognized as mediating the conflicts playing out among individuals and groups in two key ways. Initially, this informs the exigency of plays: conflicts that drive the play, whether political or psychological, now have distinctly spatial origins. Likewise, this mediation is evident in terms of resolution: the plays dramatize encounters that interrogate the spaces or spatial organizations represented in and, potentially, outside the play. Become much more than setting, urbanism comes closer to subject of dramaturgical inquiry.

Certainly the terms and tone of this inquiry differ with each dramatist, but the impulse toward inquiry originates from noteworthy commonalities, the first of which are the subjects themselves. So far, I have employed "urbanism" or "the city" somewhat generally. Instead of addressing every city or those cities with a history of theater like Chicago, Miami, or Seattle, I have limited my study to plays about New York City and Los Angeles. The reasons for this decision are many, beginning with expediency: with so many different perspectives among the playwrights about urbanism, common instances of that urbanism seemed necessary to produce coherence in the larger argument. In addition, New York City and Los Angeles were ideal choices because they represent, diachronically and synchronically, paradigms of urbanism. New York City may have the most iconic landscape in the United States. Merely mentioning landmarks such as the Statue of Liberty, Central Park, or the World Trade Center (before it was destroyed by the terrorist attacks of 2001) invoked a distinct image of urbanism even to those who had never visited New York. Probably no city has had its images reproduced on more merchandise—shirts, hats, coffee mugs—than New York City.[5] By contrast, Los Angeles invokes few images beyond the ironic trope of freeways that enable the ongoing decentering of urbanism that geographers term "sprawl." As the infamous quip about L.A. goes, "there's no there there," suggesting a perfect contrast with New York City. Most significantly, New York City and Los Angeles were center stage for the "urban drama" of the 1980s and 1990s: the rioting in Crown Heights, New York, and in Los Angeles; the crisis of homelessness and the various campaigns against the homeless; urban redevelopment and gentrification; ghettoization and suburbanization; immigration and anti-immigration backlash. Undoubtedly it was these concerns that drew the attention of so many playwrights during these decades.

If New York City and Los Angeles are the subjects, how then do we define the terms of dramaturgical inquiry? This begins from an abiding premise in the writing of the playwrights. Above all, the plays considered in this book demonstrate concerns with the ways that people live in, move through, and think about New York City and Los Angeles and, consequently, attempt to dramatically "map" moments of crisis *in* and *of* urbanism. In Aristotelian terms of plot or thought, such crises emerge in plays through moments of collision or, better yet, of contestation. In fact, most of the plays build toward and turn on a moment where characters collide with or about the urban environment: Austin from *True West* considering the hypocrisy of suburbanism;

Joe from *Angels in America* watching homosexual encounters in Central Park; Billie and Othello from *Harlem Duet* finding memories of African American triumph and tragedy in the landscape of Harlem. The plays make space (the physical locales) and spatiality (the conceptual paradigms for knowing spaces) part of the conflict experienced by the characters and, potentially, part of the interpretive activity of audiences. The urban environment becomes a field of interaction and (mis)understanding that the characters must negotiate geographically, epistemologically, and ideologically. Behind this dramaturgy is the following ambition: the search for ways to reveal how social arrangements in the city naturalize patterns of spatiality and, vice versa, how spatial arrangements naturalize sociality. So consistently do the plays stress this imbrication of sociality and spatiality that I have defined them as sociospatial drama.

The Spatiality of Human Life

Intended to be descriptive of a trend in contemporary drama during the 1980s and 1990s as well as a theoretical paradigm for considering the accomplishment of the drama, the term "sociospatial" suggests the theoretical framework behind my study. The term derives from Edward Soja's *Thirdspace: Journeys to Los Angeles and Other Real-And-Imagined Places* (1996), which begins with this claim: "We are, and always have been, intrinsically spatial beings, active participants in the social construction of our embracing spatialities."[6] Not merely important to Soja's book, this statement defines the assumptions of critical and cultural geography, fields of study that emerged in the 1970s with translations of Henri Lefebvre's books and the parallel works of David Harvey, and came to fruition in the 1980s and 1990s. Most significantly, Soja defines the interplay of sociality and spatiality in ways that suggest not a new condition but rather a new understanding of a condition: that sociality and spatiality are indelibly linked. This premise underlies much of the work in geography during the last three decades, work that has investigated and theorized the spatiality of human life.[7] Along with Soja, many have contributed to this field: Doreen Massey's study of spatial divisions of labor; Neil Smith's research of uneven development across geographical scales; Steven Feld's and Keith Basso's ethnographical studies of space, place, and identity; David Harvey's arguments about social justice and geography; Michel Foucault's theorizing of heterotopian spaces; and Henri Lefebvre's seminal works on the production of space. Summarizing the benefits of this work, Soja argues, "In what . . . will eventually be considered one of the most important intellectual and political developments of the late twentieth century, a growing community of scholars and citizens has, for perhaps the first time, begun to think about the *spatiality* of human life in much the same way that we have . . . approached life's intrinsic and richly revealing historical and social qualities" [original emphasis].[8]

In the following chapters, I draw from many of these scholars in different ways, but there are two defining concerns that guide the argument of this book. The first comes from Henri Lefebvre's *The Production of Space*, originally published in French (1974) and translated into English (1991). Distinctly Marxist in its argument, *The Production of Space* contends that organizations of space, in midcentury France, derived from and served the ends of capitalism. What is so revolutionary about Lefebvre's argument is the underlying premise: spatial patterns had social exigencies that could be assessed, understood, and changed. Standing in the way of such change, though, is what Lefebvre defined as the "double illusion" of space. The "illusion of transparency," first of all, characterizes space as "luminous, as intelligible, as giving free rein" to those who attempt to understand its iterations.[9] Read this way, space becomes self-evident, without need to question, or "free of traps" to those who inhabit its dimensions.[10] The problem with this premise is that it obfuscates the ideological origins of the emergence of ghettos, the enclosures of the countryside, the stratification of suburbanism. Along with transparency was the "illusion of opacity" that, by contrast, highlights the immutability or immanence of space or spatial patterns by endorsing their "naturalness."[11] Read this way, space becomes fixed and already defined, consequently, incapable of being interrogated. In a different though complementary way, this removes the questions of the social origins of spaces and the possibility of changing them. How do we change what is natural? On the basis of his Marxist assumptions, Lefebvre argues that both readings advance ignorance in order to facilitate capitalism. Become a defining principle of critical and cultural geography, Lefebvre's argument against the unnatural naturalization of space informs the geographers cited in this book.

Around the same time that *The Production of Space* was being published, David Harvey published another defining work for my argument, *Social Justice and the City* (1973). Here, he examines "the interpenetration between social process and spatial form."[12] Defining the first premise, Harvey draws on John Stuart Mill's "sociological imagination," or that "which 'enables its possessor to understand the larger historical scene in terms of its meaning for the inner life and the external career of a variety of individuals.' "[13] This is the historicizing of incidents, beliefs, or lifestyles that is the dominant discursive mode of analysis in many fields. Alone, however, this is insufficient for Harvey's argument and so he contrasts it with what he calls the "geographical imagination": "this imagination enables the individual to recognize the role of space and place in his own biography, to relate to the spaces he sees around him, and to recognize how transactions between individuals and between organizations are affected by the space that separates them."[14] Harvey's definition proves invaluable in two ways. First, the geographical imagination informs the methodology of the discipline: consideration of how all social interactions (personal, familial, economic, nationalistic) are mediated by the "space that separates" the actors in these interactions. No longer simply *where* events take place, space becomes, in part, *how* or *why* they take place. Second, Harvey's definition of the geographical imagination helps to initiate the discursive refutation that critical and cultural geography have advanced during the last three decades: the shifting of the emphasis away from historicization alone, as a category of analysis, and linking it with spatialization. Harvey's ambition was to advance and defend a spatial corollary to the sociological assumptions that had become the defining heuristic in most scholarship. As he maintained in 1973, "The general point should be clear: the only adequate conceptual framework for understanding the city is one which encompasses and builds upon both the sociological and geographical imaginations."[15]

A Rhetoric of Sociospatial Drama

Distinctly interdisciplinary, then, my argument draws on much of the aforementioned work from critical and cultural geography to define sociospatial drama in two complementary ways. Because the chapters are organized geographically as much as thematically, that is, about a particular element or iteration of urbanism (suburbs, ghettos, public space), they work inductively across this criticism. In other words, each chapter introduces, defines, and engages with different theoretical frameworks given its subject. Necessary not just because certain aspects of urbanism require different methodology, this approach furthermore privileges the differences among the plays included in this book while still arguing for a shared ambition. Nevertheless, the plays considered here come together under the broad, deductive principles derived from the works of Lefebvre and Harvey: the problem of the "double illusion" of space and the importance of the "geographical imagination." In many ways these two principles can be read as mirroring responses to the same issue: how to elevate space, place, or geography to heuristics in the same way that critics have long done with history. Central to my definition of sociospatial drama is the engagement of plays with these principles. Applying deductive principles to any play, much less across so many plays from such different backgrounds, produces a number of questions. How does the play confront the "double illusion" of space? Alternately, how does the play develop a "geographical imagination" internally, that is, in the characters, and how so externally, that is, with audiences? Most significant, how does the play attempt these ends not just thematically but formally?

It is this last question that led to what I have defined as a rhetoric of sociospatial drama. The term "rhetoric," as I am using it, comes from W. B. Worthen's *Modern Drama and the Rhetoric of Theater*, in which he theorizes the interplay of text, performance, and reception. Specifically, Worthen contends the dramatic text works dialectically with theatrical productions in ways that "define [...] and legitimate [...] a certain range of interpretive behavior and experience as the role that the audience performs."[16] Only tangentially concerned with the argument about genre advanced at length by Worthen,[17] I have adapted the term "rhetoric" to consider the following: how the plays represent the imbrication of sociality and spatiality in the dramatic text and how that text, potentially, becomes a blueprint that defines and legitimates the roles of audiences. Regardless of what they dramatize about New York City or Los Angeles, these plays do this, in part, through *sociospatial narratives*. The term "narrative" throughout this book includes plotting (the incidents that move the story) as well as the ethos of the work (the tone or attitude about that plot). The sociospatial narrative, then, both depicts events grounded in elements of urbanism and advocates an argument about urbanism. This advocacy occurs primarily with characters coming to some realization about the urban environment, though the plays certainly invite audiences to share this realization. But the plays address audiences more directly through *sociospatial structure*. The term "structure" here describes both the visual patterns within plays (staging in scenes) and the conceptual relations among the patterns (how genre defines staging, scenes, and to some degree spectatorship). Sociospatial structure, then, describes how plays are constituted within and across scenes in ways that potentially define and legitimate the roles of audiences.[18]

In surveying contemporary drama, I have found two defining sociospatial narratives that are linked with Harvey's geographical imagination. The first is called the "initiation narrative" because of what it shares with the *Bildungsroman*. Normally linked with fiction, the classical *Bildungsroman*[19] follows a character's growth from naivety, through maturation, and toward integration. In the dramas that employ the "initiation narrative," the basic elements of the *Bildungsroman* have become spatialized: the story follows characters who move from naiveté about the urban environment through moments of crisis that produce disillusionment with the constitution of the city and, often, the impetus for change. The narrative moves from one or both of the "double illusions" of space, through encounters that induce disruption in characters' lives, and toward renewed understanding of the organization, legislation, and inhabitance of the urban environment. Most often, this narrative's plotting follows the journey motif, with the character being thrust into New York City or Los Angeles in ways that challenge his or her epistemological or ideological presumptions. The journey is episodic—marked by encounters with those who have different experiences or knowledge of the environment—and follows the character's efforts to negotiate the physical environs and the conceptual frameworks of the city. Maturation of this character, in effect, moves toward Harvey's geographical imagination. If this narrative includes audiences, it does so through sympathy or surrogacy, or if audiences see themselves in the characters, since the interrogation of the city occurs within the play.

This internalizing of interrogation is one distinction between the "initiation narrative" and the "transgression narrative." As its name suggests this narrative begins from the violation of boundaries in the city. This violation can be spatial: going somewhere characters are not supposed to go or crossing some line intended to separate one group from another. This violation can likewise be social: doing something the characters are forbidden to do such as defying a set of normative behaviors that define the community. What brings together both forms of transgression is confrontation with the ideological mapping of space. During the 1980s and 1990s, decades imbued with conservatism, this mapping became increasingly common across any number of fault lines that the individual chapters will outline in greater depth. Needless to say, it is these very lines that the transgression narrative seeks to reveal and interrogate. Almost always, this narrative begins with characters who have already developed a geographical imagination and are attempting to pursue the implications of their discovery, by either converting others or challenging the status quo. Typically less linear than the initiation narrative, the transgression narrative becomes even more episodic because the plot often follows the push against ideological boundaries and the push back by whatever authority defends that boundary. Generally, the transgression narrative concludes with one of two possibilities: this authority crushing insurgence and compelling submission or the possibility of transformation of the boundaries, at least temporarily, defeated. If this narrative includes audiences, it does so directly. Some of these narratives try to offend audiences who may belong to whatever class or racial group that benefits from or is responsible for the boundaries. Others offer ways of channeling the outrage of audiences when they come to realize what is wrong.

Clearly complementary, the initiation and transgression narratives of sociospatial drama pursue the same ambition. They interrogate the "double illusion" of space that obfuscates the ways that urban environments are imbricated with ideological assumptions regarding what is normal and what is aberrant, about who belongs and who does not, and about authority over and access to certain spaces. Without being able to question such assumptions, there is little chance for meaningful changes in terms of identity politics or social justice. Because of this, these two narratives likewise advocate for the value of geographical imagination, of an understanding of the role the urban space plays in everyday lives. In many ways, these narratives address the same problem from different angles. In fact, elements of both narratives are found in many plays considered here, though the overall narrative of any play corresponds more closely to one or the other. Because these narratives complement each other so well, I have paired them in the subsequent chapters. Rivera's *Marisol*, Greenberg's *Three Days of Rain*, Shepard's *True West*, Sears's *Harlem Duet*, and Hwang's *FOB* all fall within the initiation narrative. By contrast, Kushner's *Angels in America*, Clark's *Lost Souls and Missing Persons*, Machado's *Broken Eggs*, Smith's *Twilight Los Angeles, 1992*, and Moraga's *Giving Up the Ghost* are all examples of the transgression narrative. In considering them side by side, we can better appreciate how contemporary drama interrogates the built environment and the social ordering of New York City and Los Angeles during the closing decades of the century.

Regardless of which narrative best defines any one play, the narratives themselves are always nested within sociospatial structures that further the aforementioned interrogation of the urban environment. Paradoxically, sociospatial structure as I have considered it in this book is simultaneously more generalized and more idiosyncratic than sociospatial narrative It is more generalized at the level of genre, which often defines how the elements of the play relate to one another conceptually and how those elements relate to audiences. One remarkable trend among contemporary plays about the urban environment is their skepticism toward realism. Dramatists as different as Tony Kushner, Sam Shepard, and Cherríe Moraga demonstrate, in their dramaturgy, an aversion to realism's fundamental principles: linearity and coherence on the one hand, verisimilitude and indexicality on the other. Dramaturgically, this aversion may have to do with how realism defines relationships among stage properties, among scenes, and with audiences: already complete and fully transparent, the realist stage demands little from audiences beyond voyeurism.[20] Sociospatially, this aversion probably has something to do with realism's privileging of indexicality and how this endorses the "double illusion" of space at the root of problems, epistemologically, about the metropolis. Because of this skepticism, the plays considered in the following chapters break with realism in two ways. By far, most of them simply reject the structural assumptions of realism altogether and borrow from expressionism or surrealism, where objects transform, spaces dissolve and reform in competing iterations, and scenes and acts violate chronological and geographical integrity. Others metatheatrically critique realism as part of its sociospatial ambitions, usually beginning realistically and then becoming increasingly unrealistic over time. In either case, the sociospatial structures of these plays privilege contestation rather than coherence, interrogation rather than indexicality.

In many ways, however, sociospatial structure is better defined by the visual patterns of staging these plays. Because this book is a study of the dramaturgy of contemporary North American drama, I have considered staging, which includes but is not limited to scenography, primarily through the stage directions, though whenever possible I have augmented this with a discussion of key productions. Unlike the genre level of sociospatial structure, this staging proves too idiosyncratic for classification and therefore I address it here only descriptively: through allegorical doubling, which involves dramatizing "interactions" of multiple characters from different time periods (usually only audiences are aware of this) in the same space, or making characters double other characters from different spaces; through split-staging, which involves bringing multiple places to the stage consecutively or simultaneously in ways that illustrate not just the contrast of places but additionally contrasts of ideology and epistemology grounded in these places; through expressionistic or surrealistic structures, which involves a dream-like movement from one space to another, often with thematic—but not logical—segues among the scenes, thereby suggesting the overlapping of geography, epistemology, and psychology. The principles behind these examples of sociospatial structure are juxtaposition and contestation: the ambition of putting two different kinds of spaces or concepts of spatiality into conflict, visually, before audiences. Although the argument has certainly been overused,[21] the connection to Michel Foucault's citation of the stage as a defining example of "heterotopian spaces" speaks to this point. Like Foucault's heterotopian spaces, the stage becomes a space where other spaces are "simultaneously represented, contested, and inverted."[22] In the very structure of contemporary plays, then, emerges the abiding ambition of interrogating urban space in ways that ultimately complement the sociospatial narratives.

The Spatial Turn of Drama

Clearly, this argument falls within the "spatial turn" in dramatic and theatrical criticism. Become popular during the last decade, this consideration of how geography, place, or space informs dramaturgy or performance suggests valuable lines of inquiry from which this book has greatly benefited. Marvin Carlson's *Places of Performance* (1989) and to a somewhat lesser extent *Theories of the Theater* (1984) established the genealogy of theater and urbanism leading up to this period. Una Chaudhuri's *Staging Place* (1995) argues for a distinct pattern of spatialized concerns in American drama during the twentieth century, though her focus is only tangentially linked with urbanism. More than anything, *Staging Place* was instrumental to the spatial turn because it argued most forcibly for developing space as a "category of analysis" for theater studies.[23] But it was the anthology coedited by Elinor Fuchs and Una Chaudhuri, *Land/Scape/Theater* (2005), that proved most important to my argument. In the introduction, Chaudhuri and Fuchs argue that the close of the nineteenth century saw a shift of consciousness toward landscape: "At the threshold of modernism, theater began to manifest a new spatial dimension, both visually and dramaturgically, in which landscape for the first time held itself apart from character and became a figure on its own."[24] In "Reading Landscapes," Fuchs further defines this premise by describing this shift in the plays of Ibsen, Chekhov, Wedekind, and others: "one can begin to see landscape itself as an independent figure: not simply a support to human action, but entering in a variety of roles, for instance, as mentor, obstacle, or ironist."[25] Importantly, Fuchs defines landscape in the same terms as critical and cultural geography: it is not a neutral container but rather an active constituent of drama. Based on this definition, they maintain that "As the [twentieth] century moved on, landscape would encroach on the traditional dramaturgy of plot and character to become a perspective and a method, linking seemingly unrelated theatrical practices in staging, text, scenography, and spectatorship."[26] In many ways, sociospatial drama falls within this trajectory.

As valuable as *Land/Scape/Theater* was for my research, the argument of this book offers significant refinements to the work of Fuchs and Chaudhuri. The first involves terminology: their use of "landscape" as the "new spatial paradigm" for theater and drama. They justify their privileging of "landscape" over "space" or "place" by arguing that landscape "permits certain distinctions that are necessary to a theorization of the new spatial paradigm."[27] According to this premise, landscape offers a precision not found in the other two terms: because "every inch of space is just another inch of space," space is too abstract; because place is "overly particular," it is too localized to be theoretically valuable.[28] Mediating such limitations, "landscape is more grounded and more available to visual experience than space, but more environmental and constitutive of the imaginative order than place."[29] Rigorous definition of terminology is certainly welcome, but this argument proves unsatisfactory in many ways. First of all, John Brinckerhoff Jackson, one of the founders of cultural landscape studies, acknowledges a basic uncertainty at the heart of this discipline. In *The Interpretation of Ordinary Landscapes,* he describes that after 25 years of trying to "understand and explain that aspect of the environment I call the landscape . . . the concept continues to elude me."[30]

Editing the volume, D. W. Meinig begins by defining "landscape" through negation: that is, in contrast to "nature" or "environment" or "place"—a sign of definitional uncertainty. If the major figures cannot define landscape without ambiguity, it seems unlikely that it offers the precision that Fuchs and Chaudhuri claim. Another problem is that those definitions that have become acceptable about landscapes imply either emplacement (being physically *in* the landscape) or exclusion (being *removed from* the landscape but providing a focal point)—but not both simultaneously. In this way, landscape becomes a snapshot of what Pierce Lewis calls an "unwittingly autobiography" of how we live in space.[31] But landscape proves less effective in theorizing interactions within and through the field of spatial relations because landscape tends to reflect a particular focal point rather than fluid and contested sociality.

I'm not arguing against the use of "landscape" in terms of theorizing concerns with space but rather against the privileging of landscape. In this study, I have privileged "space" over "landscape" and "place" because "space" includes both terms within itself. "Landscape" and "place" are specific manifestations of "space" dependent on the interplay of sociality and spatiality. In fact, I use "landscape" and "place" throughout this book, though in ways more precise. I use "landscape" to define, explicitly, the expanse of space that includes many elements—streets, buildings, parks—that are apprehensible from any single perspective. This perspective, interestingly enough, can be both geographical (where one stands in looking at a landscape) and epistemological (the frames used, conceptually, that might open up or limit what one sees). This distinction marks a secondary use of "landscape": to define how particular organizations of elements within given geographical coordinates— suburban neighborhoods, for instance—are always defined empirically *and* epistemologically, as Meinig contends.[32] Likewise, in this book I use "place" to define first a physical location within a particular landscape, such as a building, a community park, or a street corner, that is much more specific and concrete than the landscape. Along with this geographical definition, "place" is distinguished from "space" by attention to the connotations imbuing place with particular meanings, whether this meaning is cultural or idiosyncratic. This definition of place allows for better appreciation of the spatiality of human lives, and further, a way of demonstrating how particular places in that spatiality become the focal point of contestation. A good example of the distinction between "landscape" and "place" can be found in *Harlem Duet*: while the view of Harlem described by the characters represents a landscape, the focus on the Apollo Theater represents a particular place.

Another refinement to "landscape theater" guiding this study involves redressing a flaw acknowledged but not sufficiently addressed by Fuchs and Chaudhuri. In the anthology's introduction, they predict the central question that follows from their argument: "Weren't landscapes a feature of dramatic fiction and theatrical representation long before the modern period?"[33] How is the newfound interest in landscapes in the plays of Ibsen, Chekhov, and others *new*? Unfortunately, they never answer this question other than to contend, rather unsatisfactorily, that cultural thinking about landscapes underwent a change commensurate with modernism. Why did it change? How did dramatists tap into this change? What did it mean for understanding of landscapes? On the one hand, it is unfair to hold Fuchs and Chaudhuri accountable for such concerns since their anthology's ambition was to introduce the theory that would be addressed through the essays included therein. On the other hand, the argument behind "landscape theater" evidences a flaw in methodology. Fuchs and Chaudhuri identify the subject matter without defining the means of assessing how it manifests itself, why it did so, or what it might mean beyond perpetuating itself. The ways that landscape became a subject or how it informs dramaturgy and performance remains too ambiguous to function heuristically.

In this study, I have redressed this problem in two complementary ways. Definition of sociospatial drama, first of all, is always grounded in the historical, cultural, and geographical crises of New York City and Los Angeles during the 1980s and 1990s. Designed as a case study, each chapter begins by outlining, in some detail, the problems that provided exigency for the plays there: this involves working from historical documents, interviews of the playwrights, critical geography, and urban theory. The readings pursued in each chapter, then, produce conclusions grounded in specific events that were reflected in the dramaturgy of the plays. Read against one another, the chapters offer an increasingly nuanced portrait of New York City and Los Angeles in these decades from distinctly different points of view. Moreover, it is not enough for sociospatial drama to simply have plays set in either of these cities. If this were sufficient, this study would be subject to the question confronting "landscape theater": weren't New York City and Los Angeles features of drama before this period? Instead, these plays question common understandings or organizations of the urban environment in ways thematically *and* formally. Concerns about urbanism inform the storyline and structure of the plays. In many ways, a parallel emerges between contemporary drama and what August Strindberg said about modern drama a century earlier: the dramatists were making new bottles for new wine.

The Argument of the Chapters

The following chapters are organized thematically and geographically, that is, around particular elements or iterations of the urban environment and the concerns most vehemently contested during the 1980s and 1990s. Chapters 1 and 2 address complementary elements of urbanism, with Chapter 1 addressing conflicts about public space. Specifically, this chapter looks at Tony Kushner's *Angels in America* and José Rivera's *Marisol* as plays that dramatize the ideological contestation of urban space during the 1980s. In the case of Rivera, these concerns are localized in New York and include the themes of poverty, immigration, and belonging as they unfolded in Mayor Ed Koch's campaign against the homeless. In the case of Kushner, the play uses New York City as a nexus for the nationalized concerns about deviancy and normativity that were paramount during the Reagan administration. Unlike *Marisol, Angels in America* works by putting a number of spaces in conversation with New York City, most importantly, Salt Lake City and San Francisco, two competing paradigms of urbanism that suggest how public space becomes *where* and *how* concerns about identity politics and social justice are contested. In Chapter 2, the focus on elements of urbanism turns from public to constructed spaces, in particular, the architecture of New York City during the 1980s and 1990s when the cartography of the city was being reimagined. In Richard Greenberg's *Three Days of Rain* and Sally Clark's *Lost Souls and Missing Persons,* concerns about identity, family, gender, and nationality all unfold within the incoherence of the increasingly postmodern city.

Chapters 3, 4, and 5 go beyond particular elements of urbanism and consider different iterations where major conflicts were unfolding during these decades. Chapter 3 looks specifically at suburbanism through the pairing of Sam Shepard's *True West* and Eduardo Machado's *Broken Eggs.* Read together, the plays interrogate the assumptions about aesthetics and belonging communicated through the organization and policing of suburbanism in greater Los Angeles—though each from different perspectives. Chapter 4 works dialectically with Chapter 3 by considering the mirrored iteration of urbanism to the suburbs: the ghettos of New York City and Los Angeles. In particular, Djanet Sears's *Harlem Duet* and Anna Deavere Smith's *Twilight Los Angeles, 1992* examine the racial and social fault lines that erupted into riots and violence during the 1990s by considering the long history of racism and urbanism. Read together, they offer competing diagnoses of what produces urban rioting and what that rioting portends for urbanism in the United States. Chapter 5 brings together threads from chapters 3 and 4 and focuses on immigrant enclaves in Los Angeles, specifically, a Chicano barrio and Chinatown. David Henry Hwang's *FOB* considers the nature of belonging, geographical and existential, for immigrants and children of immigrants from China, while Cherrie Moraga's *Giving Up the Ghost* considers the dislocation of the Mexican immigrant and the Mexican American, both of whom are doubly disenfranchised—by ethnicity and by sexuality, with the concerns about homosexuality and transgression making links to *Angels in America*.

The contribution of this book to the spatial turn in dramatic and theatrical criticism is, hopefully, twofold. In part, this book offers an exploration of the most recent branching in the genealogy of drama, theater, and urbanism with particular emphasis on the formal innovations and spatial concerns of these playwrights. By itself, this study can potentially expand both the canon of dramatic literature (who is anthologized and taught today) and perhaps the ways that canonical writers (Kushner, Shepard, Hwang) have been considered, taught, and performed by defining sociospatial drama as a heuristic for investigating spatialized concerns about urbanism. Another part of this contribution, though, may be more far-reaching. At the beginning of this introduction and throughout, I have suggested that contemporary drama offers a new branching in the genealogy of drama, theater, and urbanism. But it is also possible that only now, with the advancements of critical and cultural geography described by Soja, critics have sufficient tools for considering how drama and theater have engaged with urbanism in its many iterations. In effect, sociospatial drama may offer a powerful heuristic for rereading this genealogy in order to discover earlier works that anticipate what has become common among contemporary dramatists and thereby suggest further lineages within the genealogy. In either case, this book hopes to advance consideration of how drama, theater, and urbanism inform one another. In 1989, at the beginning of the spatial turn in drama and theater criticism, Carlson showed "how places of performance generate social and cultural meanings of their own which in turn help to structure the meaning of the entire theatrical experience."[34] *Where* theater took place, in other words, informed *how* theater was received. Ultimately, the argument of this book reads like the corollary to Carlson's point: the performance of space, especially urban space, can generate its own social and cultural meanings that inform and transform knowledge of urbanism.

PART I

Elements of Urbanism

CHAPTER 1

"Against the Law in this City": Public Space in New York City

In the 1980s, the very nature of society was contested in the streets and on the sidewalks of New York City. One of the ways this occurred involved the homeless, whose numbers had ballooned to levels unprecedented since the Great Depression,[1] and Mayor Ed Koch's response to this growing crisis of homelessness. When homeless crowds began gathering in Grand Central Station and other public locales to escape inclement weather and avoid possible violence,[2] it became an official embarrassment. Something, certainly, had to be done. Instead of expanding social services to ameliorate this problem, Koch set about defining the homeless *as the problem.* According to Tim Cresswell's *In Place, Out of Place,* Koch's initial gambit was legislative: he passed anti-loitering laws empowering the New York Police Department (NYPD) to "remove the homeless from public space."[3] In criminalizing homelessness, Koch defined public spaces as sites where "what is right, just, and appropriate" is adjudicated in favor of middle-class New Yorkers, who found encounters with homelessness disruptive and disturbing.[4] Beyond the consequences for the homeless being rousted out of their temporary refuges, Koch's legislation challenged traditional conceptions of public space. Instead of being defined through accessibility to all citizens, public space became *where* and *about what* Koch carried out this campaign. Implicitly, he advocated a class-based vision of society through the policing of public space. When the State Supreme Court struck down this law as unconstitutional, Koch turned to propaganda and continued to assail the homeless. In a speech to the American Institute of Architects in 1988, for example, he publicly railed against them: "They're sitting on the floor, occasionally defecating, urinating, talking to themselves."[5] Become increasingly ideological, his argument was the same: he was trying to "defend" middle-class society by excising the homeless from public space.

One year later Koch, along with other public officials, was uncomfortably present for another instance of social definition being contested in public space. On December 10, 1989, parishioners of St. Patrick's Cathedral in New York City were confronted by "more than 4,500 AIDS and reproduction rights activists staging a 'STOP THE CHURCH' protest."[6] This protest was organized by AIDS Coalition to Unleash Power (ACT UP), which dedicates itself to acts of civil disobedience that (1) intend to draw attention to concerns about homosexuality, AIDS, discrimination and (2) to do this through irreverent appropriation of public space. Originating from Cardinal John O'Connor's remarks about the immorality of homosexuality and abortion, ACT UP's protest was "a carnival-like performance of guerrilla theater": protestors costumed as clowns, Catholic bishops, and nuns cavorting in the streets; a male Virgin Mary carrying a sign reading "This Mary believes in safe sex education"; a giant condom labeled "CARDINAL O'CONDOM."[7] Most significant in terms of this argument, however, were ACT UP's "die-ins": while many protestors paraded around the cathedral with mock tombstones, hundreds of others lay on the street as if dead. Bodies were outlined in paint and chalk to stress "the deadly effects of social indifference to AIDS" and literalized the premise underlying the protest: the rewriting of public space through contestation.[8] Literally and figuratively, protestors transformed this site into an interrogation of conservative definitions of belonging. Not only did Mayor Koch and future mayor Rudy Giuliani get caught up in this fight over identity politics and social justice, but so too did parishioners and passersby: they became audience and actors in this distinctly urban drama. Although public officials, including Koch, decried the protest,[9] it ironically mirrored Koch's campaign against the homeless: the ACT UP protest made its own argument about society through contesting public space.

Different experientially and existentially, of course, homelessness and homosexuality nevertheless became complementary flashpoints in the 1980s about conservative definitions of society. Behind Koch's campaign was the ambition, contends Cresswell, of using "space and place . . . to structure a normative landscape."[10] That is, his criminalization of homelessness sought to defend not only the public spaces of New York City but further the middle-class society that frequented such spaces against that which was judged wrong or inappropriate. Note the language employed by Koch when talking about the homeless publicly: it generally defines homelessness through degeneracy, marking the homeless as different from and dangerous to the middle class in ways similar to Victorian anxiety about poverty.[11] In Cresswell's reading, Koch's campaign demonstrates the ways that spaces can be ideologically contested toward definitions of society itself: the public spaces Koch was policing were both *where* and *what about* society that was being defended. Behind

ACT UP's "cathedral action," of course, was a similar ambition. Beginning from Cardinal O'Connor's remarks condemning gays and lesbians and ignoring the growing epidemic of AIDS, the "STOP THE CHURCH" protest sought to deconstruct another normative landscape. By staging the protest publicly, ACT UP turned a part of New York City, temporarily, into the battleground for the acknowledgment and inclusion of gays and lesbians. By giving the church and the media advanced warning, ACT UP ensured that the protest would receive national attention and would, consequently, bring this local contestation into the public sphere. They irreverently questioned not just the definitions of homosexuality and AIDS, but also questioned the authority of local and federal governments to make these definitions. However ideologically different Koch's campaign and ACT UP's protest may be, they both define public space as the setting and the subject of the fight for identity politics in the 1980s.

During this decade a number of dramatists recognized this contestation of public space and incorporated it into their dramaturgy, nowhere more clearly than in José Rivera's *Marisol* and Tony Kushner's *Angels in America*. Already, the two plays have been linked in criticism because of the proximity of their debut productions (two years of each other) and because of shared themes (angels and apocalypse). More important links emerge, though, when *Marisol* and *Angels in America* are read against this spatialized contestation of sociality. In fact, both playwrights have suggested links between this urban drama playing out in New York City and their dramaturgy. Shortly before *Marisol*'s debut in 1990, Rivera told Lynn Jacobson in an interview that the homeless crisis was the crux of the play, epistemologically and ideologically. "We have constructed a pretty tidy world that excludes the street," he observed, "but it's there and it affects us, and we shouldn't be surprised when it is what it is. We've chosen to ignore the street's laws, but they don't go away."[12] Hiding none of his frustration, he defined the plight of homelessness as emerging from a rather naïve or merely expedient attitude: to New Yorkers like Mayor Koch, the homeless should only be acknowledged once they intrude on their lives and then only as a problem for the tidy world of the middle class. Kushner, too, drew attention to the ways that conservatism was defining attitudes about the limits of society during interviews in this decade, speaking angrily about the indifference toward gays, lesbians, and AIDS endorsed by the Reagan administration.[13] During a roundtable discussion led by Craig Kinzer, Kushner made connections between the "cathedral action" of ACT UP—which, in Kushner's terms, "disrupted High Mass"—and *Angels in America,* implying a common ambition of "disruption" between protest and play.[14] Read together, Rivera and Kushner exemplify sociospatial concerns in the "deep structure" of their plays.[15]

Deep structure refers simultaneously to the composition and exigency of *Marisol* and *Angels in America*: How the plays were composed, and perhaps why, foreground the contestation in—and of—public space in the 1980s and into the early 1990s as defining moments in the fight for identity politics and social justice in the United States. Initially, *Marisol* and *Angels in America* do this by revealing the contestation for what it is: an attempt, by an absent authority, to defend normative definitions about society through the policing of public space. Obviously the terms of these definitions differ from one play to the next, but the premise remains consistent. The plays interrogate the naturalization of the distinctly spatialized boundaries defining the limits of society that make questioning the constitution of society difficult, if not impossible. They expose what is behind Koch's and O'Connor's comments: the ideological mapping of public space and public sphere toward conservative definitions of what is "just, right, and appropriate." Merely revealing the boundaries, however, is not enough. *Marisol* and *Angels in America* additionally stage transgressions of the boundaries because, as Cresswell has argued, transgression makes the boundaries visible and suggests alternative definitions of what is right, just, and appropriate by imagining society beyond such limits. Although *Marisol* is concerned with transgression, it corresponds more closely with the "initiation narrative." It follows the journey of Marisol Perez, a woman aspiring to the middle class, whose encounters, in Rivera's nightmarish reflection of New York, illustrate the brutality and indifference toward anything that might intrude on the tidy world of the middle class. While drawing on the "initiation narrative," *Angels in America* corresponds with the "transgression narrative" in the subplot about Joe Pitt in Central Park, which I stress here. Through Joe's spatialized struggle with his homosexuality, Kushner dramatizes the value of transgression against conservative definitions of community, city, and self. In both plays, the narratives that unfold revolve around contested definitions of urbanism.

Another way these plays register and reflect the contestation of public space is through the sociospatial structures of *Marisol* and *Angels in America*. Always in this book, discussion of sociospatial structure comes with the caveat articulated so well by Janelle Reinelt: whatever the dramatist may have written into the text about the staging or production, it depends upon the synergy of director, scenographer, and actor for actualization on the stage.[16] Nevertheless, the stage directions of *Marisol* and *Angels in America* define a sociospatial structure premised on juxtaposition and superimposition. *Angels in America,* for instance, depends frequently on split-staging, that is, the dividing of the stage between two or three scenes that unfold alternatively (with dialogue and action shifting from one scene to another) or simultaneously (with dialogue and action overlapping among scenes). Not original to Kushner's dramaturgy,[17] of course, this split-staging nevertheless proves especially valuable in visually foregrounding contestation: it stages two spaces or two conceptions of spatiality in competition with each other. Although *Marisol* never uses split-staging, it relies on juxtaposition and superimposition diachronically. The scenes in Marisol's journey are set against traditional signifiers of urbanism: a brick wall with boarded windows, a garbage dumpster, a sidewalk—each of which is redefined by the encounters that occur before them. Visually, audiences are presented with scenes they should recognize and then made to see them again—from the perspective of the homeless in Rivera's play. Considered together, the sociospatial structures of *Marisol* and *Angels in America* serve three ends. First, they foreground contestation visually and epistemologically throughout the scenes by having competing spaces or definitions of space become part of the conflict. Second, because this depiction of the conflicts is visual as much as conceptual, it invites audiences to participate in the interrogation of normative definitions. And third, it almost metatheatrically demonstrates *how* public space becomes simultaneously the setting and the stakes of the battles being fought about rights, freedoms, and belonging during the 1980s and early 1990s.

Walking Nightmares Out There

José Rivera's *Marisol* originally debuted at some remove from New York City. Along with Marsha Norman's *D. Boone* and David Henry Hwang's *Bondage*, Rivera's *Marisol* was among the highlights of the 1992 Humana Festival of New American Plays in Louisville, Kentucky. Well reviewed, this production did not realize the play's sociospatial concerns for numerous reasons. The Actor's Theatre was too small for the "sprawling and ambitious" play according to Mel Gussow's review for *The New York Times,* nor did the Festival's mounting some 11 plays over just a few short days allow for the stagecraft needed to invoke Rivera's concerns.[18] Likewise, limited casting during the Festival downplayed some of the play's concerns with homelessness: there was only one homeless person in the production (as opposed to five in the New York production the following year). Another possible inhibiting factor was stressed by Gussow: "While some Louisvillians might have been perplexed by the weird urban extremes depicted onstage, beleaguered New Yorkers may identify them as the norm."[19] Gussow's definition of "the norm" is certainly questionable given that *Marisol* includes food turning to salt, the moon disappearing, homeless people being set on fire, and an angelic siege of heaven to dethrone a senile deity. Nevertheless, he has a valid point in that something of the play's argument would have resonated more clearly with New York audiences, particularly the play's criticism of the

Koch administration, which unfolds without topical reference. When *Marisol* moved to the New York Shakespeare Festival the next year, where it was produced by George C. Wolf, it had better opportunity to realize its concerns. Reviewing this production for *The New York Times*, Frank Rich suggested that it did so through his praise for the play's willingness to tackle the social discord that ignited the L.A. rioting and his quip that "This is not a play that the mayor would want to use for a re-election campaign."[20]

Rich rightly infers the play's antipathy about municipal authority, though toward the wrong mayor.[21] Never named in the play or in interviews by Rivera about this play, Mayor Koch's campaign against the homeless during the 1980s nevertheless plays a defining role in *Marisol's* sociospatial concerns. During the interview with Jacobson in 1990, well before *Marisol* ever reached the stage, Rivera stressed that the homeless experience was the "political essence of the play."[22] Without a place literally (a home) and figuratively (in society), the homeless were hounded through propaganda, legislation, and policing during the 1980s. Throughout this campaign Koch cast himself as an absurd Dr. Stockmann from Henrik Ibsen's *An Enemy of the People* and the homeless as poisoning the waters of New York City. Koch was, to many, defending the tidy world of the middle class from the intrusion of aberrance into public space. But to Rivera, Koch's campaign suggests something considerably more cynical and more dangerous, something that he described during another interview shortly after the New York debut of *Marisol*. " 'I have been become struck in the last few years,' " he told Karen Fricker, " 'by the enormous violence that we live through on every level. There's a feeling that people have lost their way, that the basic rules of civilization have been suppressed.' "[23] Not defined explicitly, the nature of such rules can nevertheless be inferred, through other remarks by Rivera[24] and the play, in terms of Hobbesian philosophy: a form of social contract between people and their government that begins from and reaffirms human dignity and social justice. As Rivera put it in the 1990 interview, "There are walking nightmares out there that have to be dealt with—people who need help."[25] Of particular note is how Rivera's philosophy contrasts sharply with that underlying the pursuit of a normative landscape, which, in the case of Koch's campaign, begins from the suppression of the "rules of civilization." Rivera's concerns were, in part, biographical: he had an uncle die homeless.[26] But they were undeniably political: the treatment of the homeless was violence committed against individuals and civilization itself since it endorsed callous indifference toward the most vulnerable.

In *Marisol*, Rivera's ambitions are twofold: to confront the abuse of the homeless and, more significantly, to confront the ways this abuse was legitimized in cultural consciousness. The tensions between the tidy world and "the street"—Rivera's terminology—correspond with the interplay of empiricism and epistemology defined by Michel de Certeau in *The Practice of Everyday Life*. In de Certeau's terminology, the "voyeur" knows the city from the "summit of the World Trade Center," from such heights that the everyday world of crime, garbage, and poverty becomes little more than abstraction. Distance, here, is simultaneously geographical and epistemological: the voyeur does not engage in the city but remains aloof. Naturalized by the social and spatial configurations of the city (for instance, buildings with doormen or streets protected by noticeable police presence), this perspective is what Rivera questions in *Marisol*. He does so by collapsing the insulating distance between voyeur and what de Certeau defines as the "walker," or those who live down "below the thresholds at which visibility," from the viewpoint of the voyeur, "begins."[27] Though de Certeau's term describes anyone who moves about the city by walking, it becomes especially apt in Rivera's representation of homelessness since it foregrounds the contrasts to the privileges of the middle class: the homeless know the city in ways clearly different than the privileged and represent a distinctly different knowledge that the voyeur avoids. Simply bringing walkers like the homeless into consciousness, in the play and in the audience, disrupts the voyeur's tidy world by making him or her acknowledge what is excluded. In this way, *Marisol* begins from and agitates for contestation. But Rivera goes further and questions the assumptions of the voyeur, when politicized toward definition of the city. Thematized in the narrative structure, the tidy world becomes subject to questioning that suggests its complicity in creating or sustaining the "walking nightmares out there."

A Prevailing Sickness

Marisol opens with a particularly dark and threatening picture of New York City. On the subway traveling north toward 180th Street is Marisol Perez, a Puerto Rican woman on her way home from her job in a Manhattan publishing firm. She is "smartly dressed" and reading *The New York Times*—both signifiers of her middle-class status—behind which she attempts to ignore the homeless-looking man, carrying a golf club, who enters the subway car. Named Man with Golf Club, he wears filthy and torn clothing, has rags for shoes, and rambles about his "god-blessed little angel."[28] His remarks draw attention to the Angel sitting atop a ladder downstage: a young black woman with silver wings and radiating heat and light. This Angel will play a central role in *Marisol*, the conflicts of which unfold on the metaphysical level of the heavens along with the sociopolitical level of New York City streets, but for now, the Angel silently watches what is occurring below. Alone with this man on a late subway, Marisol initially pretends not to see him, but when he addresses her, she responds with practiced indifference: "God help you, you get in my face."[29] When this fails to dissuade him, she adds, "I have no money."[30] Not interested in panhandling, Man with Golf Club continues talking, with a stream-of-consciousness quality that grows in intensity: he describes sleeping his box on 180th Street and encountering his guardian angel; lamenting the news that she was leaving him; and experiencing relief when the guardian angels stopped skinheads from setting him on fire in Van Cortlandt Park. When the Man with Golf Club realizes that without this angel, he will be "a fucking *appetizer* for all the Hitler youth and their cans of *gasoline* . . ." (original emphasis), he lunges at Marisol.[31] Afraid but still angry, Marisol yells for the heavens to strike him dead but when nothing happens, he attacks her with the golf club. Before his attack lands, the Angel lets out an "ear-splitting scream" that brings the subway car to an crashing stop and throws Marisol and her would-be attacker across the car. The first to recover, Marisol shoves her way past her attacker and runs out of the subway car before the scene dims to black.

Introduced in this scene, homelessness enters the play, initially, in ways that correspond with the assumptions behind the tidy world. Man with Golf Club's presence on the subway is, first of all, an intrusion into the life of Marisol, who is trying to read her newspaper on her way home. From the moment she has to share the same space with him, she attempts to erase his presence in ways that suggest a grammar of the voyeur's behavior. Trying to pretend he's not there, she digs deeper into her newspaper so that she does not have to acknowledge him. When she can no longer ignore him, she turns to phrases intended to underscore the social and existential distance between them and, ideally, to reestablish the preferred spatial distance. Proximity initially produces aversion in Marisol, who clearly does not want to deal with this homeless man. But aversion becomes anxiety, for Marisol and for audiences, as the Man with Golf Club rambles on about angels, immolation, and credit cards. Without background, the play's audiences know nothing more than what is happening between middle-class woman and homeless man. His language, along with his blazing eyes, suggest mental imbalance if not outright madness—he becomes as much threat as intrusion. Sharing space with this homeless man—or with the homeless, since he stands in for the group here—becomes more dangerous, especially with his carrying a golf club, an object that simultaneously suggests phallic power and class usurpation. For audiences, Marisol's attempts to distance herself from this homeless man are perfectly justified and, perhaps, not aggressive enough. When he says, "I could turn you into one of me," his language suggests a terrifying thought: the erasure of the existential distance between the homeless and the middle-class.[32] During its opening scene, *Marisol,* then, thematizes attitudes toward the homeless that echo what Mayor Koch was advocating in his propaganda. Intrusion, threat, and madness become synonymous with homelessness.

Conclusions like these are, most likely, compounded during the encounters that follow. After Marisol escapes the subway, she finds herself listening to the screaming, lamenting voices through the walls of her Bronx apartment. One of them belongs to a woman who threatens to get a gun and shoot everyone in the building because her boyfriend, Mathew, has cheated on her. Making good on her promise, this woman returns to Marisol's door by mistake and is only prevented from firing inside by the Angel who again intercedes on Marisol's behalf. The next day, Marisol is nearly assaulted in her Manhattan office by another anonymous man looking for back-pay for his acting in *Taxi Driver,* an apt reference point given the moral bankruptcy and the preponderance of violence in *Marisol.* This time, it is June, Marisol's friend and coworker who intercedes and who best defines this nightmarish city: "There's a prevailing sickness out there, I'm telling you, the Dark Ages are here, Visigoths are climbing the city walls, and I've never felt more like raw food in my life."[33] The abiding question considering Rivera's remarks about homelessness is how does the opening scene relate to this prevailing sickness? Certainly, the initial encounter is of a kind with what follows: sudden and irrational violence has become the norm in this city. Metonymically, the first scene defines homelessness as a part of the whole, suggesting that homelessness, violence, and criminality are common threats to civilization. More noteworthy is the suggestion, which emerges structurally, that the homeless may be the defining cause of this prevailing sickness of this city. Since the scene with Marisol and Man with Golf Club occurs first, it invites audiences to construct a narrative about this city, a narrative that begins with the intrusion and menace of the homeless into the voyeur's tidy world and extends through incidents of appalling violence. Surely, audience sympathy is with Marisol, a woman threatened by a deranged homeless man. In any case, the first act of *Marisol* suggests that homelessness is either symptom or source of this prevailing sickness.

But this narrative, which justifies apathy or even malice toward the homeless, is exactly what *Marisol* intends to challenge. Rivera's dramaturgy invokes the assumptions of the voyeur, initially through the title character, in order to interrogate them, to show how they endorse self-serving apprehensions on urban life. This begins with making visible the assumptions behind the tidy world, something that occurs through the doubling of the first encounter with another from the beginning of act two. When the lights come up on the second act, Marisol has escaped yet another near-assault, this one by June's brother Lenny, with a golf club that she now carries as she stands alone on a street that she does not recognize. When the Woman with Furs, a well-dressed and confused-looking woman, enters, Marisol tentatively approaches. When Marisol asks "*Where the hell are we?*" and describes the landmarks now missing (a school, a bodega), the Woman with Furs speaks "as if in a trance": "God help you, you get in my face" (original emphasis).[34] Her words are exactly the same as those spoken by Marisol during the opening encounter. When Marisol continues to describe what is wrong with this landscape—lack of cars, noise, police—the Woman with Furs again echoes, precisely, the language from the first scene: "I have no money." Clearly, Rivera intends for the encounters to be read against each other. During the first, Marisol's words were perfectly logical for her situation: confronted by a homeless man who may become a threat, she tried to distance herself from him. But in this later scene, the responses of the Woman with Furs are *non-sequiturs*: they do not match the situation at all. As it becomes clear soon thereafter, this woman mistakes Marisol for a homeless person and is afraid that Marisol will attack her with the golf club. But this "explanation" only adds to the dissonance between language and situation for audiences who have watched—and probably sympathized with—Marisol for a full act and know that she presents no threat.

Alienated[35] by this doubling, the Woman with Furs's reaction becomes something open to and perhaps even requiring inquiry. Most noteworthy is the question of why she reacts this way. The way she delivers her lines, as if in a trance, suggests that the attitudes themselves are something that she had been conditioned to accept, in this case, based on how homelessness is defined in the city. It is the Woman with Furs who brings the news that the city's response to the homeless crisis is criminalization: "Homelessness is against the law in the city. I'm going to have you . . . arrested!"[36] In this legislation, the most overt reference to Ed Koch's campaign against the homeless, emerges the municipal authority's efforts to define who has authority over and access to public space. As Cresswell argues about Koch's efforts regarding Grand Central Station, this legislation conflates the crimes associated with the homeless with being homeless itself: that is, the homeless do not pose a threat simply because of the bad things that they do (like attack women on the subway) but instead are bad because they are homeless. Inherently, this condition is menacing to the tidy world of those like the Woman with Furs because it confronts voyeurs with what they do not want to acknowledge: the problems of the city. Consequently, legislation emerges to define and defend a normative landscape that excludes the homeless. No wonder the Woman with Furs reacts to Marisol with the same language used during the earlier scene: she has been conditioned to believe that the homeless are inherently threatening and that rewards are forthcoming for her help in outlawing the homeless: "I'll get big points for that."[37] Read without the menace from the earlier scene, this encounter with the homeless (here, Marisol) demonstrates how sociality and spatiality have become ideologically imbricated. But this works both ways: the later scene rereads the earlier scene, so that Marisol's reactions *before* she is attacked emerge from the same assumptions as that of the Woman with Furs. Reading and rereading one another, *Marisol's* scenes define a dialectic engagement for audiences, involving acts one and two, sociality and spatiality, play and city.

Another notable question that emerges from this encounter involving the Woman with Furs is this: what are the consequences of such conditioning? Like the former question, this one is answered dialectically, that is, by reading scenes alongside each other. Toward the end of the scene the Woman with Furs and Marisol are joined by Scar Tissue. Another homeless man, he is covered in bandages and in a wheelchair, and his presence reveals the consequences of the tidy world. The Woman with Furs says nothing about the (slightly comic) pathos of this figure; in fact, it is his arrival that triggers her announcement about the criminalization of homelessness before she runs off-stage. The irony here is palpable: the reason that this woman is well dressed is that she had been on her way to *Les Miserables* before getting lost. Although eager to see the adaptation of Victor Hugo's novel, she cannot or will not recognize the misery of someone like Scar Tissue, suggesting that denial is necessary to sustaining her tidy world. But this is just what Marisol confronts during this scene. Alone with Marisol, Scar Tissue reveals his horribly burned skin and tells its story: "I vaguely remember the sounds of goose-stepping teenagers from Staten Island with a can of gasoline shouting orders in German."[38] Marisol makes the connection, for audiences, to the opening scene when Scar Tissue talks about being hounded everywhere he went, so he decided to sleep in the park. "Van Cortlandt Park?" she asks, remembering the words of the Man with Golf Club.[39] What may have sounded like rambling about skinheads, immolation, and credit cards during the earlier scene becomes, with visual confirmation in the body of Scar Tissue, the brutal truth. More notably, after Scar Tissue tells his story, he and Marisol witness a skinhead chase, catch, and immolate another homeless person right on stage—an undeniable atrocity right in front of them. With this doubled scene come a number of dialectical conclusions about the prevailing sickness in this city. Though Marisol cannot yet accept the implications of this dialectic, it nevertheless suggests how act two introduces a counternarrative about the homeless and the city.

Sick of the Homelessness

What Marisol cannot accept, at least at the opening of the second act, goes to the play's indictment of Koch's New York City. The attacks on Scar Tissue, Man with Golf Club, and the anonymous homeless person are much more than random incidents of violence by skinheads. Instead, they are one front in a systematic campaign of intimidation, discrimination, and even genocide against the homeless in this nightmarish city. Originally, these attacks were occurring in Van Cortlandt Park, in the Bronx, which is depicted in *Marisol* as a ghetto—derelict buildings, tenement apartments—far away from the experience of the voyeur living in Manhattan. Now, these attacks are occurring, with increasing audacity, in the streets of Manhattan and Brooklyn. Become grotesque attempts to "police" public spaces of New York City, if only by default since there are no police in this world, these attacks serve some end beyond terrorizing the homeless. They are making the city "safe" for voyeurs like Woman with Furs by destroying that which disturbs their tidy world. Clearly, the rules of civilization have not only been suspended in Rivera's dramatic world, they have been thoroughly inverted. After Marisol leaves Scar Tissue, trying to get to Brooklyn to find June, she discovers a second front that corroborates this campaign. Overcome by hunger, she begins rummaging through garbage dumpsters and finds some moldy French fries but is stopped before eating them by the voice of Lenny, June's brother. "Don't eat anything from that pile," he warns, "Man who owned the restaurant on the other side of that wall put rat poison in the trash to discourage the homeless from picking through the pile."[40] Less appalling perhaps, this front is still of a kind with immolating the homeless. Beginning from the premise that public space must be defended, poisoning the garbage reveals, at best, disregard and, at worst, contempt for the lives of the homeless. As Lenny says, "God bless the child that's got his own, huh?"[41] What these two fronts have in common, then, is twofold: that the homeless are a problem for the city rather than of the city and that this problem merely requires ridding the landscape of the homeless. And this leads to the third front, which complements the first two, the city's criminalization of homelessness.

In this last front *Marisol* suggests the more disturbing conclusion about this campaign, namely, that it is sanctioned by municipal authority. Much like the Woman with Furs, whose hostility toward Scar Tissue and Marisol comes from the city's criminalizing homelessness, the shopkeepers and skinheads derive their mandate from the city. Evidence for this conclusion in *Marisol* abounds, but comes from Lenny after the encounter near the garbage dumpster. It should be acknowledged that Lenny is pregnant during act two, a condition that leaves Marisol bewildered and that suggests further questions about Mel Gussow's definition of "the norm" in Rivera's play. In any event, after the baby is stillborn, he leads Marisol to a Brooklyn sidewalk that doubles as a cemetery for the homeless, another dialectical reading, this one of space itself (more in next section). After moving slabs of sidewalk, Lenny says, "The city provides these coffins. There are numbers on them. The city knows how we live."[42] Here, the city is implicated in the moral bankruptcy of what is happening to the homeless. Knowing about the homeless being set on fire or poisoned and only supplying the means of obfuscating the consequences suggests that the city endorses the skinheads' and shopkeepers' actions. In fact, burying the homeless under sidewalks is a perfect complement to the premise of defending a tidy world: out of sight, out of mind. Better evidence of the city's responsibility, however, comes through the "huge ugly windowless building with the smokestacks and armed guards" that Marisol encounters while visiting June's apartment in act one.[43] Answers about what it is vary from "where they bring overthrown brutal right-wing dictators from Latin America" to "a federally funded torture center where they violate people who have gone over their credit card limit." But what is important is that the Woman with Furs was detained there and links the criminalization of the homeless with the building, so when she shoots Marisol, this official building becomes antecedent and authorizing symbol of the antagonism. Notably, Marisol senses something of such conclusions long before her foray into the city, as suggested by her question for the Angel in act one: "Why are they planning to drop human insecticide on overpopulated areas of the Bronx?"[44]

The answer to this question gestures toward Rivera's apprehension about the "rules of civilization" being suppressed during the 1980s in New York City. The city's proposed gassing of Bronx ghettos, the shopkeepers poisoning their garbage, the neo-Nazi skinheads immolating the homeless—all become overwhelming evidence for a most disturbing conclusion. The city depicted in *Marisol* is governed, literally and figuratively, by an ethos of exclusionary violence. Already implicit in the legislation against the homeless, this ethos becomes explicit in the diatribe by one of the skinheads toward the end of the play: "Look at this goddamn thing, this waste, this fucking parasite," snarls the skinhead, indicating Marisol, who is sleeping next to Lenny, "God, I'm sick of it. Sick of the eyesores. Sick of the diseases. Sick of the drugs. Sick of the homelessness. Sick of the border babies. Sick of the dark skin."[45] This litany begins from and perpetuates a conservative ideological definition grounded firmly in dichotomy. Defined from a privileged (distinctly white, middle to upper class) sociality, the spatiality of New York must be defended against the intrusion and threat of anything deemed "out of place." Difference becomes deviance in this ideology: "if you people want to kill yourselves, fine, do it," continues the skinhead, in a growing frenzy of indignation against anything that threatens conservative notions of society: "kill yourselves with your crack and your incest and your promiscuity and your homo anal intercourse . . . just leave me to take care of myself and my own." Notably, the skinhead's litany is not appreciably different in connotation from Koch's propaganda about the homeless in Grand Central Station.[46] Ideology, geography, and epistemology converge *in* and *about* the urban landscape of New York City, a public realm that endorses the particular worldview of the voyeur. That this social dichotomy is grounded in the spatial is evident from the skin-head's plea, "*I mean, why can't they just go AWAY?*" and her longing: "Leave me to my gardens" (original emphasis).[47] Determination to regain this pastoral vision, paradoxically, sanctions brutal force to protect the tidy world and punish threats to that world: "Stay still so I can burn you!" says the skinhead when Marisol wakes up and resists.

Certainly Rivera's use of Nazi skinheads to represent the hostility toward threats of difference and deviance in *Marisol* indulges in hyperbole and approaches the truism that many, like Bonnie Marranca, have argued often shortchanges meaningful debate about social justice in contemporary drama.[48] This is especially true when the Nazi in *Marisol* turns out to be June, who suffered head trauma after being attacked by Lenny toward the end of act one and "ended up torching half the city!"[49] But Rivera is not, primarily, suggesting moral equivalency between Nazism and middle-class perceptions, or between fascism and Koch's campaign against the homeless— though surely something of this comes across during production. Rivera's use of the Nazi here and throughout the play is more method than conclusion, specifically, a way of *magnifying*[50] the crisis of urbanism in the 1980s. In fact, *Marisol* employs a number of magnifications (angelic sieges of heaven, ecological catastrophe, fascists with gas cans) to demonstrate almost expressionistically how the rules of civilization have been suppressed and what the effect might be. When these rules collapse, the play argues, the immolation of the homeless not only becomes possible in the cultural imagination of these New Yorkers but perhaps becomes the (il)logical end of criminalizing the homeless. The language used by June-as-Nazi, after all, speaks to the assumptions underlying the preservation of a normative landscape, if not the specific means of defending this landscape in *Marisol.* When read, again dialectically, against the treatment of the homeless, Rivera's play discloses the ideological battle for control of public space that was invisible because it appeared natural. Of particular interest is what is revealed about the prevailing sickness of the city when contrasted with the Nazi's diatribe. The echoing of the word "sick" over and over links this ideology with what has brought the city to the "rim of the apocalypse," as Marisol laments during act two: the appalling failure of moral and political authority toward the present and the future of the city.[51]

Worth noting, too, is that the Nazi's diatribe makes explicit what has remained mostly implied in this argument so far: how homelessness corresponds, metonymically, with identity politics. The litany of affronts rehearsed is not limited to the homeless but includes immigrants, minorities, and homosexuals, among others. "Diseases," "homelessness," and "border babies" are conflated as uniformly odious transgressions against her tidy world. Most significant for the play would be ethnicity, something that Marisol struggles with frequently. Jon Rossini has already discussed this topic thoroughly,[52] including the definition of the Nuyorican as "a lived identity emerging out of the harsh realities of underclass life in an urban barrio."[53] Adding to Rossini, I would further emphasize that the abuse of the Nuyorican is distinctly spatialized, mostly through ghettoization, and thus offers a corollary to the exclusion of the homeless in *Marisol*. As Nuyorican, Marisol lives in the Bronx ghetto that is invoked, in the play, metonymically through the boarded-up and broken windows in the brick wall that runs the length of the backstage wall and through the crime and violence in scene three, when Marisol is nearly gunned down in her apartment. Crowded into impoverished conditions, the Nuyorican individual or family is already on the margins of society and is therefore particularly vulnerable to homelessness with the federal cuts to Housing and Urban Development (HUD)[54] and to gentrification campaigns in the 1980s. Beyond these conditions suggested in *Marisol* is the open hostility toward ethnic difference evident most clearly, prior to the Nazi's diatribe, in the Woman with Furs's response to Marisol. Much of her hostility during the scene already discussed stems from her assumption that Marisol is homeless; but, when Scar Tissue joins the two women, the Woman with Furs shouts, "This brown piece of shit is mine! *I'm* going to turn her in! Not you!" (original emphasis).[55] Though she quickly turns her hostility toward Scar Tissue as well, this initial response reveals how ethnic difference compounds the threat of the homeless. Rivera's New York City, then, is a landscape that is vehemently divided along and defended against ethnic as well as socioeconomic lines.

Divisions inscribed in the landscape, moreover, correspond with divisions in Marisol's identity. However implicitly, she understands that her Nuyorican heritage makes her "out of place" at her Manhattan job and, to a lesser extent, with her Brooklyn friends. But she wrongly believes, when she decides to move in with June toward the end of act one, that she can simply leave her ethnicity behind when she moves out of the Bronx. In her thinking, a new apartment in Brooklyn translates to a new identity in New York City. In effect, she accepts and intends to assimilate herself into the dichotomy underlying the tidy world by embracing her middle-class job and education at the expense of her ethnicity and others like her living in the Bronx. When confronted by her simulacral death—the murder of another woman named Marisol Perez—she rehearses her middle-class background as if to ward off association with this "other" Marisol Perez: "Fordham—English major—Phi Betta Kappa—I went into science publishing—I became head copywriter."[56]

Her conclusion, "I'm clean," anticipates the disapproval of immigrants as diseased by the Nazi in act two. She is trying to convince herself that she is "clean" of any remnant of ethnic difference from those like June, but she cannot escape her heritage. "I lived in the Bronx—I commuted light-years to this other planet called—Manhattan! I learned new vocabularies... wore weird native dress... mastered arcane rituals."[57] The discourse of anthropology invoked here reinforces how different she felt, with her Puerto Rican ancestry, in New York City. And what she adds after this suggests how painful the process of assimilation was to her: "amputated neat sections of my psyche, my cultural heritage." She admits here, though only briefly, how thoroughly she has internalized the social and spatial demarcations between those who belong and those who do not. Trying to hide this, from others and herself, she adds, "with no pain expressed at all—none!—but so much pain inside I almost choked on it... so far deep inside my Manhattan bosses and Manhattan friends never even suspected." This admission foreshadows the play's ending, but Marisol cannot bring herself to accept the truth here, in part because she remains invested in the allure of the American Dream and in part because what she—like audiences—faces is a daunting epiphany about the city.

What Hope, What Possibility

This epiphany is not the personal epiphany of humanism but rather a distinctly political epiphany about the nature of the city and civilization in *Marisol* that unfolds through competing narratives on homelessness: that it represents a threat to the tidy world and that the homeless are especially threatened by the tidy world. This tension between narrative and counternarrative is evident from the beginning of the play, even before the encounter between Marisol and the Man with Golf Club. In what Rossini describes as the first "scenic image" of *Marisol*, audiences are confronted[58] by the landscape of this city: a brick wall "running the width of the stage and going as high as the theatre will allow."[59] Windows in the wall are covered with iron bars or are boarded up, suggesting the dilapidated Bronx tenement where Marisol lives and a sense of the city slowly collapsing on itself. Additionally, there is graffiti on the wall, the first five lines of which read as follows:

> The moon carries the souls of dead people to heaven.
> The new moon is dark and empty.
> It fills up every month
> with new glowing souls
> then carries its silent burden to God.[60]

While hinting at something of the tragedy unfolding in this city, these lines obfuscate the harsh truth that will come onto the stage during the following acts through language suggesting both euphemism (the souls filling the moon are "glowing" and on their way to God) and naturalness (the process is cyclical, recurring every month). In any event, nothing has occurred in *Marisol* as yet that would suggest the atrocity simultaneously described and denied here. But the last two words, written in another hand and much larger than the rest, are intrusive: "WAKE UP." This irruption in the graffiti-poem and from the urban environment defines itself (the nonspecific reference is intended here, continuing the play's emphasis on dialectical reading: poem *and* play, wall *and* city) as a palimpsest "text" in need of exegesis.

Emphasized by lighting against an otherwise darkened stage, both wall and graffiti become focal points in what Susan Bennett defines as "hypothesis-building." In Bennett's theory, audiences construct silent and subconscious hypotheses about what is unfolding before them during the play, guesses "which are subsequently substantiated, revised, or negated" by what follows.[61] When audiences consider the wall, with its boarded and barred windows, they probably hypothesize a particular space as the play's locale: some run-down or abandoned urban quarter. In this case, hypothesis building serves the play's exposition by helping to establish the nature of the Bronx in the play. When audiences consider the graffiti, though, their hypotheses are probably more complicated. Without consideration of content, graffiti signals the ongoing struggle for control of urban spaces, the traces of a battle over public space.[62] Consideration of the graffiti's content suggests an almost ideological struggle between the official story of this city (order and nature) and a subversive story (outrage and rebellion) in the last lines. Signaling angry and anonymous authorship, these lines resist—and call for resistance to—the hegemonic narrative of the rest of the poem. In this case, the hypothesis building serves *Marisol's* sociospatial ambition by demonstrating the ongoing contestation in New York City long before the particulars of this contestation come on stage. Within the graffiti is the fundamental tension between narrative and counternarrative that, first of all, prepares audiences, subconsciously, for representations of the homeless and the tidy world of the voyeur that follow. Just as significantly, the tension between these narratives is already defined as distinctly spatial: the contestation within the graffiti-poem, as in the play, will play out *in* and *about* public space of this New York City. This is true in both the argument made in the graffiti (the demand that audiences "WAKE UP") and the act of writing the graffiti (spatializing this necessary epiphany). This opening scene invites audiences toward a dialectical reading of the city that will revise, negate, and finally substantiate an argument about homelessness.

In many ways, this "scenic image" puts audiences of *Marisol* in much the same position as the title character: they must confront the appalling truths of this city to understand how, by whom, and why the "rules of civilization" have been suppressed. The dramaturgical structure of *Marisol* builds on this premise. The first half of the play invites audiences toward the narrative of the homeless as intrusion or threat, beginning with the encounter with the Man with Golf Club and extending through the violence of the first act. Marisol's decision to move in with June, because they have "install[ed] metal detectors in all the buildings" on her block in Brooklyn emerges primarily from the impulse to separate herself from the city's problems.[63] And a perfectly logical impulse it seems, considering the prevailing sickness. But this narrative of the tidy world is negated and revised structurally by what happens in act two: the encounter with Scar Tissue, Marisol's discovery of the poisoned garbage, her understanding that comes from the sidewalk-cemetery where the most "fragile" of the street people are buried. Of particular note for discussing how audiences are situated in relation to this political epiphany is how Scar Tissue connects events unfolding in the play back to the lines of the graffiti poem, which, in some productions, remain against the backstage wall throughout the play.[64] Toward the end of his time on stage, he recites the language of the poem, now in prose, to Marisol: "And did you know the moon carries the souls of dead people up to Heaven?"[65] Reciting the first five lines, with minor interpolations, Scar Tissue stops short of "WAKE UP"—probably because his very presence, scarred and traumatized, expresses its own demand for audiences to "WAKE UP." Repeated through Scar Tissue, the language of complacency and euphemism becomes hollow and ironic, drawing attention to what is producing all those souls that fill up the moon rather than the assurance of "glowing" souls going to heaven. The ambition here is to make audiences confront what Marisol describes after he leaves: "my intellectual detachment—my ability to read about the misery of the world and not lose a moment out of my busy day."[66]

But recognition is not enough for Rivera's political play. The effort to make audiences "WAKE UP" to this calamity of urbanism is coupled with the discourse of praxis throughout *Marisol*. During scene four, immediately following the scenes where Marisol is nearly shot in her apartment, the Angel tells her of the impending assault on heaven. "The universal body is sick" because "God is old and dying and taking the rest of us with Him."[67] Sickness as a theme is verbalized for the first time here, connecting June's comments about the "prevailing sickness" and her later remarks, as a Nazi, about being "sick" of anything aberrant to failure of authority and responsibility in this god. So the angels will lay siege to the heavens, "And that's what you have to do, Marisol. You have to fight. You can't *endure* anymore" (original emphasis).[68] But Marisol cannot even think of rebelling, at this point, because she is too invested in the middle class. This imperative toward action recurs during the next scene, this time expressed by June: "Don't let them catch you not ready, okay? You gotta be prepared to really *fight* now!" (original emphasis).[69] Although Marisol links this remark with the Angel's warning, she still cannot bring herself to reject what she takes for granted: that her privilege as a middle-class woman is well earned and not at the expense of others. She cannot face the truth until after the cemetery and the names of those destroyed by the narrative of the tidy world. After that, she becomes the one rallying others, including audiences, toward resistance and rebellion: "We're going to find the angels," she informs Lenny and June, "And then we're going to join them. Then we're going to fight with the angels."[70] *Marisol* thematizes, in other words, the engagement that it hopes to produce through this discourse of resistance that builds toward its crescendo. When the Woman with Furs reappears, says "We can't have upheaval at the drop of a hat," and then shoots Marisol, the choice between narrative and counternarrative becomes stark and necessary.[71]

Ultimately, *Marisol*'s conclusion provides what resembles a Hegelian synthesis of narrative/counternarrative about city and homelessness. After a brief blackout followed by "strange light" bathing the stage, representing Marisol's death and rebirth, Marisol becomes witness to the battle between angels and god throughout the universe. She initially describes this battle in ways that blend metaphysical and urban concerns: "Galaxies spring from a single drop of angel's sweat while hundred of armies fight and die on the fingertips of children in the Bronx."[72] And, she suggests that the rebellion nears failure before a single homeless person comes on stage and begins "*angrily throwing rocks at the sky.*"[73] Then comes this marvelous description: "then, as if one body, one mind, the innocent of the earth take to the streets with anything they can find—rocks, sticks, screams—and aim their displeasure at the senile sky and fire into the tattered wind on the side of the angels... billions of poor, of homeless, of peaceful, of silent, of angry... fighting and fighting as no species has ever fought before."[74] Instead of menace to the voyeur's tidy world or victim of the normative assumptions thereof, the homeless become a rallying point for action to rescue this city—and perhaps any city—from the rim of the apocalypse. When the Woman with Furs shoots Marisol moments earlier, she unintentionally foments the very rebellion that city fathers, locked away in the nightmarish edifice in Brooklyn, intended to forestall. This powerful imagery of collective agency clearly suggests the end that *Marisol* hopes for, if not the means of accomplishing it: throwing out those responsible for the prevailing sickness. After the battle ends, the triumphant Angel appears next to Marisol and holds a golden crown out toward audiences while Marisol gives voice to "the first day of the new history" that unfolds from this moment forward: "What light. What possibilities. What hope."[75] All that remains for this future to be possible is for audiences to fight for it.

Where Homophobia Wins Elections

During the 1992 London production of *Millennium Approaches,* the first part of *Angels in America,* Tony Kushner made a comment about the two-part epic that would go on to garner so much acclaim: *Angels in America* was, he told Adam Mars-Jones, "about New York."[76] The London production was the third production of either part of *Angels in America.* The premiere had been at the now-defunct Eureka Theater in San Francisco in 1991, with *Millennium Approaches* receiving a full production and *Perestroika,* a work in progress,[77] receiving a staged reading. The following year, the two parts played together at the Mark Taper Forum in Los Angeles, to considerable if not complete enthusiasm.[78] A New York production was in-the-works during the London interview and would take place in 1993 at the Walter Kerr Theatre with the two parts playing in repertory. It was this production, in fact, that solidified *Angels in America* as the achievement not just of the year but of the decade.[79] Significantly, it was Mars-Jones's question about the lack of any New York production, to date, that prompted Kushner's comment on the play's topic. Worthy of consideration, this comment seemingly runs counter to the epic scope of *Angels in America,* which goes well beyond New York City, or any city for that matter, in its dramatization of the tragedy of AIDS during the 1980s. First of all, Kushner's remark never limits the play's concerns to New York City. Later in this interview, Kushner talks about AIDS and the gay community, and Ronald Reagan's administration and conservatism in the United States, especially the callousness of the administration's response—if "response" is the right word—to the epidemic. Elsewhere, Kushner talks about Mormonism, socialism, and history, all of which inform *Angels in America.* As reviews observed, the ambition of *Angels in America* is breathtakingly vast: moving between New York City and Salt Lake City, between Harper's hallucination of Antarctica and Prior's experience of heaven.[80]

The natural follow-up is clear: how is *Angels in America* "about" New York? It was not necessary for Mar-Jones to ask the follow-up since Kushner directly includes New York City in the conservatism of the 1980s: "in New York . . . homophobia can win you elections."[81] He never clarifies this remark by implicating specific levels of government, any more than Rivera does when talking of homelessness in *Marisol.* Instead, Kushner defends his indictment of New York City through contrast with San Francisco, which he defines as "the most 'gay positive'" of "all the places" he has known.[82] "It's a city where the gay and lesbian community wields an enormous amount of political power, where homophobia is simply no longer acceptable in the general political discourse." In this way, Kushner defines New York City (and San Francisco, for that matter) as a nexus for political and ideological contestation, where identity politics is not merely "public" but increasingly contested in public space. If San Francisco represents a city where contestation is now a reality, where different voices make themselves heard, then New York City represents that city where contestation has become necessary. Not just New York City alone, of course, but instead New York City as metonym for Ronald Reagan's United States. In this definition of New York City is some explanation about the deliberate delaying of the New York production: Kushner was worried—unnecessary, it turned out—about the critical and public reception of a play that confronts audiences with the often brutal reality of AIDS—in Prior's body—and the callousness of Reagan's conservatives—in Roy Cohn, the closeted and self-hating gay. Rightly or wrongly, Kushner believed that San Francisco was a more "congenial place" for the play and sounded almost relieved when San Francisco's American Conservatory Theater (ACT) mounted a revival in 1994. "I wrote the play for San Francisco . . . and it was important to me that it play [in] San Francisco."[83]

In such remarks about New York City and San Francisco emerge a number of intriguing conclusions about the dramaturgy behind *Angels in America*. Despite addressing wide-ranging concerns about politics and philosophy, religion and history, Kushner grounds many of these concerns in New York City. This suggests Kushner's recognition of how definitions of inclusion and prohibition, writ large in the national imagination during the 1980s, were most intensively felt in urban environments. Evidence of this comes from the references made by Kushner when talking about *Angels in America* during interviews. As he has done elsewhere,[84] Kushner cites ACT UP, the New York-based activist organization with the mandate of confronting the AIDS crisis through civil disobedience in the urban landscape, when commenting on *Angels in America*. In so doing, Kushner suggests the common ambitions of the activist movement, of which he was a part, and his play: both bring attention to the plight of the homosexual community by using the urban environment as ways of challenging the status quo and raising consciousness. Another common reference made by Kushner, during the 1992 interview and elsewhere, is to the Stonewall Riots of 1969: "when all these drag queens refused to be arrested and taken out of a bar—the beginning of the gay liberation movement in the States."[85] Not organized activism like ACT UP, the riots were nevertheless a defining example of civil disobedience playing out in and about the urban environment of New York during a time when closeting was a way of life for many gays and lesbians. As ways of locating *Angels in America* in the history of contestation around gay rights and politics, ACT UP and Stonewall suggest much about how Kushner's play is "about" New York City during the 1980s: it registers and represents the need for contestation during a cynical decade when homophobia, disguised as "family values," became mainstream. Beyond this, the subtext of ACT UP and Stonewall rioting informs the sociospatial ambitions of *Angels in America* considered here: all three prompted or pursued questions about authority over or access to public space (geography) and public realm (politics, ideology).

Defined succinctly, the sociospatial ambitions of *Angels in America* involve dramatizing the inscription and transgression of ideological demarcation in urban environments, specifically about homosexuality and AIDS, but possibly about anyone called aberrant by conservatism.[86] Kushner pursues these ambitions through thematic and structural juxtaposition of three cities: New York City, San Francisco, and Salt Lake City. Hardly mentioned yet, Salt Lake City proves integral to the following discussion because it epitomizes a landscape deeply imbricated with ideological values for those who have lived or are, at the beginning of the play, living there: Joe and Harper Pitt, and Hannah Pitt and Ella Chapter. Since this environment is so important to the sociospatial ambitions of *Angels in America,* this section begins with extended discussion of this city left behind as part of the travels to New York. Just as significant is San Francisco, even though this city enters the play only through description (Belize's paean in *Perestroika*) and by implication (the heaven visited by Prior in *Perestroika*) and as destination (for Harper's flight at the play's conclusion). Nevertheless, San Francisco demonstrates the possibilities inherit in transgression: of violating and overcoming the ideological values inscribed in the landscape, as a reflection of cultural values of the time, a city that epitomizes what radical postmodernism has long advocated.[87] Between these two is New York City, where most of the play occurs but an urban locale that should be read against these others because the contestation ongoing there—for Joe, Harper, and Hannah, who receive the bulk of the consideration here—is defined between these poles: both a city where norms of conservatism are enforced and a city where the liberation of transgression is possible. Considering how these characters interrogate the landscape and themselves, illustrates how the play is "about" New York. I do not intend to reduce all of *Angels in America* to this reading but instead shed new light on the play's concerns with urbanism. In many ways, *Angels in America* epitomizes the sociospatial ambitions theorized here, but is never subsumed by them.

The Godliest Place on Earth

Nearly two acts of *Millennium Approaches* are completed before Kushner locates a scene in Salt Lake City and there are, ultimately, only two such scenes. Nevertheless, this city figures prominently in the play's sociospatial ambitions because of what it suggests about the interplay of geography, ideology, and identity in the urban environment. The second of these scenes (the first is considered in the next section) opens with Sister Ella Chapter and Hannah Pitt standing on the balcony of Hannah's home overlooking a canyon in Utah. "Look at the view," Chapter says, taking a deep breath and offering her thoughts about Salt Lake City, "A view of heaven. Like the living city of heaven, isn't it, it just fairly glimmered in the sun."[88] Notably less sanguine than her friend, Hannah initially ignores Chapter's enthusiasm but when pressed she reveals the impetus beyond this scene in her gentle rebuke: "It's just Salt Lake, and you're selling the house *for* me, not *to* me" (original emphasis).[89] The conversation continues with discussion of their friendship, the housing market being off, and the wonder of the Mormon city, but never Hannah's reason for selling: the telephone call from her son, Joe, in Central Park during which he confesses his homosexuality (more below). Of particular note about this scene is that Kushner seems less interesting in audiences seeing the geography of Salt Lake City than by illustrating the epistemology of those living there. He withholds details about the city by playing the scene with a rather traditional style: both characters either facing or turned away from audiences and discussing the environment of the city below. (It should be noted that in the 1993 production at the Walter Kerr, Wolfe and designer Robin Wagner filled in some details by using backscreen projections of Salt Lake City—along with New York, San Francisco, and Antarctica.[90]) Dramaturgically, Kushner filters the urban environment through the alternating perspectives of Chapter and Hannah rather than having them move through the city. In this way, Kushner depicts Salt Lake City as a confluence of geography, ideology, and history in Mormonism.

The history of Mormonism's influence on *Angels in America* has already been considered, thoroughly, by David Savran and Michael Austin,[91] and needs only a brief summary here. After leaving New York, under the leadership of Joseph Smith and, following his death, Brigham Young, Mormons made a long, difficult journey west toward the undiscovered country of Utah. Along the way, they found themselves hounded when they tried to settle, most appallingly in Missouri, where the governor "decreed that they must be 'exterminated' or expelled from the state."[92] When they arrived on the shores of Salt Lake, the city they founded would be infused by the same premise of Frederick Jackson Turner's frontier thesis—renewal, rebirth, and regeneration—though inflected with dense layers of theology. More significant than the history itself, for this argument, is how this history became encoded in the landscape of Salt Lake City. In *Senses of Place,* Miriam Kahn argues that "places capture the complex emotional, behavioral, and moral relationships between people and their territory. They represent people, their actions, and their interactions and as such become malleable memorials."[93] Nowhere is this more evident than Salt Lake City, where the landscape is interspersed with monuments meant to mythologize Mormon history. Along with Joseph Smith and Brigham Young Monuments, there are the Seagull Monument, the Mormon Pioneer Monument, the Eagle Gate Monument.[94] Such memorials inscribe the history of Mormonism in the city itself and help define Mormon spiritual life. They continually remind those living there of where they come from and *who they are,* an instance where geography, history, and ideology converge. No wonder Chapter cannot help rhapsodizing about the wonder of Salt Lake City, the "godliest place on earth."[95] As Kahn argues, "The landscape surrounds the people with a sense of shared history rooted in the past and memorialized in the present through shared symbols. It provides a focus for feelings of common identity as well as a charter for moral action."[96] This point is telling in *Angels in America,* since Salt Lake City was imagined according to a distinctly utopian historiography.[97]

How much of this background is apparent during production is debatable, particularly since the stage directions never call for dramatizing any of the landscape of Salt Lake City. But the scene between Chapter and Hannah nevertheless defines the key element of Kushner's Salt Lake City: the utopianism imbricating this city. Although Chapter admits performing some of her enthusiasm as part of her sales pitch when confronted by Hannah's no-nonsense demeanor, she feels a profound sense of belonging in Salt Lake City that represents the attitude among the Mormons envisioned in the play. Hannah's unresponsiveness toward the view or the city is marked as being out of character for Mormons. In the final moments of this short scene Chapter reminds her of how Mormons define themselves through the city by invoking its description as the "home of the saints" and its promise as "the spring of sweet water in the desert, the desert flower."[98] This definition stands in stark contrast with her description of New York, "All they got there is tiny rooms," which suggests both confinement and isolation.[99] Underlying the utopianism of Salt Lake City, then, is dichotomy: the definition of Mormon religion, society, and city as idealized like that new City on the Hill that may have supplied the impetus for the Mormon exodus from New York. Anything outside this city is potentially a threat to the city, as Chapter illustrates with her remarks: "Every step a Believer takes away from here is a step fraught with peril. I fear for you, Hannah."[100] This utopian closure, which is geographical and ideological, defines the limits of belief and belonging for Mormon society and suggests an analogy to the identity politics of 1980s United States. In adding "Stay put. This is the right home of saints," she not only repeats the utopian definition of Salt Lake City, she uses language strikingly similar to Edward Casey's argument that "staying in one place" proves integral to definition of place.[101] Staying put means protecting oneself from the world beyond this utopianism; it further suggests protecting the utopianism from the outside world.

Anyone Could Come By

But all this demands a question: why do Kushner's Mormons leave their sanctuary of Salt Lake City for the wilds of New York City? Like Joe and Harper, Hannah leaves this Mormon city, initially to help her son during his crisis of sexuality, but during the epilogue, some five years later, Hannah has settled into New York City. Why? Answering this question means addressing another question suggested during the conversation between these women: what sustains the utopianism of Salt Lake City in *Angels in America?* Between warning Hannah against New York and reminding her of the wonders of Salt Lake, Chapter offers her a cigarette and receives Hannah's pointed reprimand: "Not out here, anyone could come by."[102] Hannah rejects the cigarette not because she has deeply felt reservations about violating the Mormon prohibition against tobacco. In fact, she takes a furtive drag a second later. Instead, Hannah admonishes Chapter for this public indiscretion—they are standing on her balcony—because of the possibility of *being seen violating* this prohibition. She knows full well that particular social behaviors—including Chapter's smoking, Harper's drug addiction, Joe's homosexuality—are not only prohibited under Mormon theology, these prohibitions are enforced through the communal, even panoptic, policing of public space. If someone from her Temple were to see her smoking, the news would surely work its way up the religious ladder until she were held accountable. Not an alarmist, Hannah nevertheless recognizes what Michel Foucault theorized in *Discipline and Punishment*: because she is continually visible, she is subject to authority, here, that of Mormonism. Just the possibility that they might be seen is enough to temper behavior, though not prohibit it altogether. Nevertheless, the public sphere of Salt Lake City includes the observation and regulation of social behavior, any transgression of which can be punished.

During this scene, Kushner introduces the sociospatial significance of Salt Lake City in *Angels in America*: the momentary transgression of Hannah and Chapter reveals the imbrication of geography and ideology within this urban environment. This city is encoded with ideology, derived from Mormon theology, which continually exerts pressure on citizens of Salt Lake City. If not already evident through the monuments that define the city as "place" for Mormons, this ideological encoding informs the urban planning of Salt Lake City. Like most Mormon cities, it is built on a grid that spirals away from the Temple located at the center of the city. Streets are numbered upward and directionally according to distance from the Temple: 100 East Street or 300 South Street (though streets can have honorary names: Rosa Parks or Martin Luther King). This grid establishes a legible landscape, one that can be easily negotiated by orienting oneself in relation to the landmark of the Temple. But this orientation is simultaneously geographical and ideological: Mormons moving through the city are always reminded by the street numbers of their distance—literal or figurative—from the heart of Mormon life. Of course, the scene between Hannah and Chapter does not include these details about Salt Lake City, though they could be suggested by the use of back-screen projections. Nevertheless, this confluence of geography and ideology certainly informs the scene. Hannah's initial reaction to the offered cigarette and her "Put it away now," after taking a drag, are clearly informed by her awareness that wherever they are in Salt Lake City, while in public, they are always under the scrutiny of Mormon theology. Part of the reason Hannah assumes that someone coming by would report their transgression is because public space in Salt Lake City is so imbricated with ideology that reminds citizens of their coordinates in Mormon society. Although Chapter transgresses during this scene, she may be more aware of the interplay of geography and ideology in Salt Lake City, as implied in her repeated definition of the city: "the right home of saints."

In this inscription of ideology in the urban environment begin to emerge answers to the questions posed about Salt Lake City in *Angels in America*. The utopianism loudly trumpeted by Chapter during the scene is sustained by the ideological demarcations and prohibitions within the city, which correspond with Cresswell's argument about normative landscapes. Ideology contributes to normativity in three complementary ways: it defines "(1) what exists and what does not exist; (2) what is good, just, and appropriate and what is not; and (3) what is possible and impossible."[103] A corollary to the demarcations of geography, which define the limits of where people can go, ideological demarcations define the limits of what they can believe or how they can behave. Anything deemed "out of place" in Mormon society is, at least theoretically, excised from the city. Instead of the connotations of freedom, diversity, or even civic forum, the public space in Kushner's Salt Lake City becomes the means of controlling citizens. It becomes a form of social ordering intended to control the "sin" that Chapter remarks is everywhere by defining it beyond not just questions of ethics, but further, epistemological possibility.

Admittedly, the cigarette is a minor transgression in the scheme of things, but the anxiety it induces suggests two things about the social ordering at work in Salt Lake City. First, it gestures toward transgressions far more serious, like Harper's addiction to valium or Joe's impulses toward homosexuality. This scene primarily defines transgression as a violation of social ordering instead of defining the nature of transgression. Second, the attention placed on such a minor transgression implies the necessity of exerting continual authority. Transgression of any kind threatens authority because it makes the demarcations questionable rather than naturalized. Underlying the utopianism[104] of Salt Lake City, then, is authoritarianism.

Conclusions like this are, admittedly, rather wide-reaching for this brief scene between Hannah and Chapter; but further evidence comes from the Mormon characters living in New York. Long before *Angels in America* begins Joe and Harper Pitt have left Salt Lake City, but to some degree, it never leaves them. During Joe's struggles with his burgeoning homosexuality, he demonstrates how deeply his identity politics was informed by his childhood. When confronted by Harper about his night walking, the truth of which she has already guessed, Joe cannot bring himself to even acknowledge his transgression, which has been only voyeuristic to this point.[105] Harper, too, evidences something of her childhood in Salt Lake City, though in different ways. Rather than holding fast to Mormon beliefs, she rebels against their surrogates in New York City: she becomes anxious about symbols of authority, such as the "schizophrenic traffic cop" on Atlantic Avenue, and indulges in drugs and hallucinations to escape reality.

Despite their competing reactions to the social ordering that informs their attitudes about sex, politics, and authority, Joe and Harper both evidence what Cresswell, drawing upon Gramsci, argues regarding people inhabiting normative landscapes: they develop "permanent *dispositions* embedded in their very bodies" toward the ideological values, or "doxa" (original emphasis).[106] In this, the authoritarianism of Salt Lake City is most potent because it defines its values as "natural" or "normal" so that they extend beyond spatial coordinates. Salt Lake City, in other words, informs how Joe and Harper read New York City. This is most evident during the argument when Harper tries to get Joe to admit what he is doing during his walks. When Joe uses words like "decent" and "correct," Harper interrupts: "No, no, not that, that's Utah talk."[107] The conflation of geography and theology epitomizes much about Salt Lake City. And it answers the original question about this city: the Mormons leave because Salt Lake City is "a hard place," as Hannah says, that "wears a body out."[108]

Defined as "Utah talk" during this scene, this social ordering of the urban environment is not limited to Salt Lake City in *Angels in America*. Instead, it demonstrates the process that Kushner saw happening across the United State during the 1980s: the exclusion of homosexuals, or anything deemed "out of place," from the normative landscape being constructed politically and rhetorically by the Reagan administration. In New York City and other cities across the United States are essentially the same ideological demarcations and prohibitions found in Salt Lake City. In *Angels in America*, Kushner provides this homophobia with a particularly cynical, though complicated, face in Roy Cohn. Stephens Bottoms has discussed the dramatization of the historical figure, including the biography that is telling here: Cohn's "life-long manipulation of legal and political power was directed toward ruthlessly reinforcing the conservative notion of American identity as something coherent and unified, built around the WASP-ish notions of individualism, capitalism, and family values."[109] I have little to add about Cohn, except to suggest that he provides the link between New York City defined by homophobia, despite his homosexuality, and Salt Lake City. Closeted and self-hating, Cohn not only epitomizes the consequence of the ideological mapping of the public sphere but further contributes directly to it. In *Angels in America*, he is the face of Reagan's conservatism, a secularization of what defined Salt Lake City. Salt Lake City, then, becomes Kushner's spatial equivalent of Bertolt Brecht's Thirty Years' War in *Mother Courage*: a way of defamiliarizing what is in front of audiences, in this case, the homophobia defining New York. The forces of conservatism represented in Cohn were creating a normative vision of America with agonizing consequences: the painful denial of self (Joe Pitt) and the appalling dismissal of crisis (the AIDS epidemic).

Transgress a Little, Joseph

Angels in America resists this vision of America, sociospatially, in complementary ways. The first involves the trope of movement, which unfolds across overlapping scales: movement between cities and within cities, across time and to heaven, between hallucination and reality. As Arnold Aronson notes, the play's "dizzying array of settings through which the spectators must be led on their theatrical journey" exerts considerable demands on designers.[110] But this movement among the 60-odd scene changes helps militate against those demarcations of normativity in public space and the public sphere in the Reagan decade. Directly, it rebukes the mandate of "staying put," introduced by Sister Chapter and repeated during Prior's journey to heaven in *Perestroika*. In *Angels in America*, movement contrasts with stasis on many levels—history, geography, and ideology—but all inform the question of identity politics at the play's core. Moving freely from place to place *Angels*

in America introduces, almost structurally, the two-sided trope of dislocation. On the one hand, dislocation invokes the pangs of loss when one leaves
behind the associations, connections, and attitude used to locate oneself in
that place; this is especially important with the Mormon characters leaving
Salt Lake City. On the other hand, dislocation involves the liberating potential of discovery, both the discovery of new ways of locating oneself in new
places (here New York City) and the effects, emotional and epistemological,
of this new location. Despite Chapter's definition of New York as just "little
rooms," the Mormon characters relocated there find new and often daunting
freedoms—of movement and of self-definition. Joe finds echoes of and, paradoxically, escape from the demarcations of Salt Lake City, which compel him
to confront conservative definitions and, temporarily, to discover the possibility of life beyond these limitations. All this leads to the more noteworthy way
Angels in America resists conservative America, as Cohn teases in *Millennium
Approaches*: "Transgress a little, Joseph."[111]

Although Roy Cohn is an improbable source,[112] the possibility of trans-
gressing "a little" proves integral to the sociospatial ambitions of *Angels in
America*. Before addressing how, it is necessary to define transgression as it
relates to the imbrication of geography considered thus far. As Cresswell
argues, transgression "breaks from 'normativity'" and "offend[s] the subtle myths of consensus."[113] Transgression means, most fundamentally, going
somewhere or doing something that is not allowed—in this case, according to ideological definitions of normality or naturalness. During the scene
with Hannah and Chapter, transgression involves smoking, which could be
observed, reported, and punished. Notably, this transgression takes place *in
public* and will be *recognized as a violation of norms,* two defining aspects of
transgression. On the most basic level, then, transgression reveals the ideological boundaries inscribed in the society, here, the public realm of Salt
Lake City. Unto itself, this revelation is valuable in that it illuminates what
would otherwise remain hidden through the myth of naturalness: the social
ordering wearing out the body and the mind of Mormons. Beyond this, transgression further represents a threat to normativity. "Transgression . . . . causes
a questioning of that which was previously considered 'natural,' 'assumed,'
and 'taken for granted.'"[114] Once transgressed, what was "normal" now
becomes what is enforced according to political or ideological authority.
Breaking with that authority is still wrong, but now possible, so that during the short term "deviations from the dominant ideological norms serve
to confuse and disorientate" and in the long term they "reveal the historical and mutable nature of that which is usually considered the way things
are." *Angels in America* considers transgression—disruption, questioning, and
escape from normativity—through Joe's struggle with his homosexual desires.

This consideration unfolds on two levels: Joe watching and committing transgressions, and audiences watching these transgressions.

In *Angels in America* Central Park becomes synonymous with transgression. Hidden by the twisting paths and thickets of the Rambles, on the north shore of the lake in Central Park, gay men meet anonymously for sex as depicted in act two, scene four of *Millennium Approaches.* Leaving the hospital anguished by Prior's worsening condition, Louis visits the Rambles for just this purpose. After a few moments of loitering, an anonymous man approaches and asks, "What do you want?"[115] Already encoded with connotations of casual sexual encounters in the gay community,[116] this location supplies all the exposition necessary. This man, like Louis, comes to the Rambles for obvious purposes. Needing punishment for abandoning Prior in his time of greatest need, however, Louis answers the man through the discourse of sadomasochism: "I want you to fuck me, hurt me, make me bleed." Delivered without enthusiasm, Louis's language is certainly shocking to particular cross-sections of society during the 1980s. Although the play does not endorse this specific liaison (Louis must display bruises of punishment before he is welcomed back among his friends), this scene illustrates the sort of transgressions against conservative notions of sexuality and identity that *Angels in America* does endorse. And if Joe's frequent walks are any indication, these sorts of encounters are more the norm than the exception. Noteworthy is that such encounters are doubly hidden: they occur in Central Park and not all of New York, and in the Rambles, not all of Central Park. It would be overstating the case to say that New York City invites such encounters in direct contrast to Salt Lake City. But it seems appropriate to say that New York City contains pockets of resistance to the conservatism typified by the depiction of Salt Lake City, which delimits the behaviors that are allowed or even possible. Considering New York City against Salt Lake City, then, means considering what they have in common (homophobia and conservatism) and how they differ (what transgressions regularly take place). In *Angels in America,* the Rambles of Central Park becomes where ideological boundaries defining normativity are contested.

The contrast with Salt Lake City emerges thematically and structurally with the story of Joe Pitt. Although drawn to Central Park because of such encounters, Joe is initially troubled by his voyeurism. He believes that this sort of behavior is not just sinful but additionally unnatural, thanks to Mormon theology, or any conservatism, defining the limits of normality. When confronted by Harper's question, "Are you a homo?" after another walk, Joe cannot bring himself to acknowledge words like "homo" or "homosexual" during the ensuing argument. At first, he denies her accusation, couched as a question, but eventually responds by reaffirming the definitions of decency and correctness of Mormonism. "Does it really make a difference? That I might be one thing deep within, no matter how wrong or ugly that thing is, so long as I have fought, with everything I hate, to kill it."[117] Brought to the surface as marital strife, Joe's struggle is nevertheless deeply informed by identity politics in Kushner's New York City. During his short time there, Joe tries to observe the Mormon boundary that defines what is decent and correct. If there is tension about a cigarette in Salt Lake City, there is absolute disbelief and horror about homosexuality there. When Joe calls Hannah, still in Salt Lake, she responds by saying he is "being ridiculous" and hangs up. This is, in part, because the concept of homosexuality is so unnatural in Salt Lake City, where Joe and Hannah would be constantly reminded of their distance from the Temple. Living in New York City, Joe finds this boundary increasingly confused (in his mind) and contested (in the Rambles) in ways that induce, initially, serious internal struggles. Certainly the ulcers he medicates with Pepto-Bismol evidence his body's reaction to the psychological struggle involved in watching homosexual encounters in the Rambles.

The more transgressions Joe witnesses during his walks, however, the more capable he becomes of leaving behind conservative definitions of decency and correctness attendant with Salt Lake City, as evidenced by his calling Hannah from Central Park in act two, scene eight of *Millennium Approaches*. "CENTRAL PARK! . . . What on earth are you doing in Central Park at this time of night?" she demands.[118] Although the purpose of the telephone call is otherwise, Joe initially consoles Hannah with the assurance that "I come here to watch, Mom. Sometimes. Just to watch." But just watching transgressions offers threats to normativity because they denaturalize the ideological mapping of the urban environment: instead of being "normal," the demarcations become merely one "reading" of behavior and place. The encounters that Joe witnesses become what Cresswell describes as "heretical readings" of this place: readings that challenge "norms" by both violating the prohibitions and making such violation more likely. "Because this reading is particularly visible," he contends, "heretical readings draw attention to themselves. People acting 'out of place' suggest different interpretations" of that place, and of the behavior possible in that place.[119] In this way, Central Park becomes contested not just geographically (against the rest of New York City and Salt Lake City, through the split-scene), but further, epistemologically (in Joe's understanding of homosexuality, conservatism, and decency). Most significantly, Cresswell argues that heretical readings of public space offer the possibility of challenging the interplay of geography, ideology, and epistemology: "If enough people follow suit [with what is observed], a whole new concept of normality may arise."[120] Perhaps realizing this, Hannah urges Joe to go home to his wife, to the domestic sphere that is heavily encoded with heterosexuality and conservatism, at least for Mormon characters. But Joe will not go home—at least figuratively—because he has witnessed more than the acting out of homosexual desire during his walks through Central Park. He has witnessed the breakdown of boundaries necessary to acknowledge and pursue that desire. Because of this, he finally brings himself to admit, in Central Park, what cannot be imagined in Salt Lake City: "Momma. I'm a homosexual, Momma. Boy did that come out awkward. (*Pause*). Hello?"[121]

The humor notwithstanding, Joe's self-discovery suggests much about the sociospatial ambitions of *Angels in America*. In moving through New York City, Joe finds the possibility of moving beyond Salt Lake City, or perhaps, beyond what that city represents about the United States. Joe's watching homosexual encounters in Central Park invites him to recognize how his beliefs and behavior were regulated by conservative ideology—and not nature or normality. Making this distinction, initially in the urban environment but ultimately in national dialogue about homosexuality, AIDS, and difference, is central to the ongoing fight for identity politics and social justice. Joe himself acknowledges this recognition after starting his affair with Louis, which has its beginnings, not incidentally, on a Central Park bench at the end of *Millennium Approaches*. In *Perestroika,* while sitting on Jones Beach and listening to Louis go on about his guilt, Joe consoles him with these remarks: "You have to reconcile yourself to the world's imperfectability by being thoroughly *in* the world but not *of* it" (original emphasis).[122] This distinction between *in* and *of* the world is striking for Joe, who had internalized so thoroughly the utopianism of Mormonism during the first half of *Angels in America*. During this scene he seems not only capable of recognizing "Utah talk" as culturally determined, but further, liberated by the knowledge. As evidence of this, he unzips Louis's pants and slides his hand inside and says, "The rhythm of history is conservative. You have to accept that. And accept as rightfully yours the happiness that comes your way."[123] Not the language of Marxist revolution, admittedly, Joe's remarks still suggest that he has begun to move beyond "Utah talk." More significant than the language is the gesture: just putting this public transgression alongside Hannah's anxiety about the cigarette shows how New York City becomes setting and subject of contestation in *Angels in America*.

Come Here . . . Just to Watch

The sociospatial ambitions of *Angels in America* derive from the premise underlying ACT UP and Stonewall: transgression in public space, when witnessed, can induce transformation of consciousness in the public sphere. Kushner pursues this thematically and structurally through the contrast of

Salt Lake City and New York City. Thematically, this unfolds through the events surrounding Joe's coming out, which emerge from transgression and then become transgression itself during the early scenes of *Perestroika*. Building on the brief transgression in Salt Lake City, the cigarette passed between Chapter and Hannah, the play suggests how transgression leads to self-discovery in New York City, where heretical acts in the landscape interrogate definitions of normality. Contestation occurs in both urban environments but results in transformation only in the latter. This transformation is deeply personal for Joe, a reimagining not just of definitions of decency and correctness but additionally of his entire identity—but this transformation never becomes political. In fact, Joe's faith in Reagan's United States remains unfaltering even during his affair with Louis, a point underscored during their turbulent breakup.[124] Nevertheless, *Angels in America* denaturalizes the conservative definitions of normality by demonstrating how they are products of particular environments, through Joe's struggle against "Utah talk" and his exploration of sexuality in Central Park. Scenes like act one, scene four (Louis and Prior talking intimately about their relationship); act two, scene five (Prior and Belize in Prior's hospital room joking about sex); or act two, scene seven (Louis and Joe flirting outside the Halls of Justice) all contrast significantly with act two, scene ten (Hannah and Chapter in Utah). More importantly, Kushner develops this premise—transgression inducing transformation—structurally through the split-scenes that he employs. There are many of these scenes in *Angels in America*, including act two, scene eight. In these scenes Kushner stages different locations, encoded with ideological connotations, simultaneously. Thereby, he depicts the indisputable difficulty and yet liberating possibility of transgression in two complementary ways.

During the initial scenes of *Millennium Approaches*, the split-scenes tend to literalize Joe's internal struggle with "Utah talk" through the dramatic form. This tendency is best exemplified by act one, scene eight, which is divided equally between the living room of Joe and Harper and the bedroom of Louis and Prior. Beginning with Harper's question about Joe's whereabouts during another of his walks, the scene initially follows the argument about the failing of their marriage due to Joe's distance and Harper's isolation and culminates with Harper's question: "Are you a homo?"[125] With Joe's denial—"No. I'm not"—this side of the stage falls "silent," with actors motionless or continuing through pantomime, and Prior and Louis begin without any reference to the other scene occupying the stage. At first, Louis talks about life and afterlife but the conversation moves toward Prior's disease that marks him—during the 1980s—as homosexual and considers questions of love and abandonment before returning to the argument of Joe and Harper. When this first shift occurs, at the moment of confrontation between Joe and Harper and within Joe, the structure of the scene conveys much about the nature of the conflict, both internally and socially. What Joe confronts here and throughout *Millennium Approaches* is the dichotomy between normativity and aberrance inscribed in Salt Lake City and his psychology. Jungian shadow to Joe's denials of homosexuality and his subsequent admission of something "wrong or ugly" living inside him, the scene with Louis and Prior reflects that which Joe cannot admit about himself, and simultaneously, it reflects that which Reagan's conservatives cannot acknowledge about the United States. The Prior/Louis scene dramatizes a number of important concerns for normativity and aberrance. First, it represents the (im)possibility of homosexual desire and love, a visualization of the trope of closeting. Second, this scene offers evidence of normative boundaries inscribed geographically, between the scenes, which are separated not just by city blocks of New York but further by the ideological coding of Central Park and Salt Lake City. Third, the scene illustrates the internalization of this dichotomy for Joe and the conservative perspective.

The dramaturgy behind this split-scene and elsewhere mirrors Joe's psyche, thoroughly divided between what is decent and correct on one side (Harper and Joe) and what is wrong and ugly on the other (Prior and Louis). The boundary is fundamentally moral: a demarcation of space that defines and defends what is appropriate, right, and possible according to "Utah talk." Because the split-action unfolds sequentially, with the couples taking turns in their interactions, the dramaturgical structure initially suggests that this boundary is robust, if not inviolate. But the very presence of Louis and Prior, visible even when not performing, in this scene about decency and correctness implies the impossibility of obscuring homosexuality completely, for Joe or for the president whom he admires. Instead, the juxtaposition of the two scenes—each encoded with competing ideological values—illustrates the ongoing contestation of those values within the urban environment. If *Angels in America* is "about New York," it is not just about the problems of homophobia in New York described by Kushner but further about the possibility of challenging that homophobia through pockets of transgression. This is precisely what many split-scenes index in Kushner's play. In the scene discussed here thus far, this indexing occurs predominately in terms of domestic concerns: with the scene between Prior and Louis intruding on and prompting—at least indirectly—much of the conflict between Harper and Joe. In scenes like act two, scene four the concerns extend toward political and public spheres. Another split-scene, this scene opens on Joe and Roy in an upscale bar and Louis and the anonymous man in the Rambles. Beginning with Joe and Roy, the scene initially dwells on Salt Lake City and how difficult it is to live according to standards of behavior there and then turns to national conservatism, including the influence of Joseph McCarthy on Roy's life. Intruding on the conservatism of this scene are Louis and the anonymous man, who act out their abortive sexual encounter without concerns about the ideological boundaries defined in the previous scene. On the one hand, this intrusion reads against the scene with Roy and Joe, suggesting something of Roy's real motives in mentoring Joe. On the other, it dramatizes the transgression in and of spaces playing out across the environment of New York City.

The transgression foregrounded structurally by *Angels in America* is noteworthy on two fronts: it reveals the ideological boundaries in society that would otherwise be naturalized and it illustrates the possibility of new definitions of what is allowed, appropriate, or normal. This is true in *what* is dramatized in Kushner's play: Louis and Prior in bed, Louis and man in Central Park, Prior and Belize in a hospital room. More significant, perhaps, is *how* this transgression is dramatized in *Angels in America.* Although early split-scenes usually unfold sequentially, with clear boundaries dividing them, later split-scenes have more ambiguous boundaries and tend to confuse distinctions between locales and conversations. The best instance of this occurs in act two, scene nine of *Millennium Approaches,* the New York scene following Joe's confession about his homosexuality to Hannah. During this scene, Joe has returned to his apartment with Harper while Louis is visiting Prior in the hospital. The first two lines of dialogue belong to Harper and Joe: "Oh God. Home. The moment of truth has arrived" and "Harper."[126] But this moment is interrupted by the dialogue between Louis and Prior: "I'm going to move out," Louis says; "The fuck you are," Prior responds. Then back to Joe and Harper for two more lines, and back to Louis and Prior, again and again throughout. Since both scenes revolve around abandonment, they overlap so that the pleas of one scene (made by the abandoners Louis and Joe) sound as if they are answered by the incensed rejoinders of the other scene (Prior and Harper). In the stage directions for this scene, Kushner describes the effect for which he is striving in the dramaturgy: "This should be fast and obviously furious; overlapping is fine; the proceedings may be a little confusing but not the final results."[127] Confusing certainly in terms of who is asking, saying, or answering whom or what, but furthermore confusing in terms of transgression as defined by Cresswell. This occurs within the structure of this scene, in which the divisions that seemed durable previously, now become frayed, so that the actions in the scenes spill over into each other and the boundary between spaces in the play is contested verbally, visually, and ontologically. During this scene in which Joe—though only temporarily—overcomes the boundary dividing homosexuality from normativity (his affair with Louis follows thereafter), the form of *Angels in America* exemplifies and endorses this transgression of boundaries.

Beyond this, the transgression of boundaries during this scene, potentially extends the liberating possibility of transgression toward audiences. After all, the effects of witnessing transgression are not limited to characters of the play. Transgression can "disrupt the patterns and processes of normality and offend the subtle myths of consensus," here, about conservative definitions of behavior and belonging, and produce new definitions of normativity.[128] While Kushner is careful not to ascribe transformational power to the theater,[129] this possibility of transgression correctly describes the "results" sought during this scene and throughout *Angels in America*: the possibility of audiences watching these transgressions in public space (theater) undergoing a transformation of consciousness in the public sphere (society). During the 1994 revival of *Angels in America* at the American Conservatory Theatre in San Francisco, according to Janelle Reinelt, Mark Wing-Davey's production pursued these ambitions in the split-scenes. "Wing-Davey reframed these scenes as interconnected and uncontainable (actors 'violated' one another's stage space to produce this effect of overflowing boundaries), staging the dissolution and blending of identities" across these boundaries.[130] If staged according to this implicitly sociospatial ambition, *Angels in America* challenges audiences to acknowledge and interrogate boundaries that divide and determine, to participate imaginatively in the play's transgression of boundaries. Of course, producing this result is certainly not easy, as Reinelt's remarks about the New York production under the direction of George C. Wolfe show: "Wolfe staged the 'split screen' scenes in *Millennium* as simultaneous but discretely separate scenes in stable space," and thus missed an opportunity that I would argue is central to the political, even epic, ambitions of *Angels in America*. In realizing this endorsement of transgression through production, Wing-Davey invited audiences to go beyond Joe's failure to move permanently beyond conservative dichotomy, as evidenced in act five, scene eight of *Perestroika* when Joe attempts to come back to Harper, Mormonism, and heterosexuality in another split-scene shared with Louis and Prior. This failure does not indicate rejection of transgression, only acknowledgment of its difficulty. The best evidence for this is that Harper leaves behind Joe, in this scene, to go to San Francisco.

Where Homophobia is No Longer Acceptable

It is fitting that in closing, discussion of *Angels in America,* dramatically and theatrically, leads back to San Francisco. Importantly, there is no scene in the city of San Francisco despite the 60-odd changes of location in the two-part epic. Instead, San Francisco is invoked three times in *Angels in America*:

act three, scene five (an argument between Belize and Roy, after Roy has been hospitalized); act five, scene five (Prior's journey to Heaven, which is described as a "City Much Like San Francisco"[131]); and act five, scene ten (Harper's midnight flight to San Francisco)—all in *Perestroika*. (The last of these is a three-way split-scene with Harper on the plane, Louis and Prior in the hospital, and Joe alone in Brooklyn.) In all three, San Francisco is invoked, visually or verbally, during conflicts regarding movement, freedom, and progress: Roy's attempts to make Belize, an African American and openly gay man, feel that he does not belong in the hospital room or the United States envisioned by Roy; the Angels' efforts to convince Prior to choose stasis rather than progress for humanity; Joe's attempt to come back to Harper and heteronormativity after his breakup with Louis. Each time, San Francisco emerges in explicit contrast to and perhaps as implicit remedy for "Staying put," whether metaphysically, politically, or personally. Certainly not incidental, this contrasting of San Francisco and stasis no doubt emerges from Kushner's definition of this city in interviews. During the Mars-Jones interview, for instance, Kushner describes when Governor Pete Wilson, a Reagan politician if there ever was one, refusing "to sign a law legitimizing gay and lesbian domestic partnership."[132] With echoes of Stonewall, gays, lesbians, and others rioted, leaving "the state building . . . completely trashed." To Kushner, San Francisco represents where contestation of urbanism is not merely possible—as it is elsewhere—but commonplace. On the one hand, then, San Francisco represents a city where political will and personal indignation flare when confronted with the homophobia of Reagan's America; on the other, something magical, like "Oz."[133]

There is something of these competing faces of San Francisco in Belize's description in Roy's hospital room, which defines the subsequent invocations of San Francisco in *Perestroika*. During another of the fractious interactions of Belize and Roy, when Roy is particularly doped from pain-killers and dreading the future, he asks "What's it like? After? . . . This misery ends."[134] Roy is talking about what is happening to his disease-ravaged body, but the question just as easily describes how he has to hide his disease (become "liver cancer") and remain closeted, particularly when the question is considered against Belize's answer: "Like San Francisco." Probably the most lyrical passage of *Angels in America* is his description: "Big city, overgrown with weeds, but flowering weeds. On every corner a wrecking crew and something new and crooked going up catty-corner to that. Windows missing in every edifice like broken teeth, fierce gusts of gritty wind, and a gray high sky full of ravens."[135] In the streets can be found "piles of trash, but lapidary like rubies and obsidian and diamond-covered cow spit streamers in the wind." After

Roy interrupts with an image of Reaganite authoritarianism and capitalism, a dragon atop a horde of treasure, Belize goes on unfazed: "And everyone in Balenciaga gowns with red corsages, and big dance palaces full of music, and lights and racial impurity and gender confusion." This San Francisco enters the play in direct contrast to Salt Lake City and New York City: a description that confounds those demarcations and dichotomies underlying Reagan's America evident in those other cities, and embraces transgression geographically, demographically, and even ontologically. It is a city of trash where the trash is precious stones; a city where buildings have been wrecked—echoes of the 1904 earthquake—but are already being reimagined and rebuilt toward something new and "catty-corner[ed]" to what was there before; a city where confusions of identity joyfully reign: "And all the deities are creole, mulatto, brown as the mouths of rivers" Belize almost sings.[136] To Cohn, it is hell, but to Belize, heaven. More significantly this invocation of San Francisco—part political reality, part Oz—is where contestation of norms has become, paradoxically, the norm and where movement, freedom, and progress have become thankfully possible.

In Harper's midnight flight to San Francisco emerges the trajectory of Kushner's argument about Reagan's United States. Moving from Salt Lake City to New York City Harper, like Joe and Hannah, knows more freedom and movement, becomes able to discover more about herself and slowly move beyond the conservatism of "Utah talk." Moving from New York City to San Francisco furthers this trajectory in what she moves toward as exemplified in Belize's paean. What she finds there must be deferred beyond the play for two reasons: because the cultural and cognitive transformation sought by *Angels in America* had not occurred in the early 1990s and because it is this ambition that must be extended to audiences if Kushner's play is to be politically efficacious. But the play imagines what could come from this movement, metaphorically, from the conservatism of Salt Lake City toward the liberalism of San Francisco during the epilogue, five years following Harper's flight. This scene offers a compelling glimpse of New York City with the gathering of Prior, Louis, Belize, and Hannah before the Statue of Bethesda in Central Park. Beyond the interesting figures who compose this grouping (gays, drag queens, Mormons) is where it takes place: in public space and during the day. Set against the fall of the Berlin Wall and the potential in perestroika, this scene imagines these changes at the local level, in New York City, where such gatherings become increasingly possible—and perhaps empowering—with the fading of the specter of Reagan and his venomous brand of conservatism. In this gathering are the means and the ambition behind the sociospatial ambitions of *Angels in America*: public space redefined through contestation and now the site of further contestation simply by bringing the discussion of homosexuality and AIDS into the public sphere. Hannah comes to represent the possibility of transgression begetting transformation, as she has settled into New York City life and has moved beyond the burden of Salt Lake City. This is not quite "Oz": Joe is conspicuous in his absence. But it is still progress, even if only the "painful progress" Harper described in act five, scene ten.[137] Progress that begins and unfolds in the public space of New York City.

CHAPTER 2

"City, Bad Place": Architecture and Disorientation in New York City

How do people negotiate the city? This was the animating question behind Kevin Lynch's *The Image of the City*, which helped define a distinctly urban cartography. Written in 1960, Lynch's book reports a study of three U.S. cities with different landscapes and different modes of negotiating these landscapes—Boston, New Jersey, and Los Angeles. A combination of geography and anthropology, this study considered the "apparent clarity or 'legibility' of the cityspace," by which Lynch means how easily the city's "parts can be recognized and be organized into a coherent pattern."[1] Considering the many questions of apprehension and coherence therein, Lynch makes two significant contributions to contemporary urban study. First, he codifies those aspects of the urban landscape—paths, nodes, landmarks[2]—that enable topographical legibility, that is, he gives contemporary geographers a discourse for discussing conceptual ways people negotiate cities. In so doing, Lynch adopts the trope of landscape as text with its culturally determined and thus learnable grammar and syntax—much as Fuchs and Chaudhuri do in *Land/Scape/Theatre*.[3] Complementing this study of urban geography in *The Image of the City* are interviews of the inhabitants of these cities that attempt to determine how they construct the "environmental image" they employ in negotiating the city, an image making possible the "harmonious relationship between himself and the outside world."[4] The ambition of the study is twofold. Primarily, it seeks to determine what constitutes a legible city, or a city "that could be apprehended over time as a pattern of high continuity" among buildings, streets, neighborhoods, et cetera. Also, this study proposes ways of developing environments that would avoid "the mishap of disorientation," which corresponds with illegibility, the experience of uncertainty "and even terror" attendant with becoming lost.[5]

A milestone in urban studies, *The Image of the City* implicitly marks the transition from modernism to postmodernism in the study of geography. Much of the discourse defined by Lynch and, more importantly, the underlying assumption of interplay between place and perception have influenced the current generation of critics in cultural and critical geography. In *Postmodernism, or the Cultural Logic of Late Capitalism*, Fredric Jameson references Lynch in chapter 1, although his argument famously pursues the aforementioned interplay through the negative: from the premise that people have lost the capacity for apprehension. Specifically, Jameson argues, "We are here in the presence of something like a mutation in the built space... a mutation in the object unaccompanied as yet by any equivalent mutation in the subject."[6] His evidence ranges from the Bonaventure Hotel in Los Angeles to the Beaubourg in Paris or Eaton Centre in Toronto: buildings that undermine our capacity, visually and conceptually, to locate ourselves in a coherent environment.[7] Lynch's worst anxiety come to fruition. Without referencing Lynch directly, David Harvey nevertheless engages with assumptions of *The Image of the City* about the grammar of urbanism when, in *The Condition of Postmodernity*, he defines contemporary architecture as "fragmented, a 'palimpsest' of past forms superimposed upon each other, and a 'collage' of current uses, many of which may be ephemeral."[8] The concerns with this postmodern environment are evident in the criticism of Michael Sorkin, Jean Baudrillard, Celeste Olalquiaga, and Edward Soja. Offering different interpretations of cause and effect of this postmodernity, they nonetheless begin from the central irony of contemporary urbanism: the landmarks Lynch used to map the city induce, instead of prevent, disorientation. Hence Jameson's remarks about hyperspace, which "has finally succeeded in transcending the capacities of the individual human body to locate itself, to organize its immediate surroundings perceptually, and cognitively to map its position in a mappable external world."[9]

Tensions between geographical legibility and illegibility, or epistemological orientation and disorientation, inform the plays considered in this chapter: Richard Greenberg's *Three Days of Rain* and Sally Clark's *Lost Souls and Missing Persons*. Instead of reading landscape to show the ways it is ideologically contested, like *Marisol* and *Angels in America*, the plays of Greenberg and Clark highlight the frustrated act of reading the illegible environment and the consequences of such abortive attempts. Not principally political, the conflicts in these plays are empirical and epistemological for characters trying to locate themselves, literally and figuratively, in the city. *Three Days of Rain* and *Lost Souls and Missing Persons* stress the breakdown of anything resembling the "environmental image" defined by Lynch: the coherence among buildings, the architecture, and the neighborhoods that allow people to negotiate the city freely. The urban landscapes they represent are clearly those of Jameson, Harvey, and Baudrillard more than Lynch. Although much of the criticism about postmodern architecture centers on Los Angeles, the plays considered here take place in New York City and respond, implicitly, to the profound changes in urbanism, culture, and architecture that have occurred during the decades between the publication of *The Image of the City* and *Postmodernism, or the Cultural Logic of Late Capitalism*. Nowhere are these changes more noticeable than in Times Square, the buildings of which have been transfigured—in the urban renewal of the 1980s and 1990s—into something like enormous television screens. Images multiply and compound themselves, or flow freely across glassy exteriors in ways that fascinate and confuse onlookers. In *Three Days of Rain* and *Lost Souls and Missing Persons*, New York City becomes, at once, subject and source of frustrated efforts to resolve the fragmentation of the built environment. More significant may be how the plays represent disorientation as less of a "mishap," as per Lynch, to more of a fundamental condition in the postmodern metropolis, which characters cannot successfully negotiate.

Before considering how the plays pursue the tensions between legibility and illegibility, orientation and disorientation, it is worth clarifying how the term "negotiate" is employed in the following pages. First of all, to negotiate means the ability to know geographically where one is within the topographical coordinates of any city and to be able to navigate, with however much difficulty, the said coordinates. It means moving from point A to point B without noticeable unease or confusion because the city evinces legibility through familiar landmarks. Although built upon the grid, New York City has become—at least in these plays—a city increasingly lacking definite coordinates. Here, the architecture defined by Jameson and Harvey comes into play in the definition of negotiation. The ways the buildings themselves are constructed destabilize the relationship between the building and the surrounding area, making it more difficult to negotiate the city's landscape. As with the moment in Rivera's *Marisol*, when the title character wonders aloud, "The Empire State Building? . . . *what's it doing over there?* It's supposed to be south. But that's . . . north . . . I'm sure it is . . . isn't it?" the characters in *Three Days of Rain* and *Lost Souls and Missing Persons* find themselves confused and frustrated by the landmarks of the city (original emphasis).[10] This confusion in Rivera's play is explained by metaphysical crisis,[11] but not in the plays of this chapter. Here, it emerges from the topography itself. Implicit in the confusion thematized by Rivera, of course, is the link between geography and conceptuality: the environmental image that Lynch argued produces stability in the urban text and enables negotiation. Another part of the definition of negotiate used here, then, is conceptual: it extends beyond the geographical to the cognitive and cultural definitions of urbanism. To negotiate describes the efforts to find a sense of belonging—the combination of purpose and place— that groups find in any community, a community grounded in a particular location. Complementary definitions, they will be pursued in the following chapter.

Deeply concerned with the growing illegibility of urbanism during the 1980s and 1990s, *Three Days of Rain* and *Lost Souls and Missing Persons* tell stories of disorientation, initiated from or exaggerated by postmodernity. In fact, they represent conflicts and crisis that stage what has been theorized by Jameson, Harvey, and Olalquiaga about personal confusion and cultural disintegration. In so doing, they expand the definition of sociospatial drama, thematically, beyond ideological contestation of authority and toward the empirical and epistemological collisions with the built environment itself. Not merely object of contestation, then, the city becomes subject of contestation: testing the capacity of characters to negotiate a postmodern city. Individual buildings, like Janeway House in *Three Days of Rain,* demonstrate all the irreferentiality of the Bonaventure Hotel or Eaton Centre so thoroughly discussed by Jameson. Trying to comprehend this building, visually or conceptually, undermines not just what the characters think they see before them but what they know, or even better, the classical ideas of perspective. There is no point, literal or figurative, from which Greenberg's characters can construct an "environmental image" that locates them within a greater field of coordinates. Because of buildings like this, the city becomes increasingly difficult to negotiate, which brings us to the New York City represented in *Lost Souls and Missing Persons.* In this city, Clark's protagonist becomes lost in the maelstrom of buildings, neighborhoods, and streets—multiplying and compounding, flowing liberally into one another like the images on the buildings of Times Square—implying collapse between sign and referent, between building and image itself that produces psychological or existential crisis. But it is worth noting that *Three Days of Rain* and *Lost Souls and Missing Persons* tell their stories about postmodern urbanism from noticeably different perspectives: the former, from that of the New Yorker returned from years abroad; the latter from that of a Canadian tourist on vacation. Such differences are important to how New York was being represented and read by U.S. and Canadian cultures in these decades, and therefore, will receive consideration.

More intriguing than such complementary thematic concerns is how these plays attempt to extend this disorientation of postmodernity toward audiences. Toward this end, Greenberg and Clark disavow the traditional narrative structures of realism or naturalism in favor of more episodic structures. In *Angels in America,* it is possible to follow Joe's progress, literally and figuratively, through the landscape of New York toward the liberation of transgression. Not so in *Three Days of Rain* and *Lost Souls and Missing Persons,* neither of which unfolds through causally related incidents, nor toward decisive resolution. Instead, the plays move back and forth across time and space with only ironic regard for Aristotelian unities. This incoherence of plot, action, and structure metonymically recreates something of the postmodern landscape encountered by characters in the play. Never taking this landscape for granted—in this case, assuming its stability or legibility—the plays of Greenberg and Clark depict it as something continually in need of exegesis. But, they simultaneously frustrate exegesis by closing off avenues of interpretation or by doubling back on conclusions previously reached. This episodic structure often demands much attention and effort from audiences to follow and understand—to negotiate, in effect—the storyline or multiple storylines unfolding therein. *Three Days of Rain* and *Lost Souls and Missing Persons,* in effect, make it difficult for audiences to find their way through the play's terrain and thus have the potential to induce—through the very structure of the play—some of the same concerns considered by Jameson, Harvey and others. Specifically: how do people negotiate the city? What happens when the landmarks necessary for negotiation induce confusion instead of coherence? What is the link between geographical, epistemological, and existential disorientation—in particular when cities evidence a "mutation" of space?

The Story of a Moment

These are precisely the questions considered in Richard Greenberg's *Three Days of Rain.* Originally commissioned by the South Coast Repertory Theater in Costa Mesa, California, and produced there in 1997, the play moved to the Manhattan Theatre Club later that year. There, it won acclaim from critics and was a finalist for the Pulitzer Prize won by Paula Vogel for *How I Learned to Drive* in 1998. In the years following, *Three Days of Rain* has been revived at the San Diego Repertory Theatre in 1998, at the Park Theatre in 1999, and most recently back in New York under the gimmick of Julia Roberts making her debut on Broadway.[12] Reviews of the play have consistently described it as a character study in part because there is little plot and because the story represents family struggles within and across generations. Without disagreeing with this summary, I will stress a qualification in the following pages: Greenberg's dramaturgy grounds this study of character in the postmodern landscape of New York City, something that he would continue doing, to lesser degrees, with *The Dazzle* (2002) and *The Violet Hour* (2003). Plainly interested in the intersection of existential crisis and postmodern urbanism, Greenberg foregrounds such concerns from the beginning of *Three Days of*

Rain. When the lights come up, the protagonist Walker, a young man recently returned to New York, initially draws attention to those city sounds indicated in the stage directions (a car alarm, the hum of traffic), and then thematizes the play's concerns through an almost lyrical evocation. "No end to the sounds in a city . . . Something happens somewhere, makes a noise, the noise travels, charts the distance: The Story of a Moment."[13] After a momentary pause, he adds, "God I need to sleep." Irony aside, Walker suggests how interpretation (attempting to make sense) of the urban landscape will play a central role in the story that will follow as well as his desire to find some moment of purchase from which to make sense. More than that, this moment defines New York as a locus of sound and sense, geography and epistemology, demanding interpretation.

Dramatizing two generations of the Janeway family (Walker in 1995, the play's present; and Ned in 1960), the play highlights their efforts to negotiate the "story" of two New York City locales. The more remarkable of these is Janeway House, an award-winning building designed by Ned, Walker's father, decades before and that Walker stands to inherit following his father's recent death. A building full of glassy surfaces in "the desirable part of Long Island," Janeway House was the product of the partnership of Ned Janeway and Theo Wexler.[14] "That house is deemed now, by those that matter," explains Walker during the opening, "to be one of the great private residences of the last half century." Described in reviews as a combination of Frank Lloyd Wright and Philip Johnson, Ned Janeway was a quiet visionary in architecture whose work not only brought acclaim but perhaps triggered new trends in architecture.[15] In his private life, though, Ned endures great disappointment: "his partner died shockingly young, and my mother grew increasingly mad, and my sister and I were there so we had to grow up," Walker explains.[16] Designing Janeway House, which has elements of a Frank Gehry design (the contrast to Wright and Johnson notwithstanding) was no doubt bittersweet to Ned, who used to sit on Central Park benches and sketch the city's skyline for the beauty of it. For Walker, the house commissioned by his grandparents and designed by his father, promises that which he has most desired in his life—a moment of purchase, or borrowing Lynch's term to define one of the key tropes of *Three Days of Rain,* a landmark by which he can existentially negotiate both the city of his youth and his family's history within the city. What he wants is something that can provide continuity and coherence against the uncertainty of his family life. At least this is his hope at the beginning of the play, but he will discover the irony he has suggested: that this building will provide no more than a "moment" of purchase against the uncertainty and irreferentiality of life.

Although Janeway House is the locus of the complicated desires of Walker and Ned, it never appears in *Three Days of Rain* except through diegesis. The play's action—act one in the present and, with little regard for chronological integrity, act two in the past—is limited to the Manhattan apartment shared by Ned and Theo in 1960. Unadorned, outdated, and dinghy to the point that Nan, Walker's sister, cannot imagine why their father, much less Walker, kept it, the apartment nevertheless supplies some continuity between the play's acts. A landmark, perhaps, for audiences watching a play that violates the typical chronology of narrative realism? Walker learns about the apartment only after returning to New York from Italy for the reading of his father's will, when the family lawyer mentions it offhandedly. But Walker embraces it, with the wry irony that exemplifies his personality, as his inheritance—a joke that comes to fruition when Pip, the son of Ned's partner, inherits Janeway House. Suddenly, Walker is obsessed by the question of who really designed Janeway House after the reading of the will (there are hints that Pip's father may have done it). Walker turns to the apartment or, more accurately, to his father's journal found there, for his answers. This journal thematizes the trope of reading or interpreting a text already suggested during Walker's introductory remarks about the city's sounds. The story of the first act revolves around Walker's efforts to read the journal, read the apartment, and ultimately read the city that he thought he knew for evidence of who he is or where he belongs. In effect, Greenberg establishes a nexus among journal, apartment, and Walker that thematizes the underlying sociospatial ambition of the play. Walker's exegesis becomes the trope of act one: an interrogatory, interpretative, and ultimately frustrating engagement with objects found in the urban landscape and the landscape itself.

Solids and Voids

Early in the play and immediately after introducing the journal, Greenberg extends this engagement toward the built environment of the play, specifically through Walker's and Nan's efforts to describe Janeway House. Acknowledging her uncertainty regarding what makes the building remarkable, Nan draws on what she knows of the traditional discourse of architecture: "it has something to do with the fenestration," that is, the arrangement of windows.[17] "Not really," Walker says, beginning the pattern of interruption that typifies their exchange. But Nan continues as if not hearing: "and the solids and the, the alternation of solids and—" before becoming too uncertain, even confused, to finish her thought. Walker then fills the elision, though there is no certainty that this is the *right* word for what Nan intended or what correctly describes Janeway House: "*voids*—the solids and the voids" (original emphasis). But what is certain is that Walker and Nan are having considerable difficulty with finding a language to describe and thereby define the architecture of the building; in this, they illustrate the ongoing "crisis in terminology" in urban studies defined by Sharpe and Wallock.[18] The nature of urban forms has changed so drastically in the twentieth century that it has, perhaps, exceeded the capacity of discourse to define, interpret, and understand these forms. Changing strategies, Walker and Nan turn to figurative language to try to "read" the architecture for audiences, but in so doing create further distance between sign and signifier, and between subject and object. "All the glass, the house is a prism," Walker offers.[19] Building on Walker's metaphor, Nan adds, "—and there's a different kind of light in every room, and at every hour—and the rooms themselves have something liquid about them, something that changes." This metaphor initially proves effective but Nan's borrowing it underscores the limits of figurative language when, halfway through, the metaphor begins to fail when she describes the light as liquid and the rooms as changing. They then turn to allusion: "Goethe— Goethe... defined architecture as 'frozen music.'"[20] But this hardly resolves their dilemma, in particular because they are not sure it was Goethe who said this: at least "some famous German," adds Walker.[21]

Along with Walker's history of the family home, this is how Janeway House enters *Three Days of Rain*: through frustrated efforts at describing it. This is because Greenberg is less interested in what the building looks like, which could easily be demonstrated by including it in the scenography, than he is with the building's effect upon onlookers. Designed and built in the 1960s, Janeway House nonetheless has much in common with the architecture of the 1980s that Jameson found so disturbing. One useful comparison is with the "freestanding wall of Wells Fargo Court" in Los Angeles, "a surface which seems to be unsupported by any volume, or whose putative volume (rectangular? trapezoidal?) is occurally quite undecidable."[22] It is not that Janeway House represents or resembles the Wells Fargo building or the Bonaventure Hotel, another likely comparison. But rather, that Janeway House speaks to the same effect in the urban environment: a building that confounds knowledge of how shapes, depths, textures become a coherent image. Walker and Nan stress, through what they can name, the slippages and elisions in the building, the refusal of the object to approach coherence. Additionally, what they cannot describe further reveals correspondences: the building belies comprehension visually or conceptually; they cannot find a language to define it. And Greenberg communicates this effect through their struggle to describe Janeway House: Walker and Nan continually interrupt and overlap with each other in their efforts at description in ways that do not endorse any compound image. Instead, each interruption or emendation takes them—and the audience, which is dependent upon them for understanding—further away from coherence. Their language becomes more fragmented, adding reference, trope, and description one on another in such ways that destabilize the narrative image they are trying to produce. In effect, Greenberg transforms ocular instability into linguistic incoherence—through interruption and elision, through trope and description, through monologue and dialogue—to thematize the effect of postmodernity.

Introduced through this *non*description of Janeway House, this postmodernity extends toward the urban landscape of New York City, a landscape that interrupts rather than informs, confuses rather than confirms empiricism and epistemology. This becomes evident following Pip's inheritance of Janeway House during an offstage scene, a turn-of-events that sees Walker storming out of the lawyer's office and wandering the city much of the night. When he returns to the Manhattan apartment, he describes what he considers, only half-jokingly, a noteworthy discovery during his walking: "I found the last extant wine and—unless it's the first *retro* wine and—anyway" (original emphasis).[23] Once again, when trying to describe the buildings or the built environment, Walker's narrative is marked by interruption and emendation, further evidence of the difficulty with trying to describe, define, and understand this city. About this specific story, Walker finds himself pondering, at least momentarily, whether what he found was a real wine shop—locally owned, before the proliferation of supermarkets, big-box stores, and mass consumption—or a copy made to blur the distinction between real and retro. This distinction is more than a matter of taste since the former presumes coherent connection to the past while the latter erases the connection and redeploys the object as commodity. Here and elsewhere, Walker finds himself caught up in what Celeste Olalquiaga describes as the "referential crash" of postmodernity.[24] Arguing that contemporary architecture has increasingly replaced the "fixed reference point" with "obsessive duplication," Olalquiaga contends that the built environment of the postmodern city produces the paradoxical confusion of "being in all places while not really being anywhere at all."[25] The confusion is spatial and epistemological, a breakdown of referential coordinates in the surroundings. Olalquiaga offers the example of the shopping mall where "homogeneity of store windows, stairs, elevators, and water fountains, causes a perceptual loss" leaving people "wandering . . . in a maze."[26] But the same consequence can occur in the postmodern city, where simulacra collapse past and present, real and retro, and consequently produce confusions about *where, when,* and even *who* individuals are.

This last point is crucial to Walker's forays into the city. Long before the play begins, his life has been one of confusion and uncertainty, probably as far back as his mother's suicide attempt, which he witnessed. He feels like he has never had a home, never had a place of belonging because he has associated his father's designing buildings with the breakdown of the family, and rightly so. The more famous his father became as an architect, the worse the family suffered from isolation, acrimony, and madness—some clear O'Neillian echoes.[27] As his name suggests, Walker is among the "nomads" described in Peter Marks's review of the Manhattan Theatre Club production, wandering from place to place without any sense of home.[28] In fact, Walker often allows himself to become "lost"—more of a game than a reality—so that someone will have to "find" him and provide the reassurance he needs. But hidden in this game is real anxiety about place, identity, and purpose. When no one finds during the years before his father's death, "I started to believe you had forgotten me," he tells Nan, "I don't mean as in 'ceased to care.' I mean as in, 'couldn't place the name.'"[29] When asked why he wanted to inherit Janeway House so much when he had not been near it in years, his answer reveals much about the perilous correlation among place, perspective, and identity suggested in *Three Days of Rain*: "Because I don't live anywhere," he admits in a rare moment of sincerity.[30] Walker intends to use Janeway House as a landmark, figuratively speaking, by which he could orient himself in space (the actual building) and history (the familial and artistic legacy of his father). What he wants is something close to what Lynch describes: that places contain memories, which supply the foundation for community and continuity. But Steven Winn, writing about the San Diego Repertory production, pinpoints the irony: "He's a lost soul, the son of an architect longing for a house to call home."[31] This is why Walker returns to New York and becomes so invested in Janeway House: he hopes it will help him to negotiate, epistemologically and existentially, the troubled terrain of his life.

But Walker's encounters with the built environment of New York City exaggerate rather than placate his fear about becoming lost. When Pip inherits Janeway House, Walker loses not merely the home where he could have lived on Long Island but further the history he had taken for granted throughout his life: the story of his father designing the building. Suddenly without this landmark, Walker is compelled to doubt his relation to the referential coordinates of his life: his father, this building, and the city itself. When he wanders the city after leaving the lawyer's office, he finds little solace among the buildings and streets that he knows well. "I was—every corner of this city—it was—I . . . couldn't stop moving," he tells Nan, "I tried to calm myself. I got . . . coffee at a couple of—that was a bad idea—and I ended up counting the Wexler Janeway buildings I passed; that was no help at all."[32] Looking for some connection within or to the city that he has always loved, Walker has no difficulty getting from place to place because of the profusion of buildings designed by his father and Theo, his father's partner. What is true about geography, however, is not true existentially. The more of these landmarks he passes, the more confused and confusing the city becomes because the buildings remind him of what he has lost, at least conceptually, with Janeway House. Once, Wexler Janeway buildings provided ways of locating himself in the interplay of family and city. Now, they have become as difficult to comprehend as the architecture of Janeway House. He can't orient himself in the city or his life and finds himself walking all night without direction and without hope of finding what he most wants. In his retelling of the night, which is marked once more by interruption, elision, and emendation, Walker unintentionally reveals the difficulty posed by the city that he thought he knew: the inability to make sense of the whole, or to construct and comprehend what he described at the beginning of the play as a "story" of the "moment."

Only as Simulacrum

Mentioned already, Walker's inarticulateness when talking about the city suggests, as a common trope of postmodernity, correlation among the built environment, epistemology, and existential condition. It is the nature of this correlation that proves crucial to the sociospatial concerns in *Three Days of Rain*. On the one hand, the city functions as Rorschach test for Walker: he finds disorientation when considering the architecture or buildings because that is what he brings to the process of apprehension. In this way, the built environment simply mirrors his internal condition. On the other hand, the play suggests that the irreferentiality of the built environment can exaggerate, if not provoke, the experience of disorientation. In fact, Walker's initial monologue, which provides the history of Janeway House, introduces this destabilizing effect of postmodernity in ways that exceed idiosyncrasy. "Everyone's seen that one picture, *LIFE Magazine,* April of '63, I think, when it looks lunar, I mean, like something carved from the moon, mirage-y [*sic*]— you remember that photo?"[33] After another pause, he continues, "People have sometimes declined my invitation to see the real place for fear of ruining the experience of the photograph." The New Yorkers described here do not differentiate between the aesthetic experience of what is "real" and false or, more remarkably, the ontological distinction between reality and falsity, original and copy. One is as compelling—if not as real—as the other. This confusion emerges from the proliferation of images in magazines like *LIFE* that produce epistemological or ontological ambiguity. The photograph published in *LIFE* is somehow more satisfying than the original in this landscape of simulacra where true and false collapse and confound distinctions of history, geography, and ontology, very much like the uncertainty Walker felt when trying to distinguish "real" from "retro." In *Three Days of Rain,* then, Janeway House is doubly linked with the collapse of referentiality: in how it is architecturally constructed, and again, in how it informs the city's culture of postmodernity. If Janeway House metonymically represents New York City, then it is not difficult to imagine Walker asking in earnest the question posed by John Lechte, "What is this architecture that can barely be described and named—which may only exist as simulacrum?"[34]

Another question, posed by Walker, further explains this correlation among built environment, epistemology, and existentialism. While describing the history of Janeway House, Walker asks, "you remember that photo?"[35] Breaking the fourth-wall is a practice so common today that it hardly warrants consideration, but here it does prove noteworthy in how it extends the ontological confusion thematized in the play toward audiences. In asking audiences if they "remember" the photo, Walker invites them to think back to covers of *LIFE Magazine* that they have seen, covers that were not only familiar but that served as much as cultural memory or archive before the Internet. While this is complete speculation, it is likely that many members of the audience found themselves, upon Walker's prompting, attempting to remember covers of *LIFE* with anything like Janeway House. In this gesture, *Three Days of Rain* blurs the ontological demarcation between dramatic world and world dramatized. From inside the play (the copy of the real) comes reference to a magazine (another copy of the real) in the world beyond the play (the real) about a building (the not real) that only existed within the play. In effect, Greenberg establishes a nexus among play, magazine, and image—paralleling that of journal, apartment, and history—and invites audiences to negotiate meaning from this thorny referentiality. Landmarks like Janeway House or *LIFE* become epistemologically destabilizing, which makes it harder to "know" what is "real" or "not real," even if only temporarily, and puts pressure on the ways of making meaning. By blurring distinctions between real and false, original and copy *Three Days of Rain* pursues a double ambition. First, it comments on the profusion of images circulating without referents in postmodern culture and perhaps catching unsuspecting audience members in the attendant referential crash felt by Walker. Second, the play foregrounds the nature of the crisis for Walker: the landmark he intends to use to establish coherence in his life is deeply imbricated with—perhaps the source of—disorientation.

What, then, can be made of the Manhattan apartment where the action takes place? The syntax of juxtaposition in *Three Days of Rain* (past and present, fathers and sons) highlights the significance of the apartment in contrast to Janeway House. Not surprisingly, Walker becomes obsessed with the apartment from the beginning and even more so after losing Janeway House to Pip, in part because it is his last link to his father's life and in part because it makes for such a striking contrast. Producing no startling visual effects, no miracle of the light, the apartment suggests a source of stability in the play that geographically links Walker to his father's life. Of course, the same is true in relation to audiences since the play observes the unity of space suggesting, again, stability against disorientation in a play that otherwise linguistically and structurally resists coherence. But this geographical continuity provides little refuge against the disorientation of postmodernity. When Walker recalls his first days in the apartment, in fact, his description reveals the same illegibility inside the apartment as elsewhere in the city. "This place is so nothing," he tells Nan, "I couldn't imagine why they kept it. I paced the floor for two days, screaming at the walls: 'Speak! Speak!' "[36] Understanding that geography encodes and potentially expresses historical or cultural messages about its occupants, Walker endeavors to "read" the apartment in much the same way that he and Nan try to "read" Janeway House. Walker tried to get the apartment to disclose secrets about his father's life before his marriage, family, and fame, and Walker latches onto whatever conclusions he can guess. "This must have been Ned's and Theo's studio," he says, suggesting the nature of the previous occupancy.[37] "They must have designed the house here, don't you think?" he asks, joining speculation with observation.[38] He demands his family history from the cracked walls and forgotten furniture because he believes that they can provide what Janeway House no longer can, or never could: the continuity and stability necessary to overcome feelings of disorientation.

But the apartment yields only his father's journal, which thematizes and problematizes Walker's attempted reading of the apartment, Janeway House, and New York more generally. "It seems to cover *everything*," Walker says excitedly: "when they built the house, everybody getting married, births, institutionalizations" (original emphasis).[39] Such milestones in this family's life provide Walker with possible landmarks by which he can define himself. But the journal is "written in cipher." Walker can make out some details from his father's life, just as he can name elements of Janeway House, but he cannot resolve these details into a coherent narrative. The best he can do, in fact, is *mis*interpret the cryptic entry "Theo dead. Everything I've taken from him" as Ned's confession that it was Theo who really designed Janeway House consequently explaining (incorrectly) Pip's inheritance of the house.[40] The entry was instead referring to Ned's winning Lina from Theo during the three rainy days named in the play's title. This faulty conclusion by Walker temporarily resolves the disorientation that he feels about his life, but the apartment's "secrets" further distance him from any place, literal or figurative, that belongs to him or to which he belongs. Walker's efforts to decode the journal's cipher suggest an intriguing, but ultimately frustrating, intertextuality that reinforces the disorientation of postmodernity. He attempts to read one text (the journal) as a way of understanding another (the apartment, or Janeway House), but these texts confuse and even collapse the explanatory referentiality necessary to reveal the truths he seeks. Like the journal, the apartment transmits messages about belonging and disorientation that Walker, Nan, and perhaps even audiences cannot easily, or even ultimately, resolve. The Manhattan apartment and the secrets disclosed therein compound, rather than relieve, the disorientation that follows from the interplay of built environment, epistemology, and existentialism in *Three Days of Rain.*

No Pattern . . . Just Traffic

What is intriguing is how the inverted chronology of *Three Days of Rain* (act one in 1995, act two in 1960) extends disorientation, structurally, toward audiences. This inversion implies more than mere reversal of temporal periods—present followed by history—although Harold Pinter's *Betrayal* has demonstrated the dramatic possibility inherent in such reversals. Instead it is that the two acts of *Three Days of Rain* thoroughly destabilize the conclusions of each other in ways that disavow denouement. When Walker misreads his father's cryptic entry about Theo, he believes that he has discovered the authoritative moment—however embarrassing—of his family history: that Ned unfairly took credit for Theo's design. More important is how strangely contented Walker is with the knowledge of his father's presumed arrogation. He burns the journal as if bringing that history, along with the uncertainty that has always troubled him, to a rather melodramatic resolution. But the second act makes ironic this Hedda-Gabler-like gesture. Act two reveals, first of all, that Walker's father did design Janeway House just as was believed. Additionally, this act exposes Ned's partner, Pip's father, to be little more than a dilettante when it comes to architecture: given to romantic declarations about beauty but little talent for design and even less determination to realize an architectural vision. And finally, it dramatizes the awkward romance of Ned and Lina, which supplies a stark contrast to Lina's attempted suicide and subsequent institutionalization later in life, two events that have scarred Walker. And the second entry from the journal, "April 3rd to April 5th: Three days of rain," proves misleading as well.[41] While Walker took it as evidence of his father's pedestrian sensibilities, it denoted Ned's happiness about those three rainy days spent with Lina. Thematically, then, such entries underscore the indecipherability of Ned's journal and suggest that meaning may be entirely idiosyncratic. "I'll know what it means," Ned tells Lina when she reads this last entry over his shoulder.[42] But Ned's certainty further highlights the *un*certainty and faulty conclusions from Walker that precede this scene— but follow it temporally. The second act of *Three Days of Rain*, then, unsettles the conclusions Walker—and, most likely, audiences—may have tentatively reached during the first act.

This second act, though, is anything but the Rosetta Stone for *Three Days of Rain*. Unlike the narrative closure sought by realism, from which Greenberg's play may initially seem derived, the play never resolves the loose ends of the first in the second. If anything, act two envisions a future—and a city—already ironized by act one. During the rainy days that marooned Ned and Lina in 1960, he mentions eavesdropping on conversations while walking through the streets in search of coffee and experience, and walking far out of his way to hear and see more of the city "because it was all so . . . pleasant."[43] With Lina's prompting, he describes his dream of becoming a *flâneur*, like a character out of Balzac's Paris: "Someone who . . . idles through streets without purpose . . . except to idle through the streets."[44] This fantasy depends on several assumptions, particularly the socioeconomic privilege necessary to indulge in wandering the city, a point Ned acknowledges when he says of the *flâneur*: "He has no work . . . if he's the real thing."[45] More noteworthy is that Ned's dream presupposes the legible city described by Lynch, the city that evinces "high continuity with many distinctive parts clearly interconnected" throughout different regions.[46] With this continuity, "the perceptive and familiar observer could absorb serious impacts without disruption of the basic image, and each new impact would touch upon many previous elements." In this city, the encounters cherished by Ned would accumulate, revealing more and more of the city without ever threatening the coherence of the city's image; in fact, the more observations made, the more the city becomes a text to be read, understood, and enjoyed. Though becoming "lost" provides much of the romance of the *flâneur*, it is becoming "lost" in one's observations that defines this experience of idling in streets. Ned can imagine nothing better than to be this "vagabond prince," to be what he calls simply "a walker" during his conversation with Lina, consequently explaining the origin of their son's name.[47]

Notably absent from Ned's description of the *flâneur* is the possibility of becoming lost in the ways defined by Lynch: that combination of "geographical uncertainty" and "overtones of utter disaster."[48] This, of course, is precisely what pervades the act already performed for audiences of *Three Days of Rain*. Walker has become *what* his father imagined during those rainy days in 1960 but certainly not in the *way* he imagined it. "He just . . . walks, you see," Ned tells Lina, the words echoing into the (theatrical) past and the (chronological) future of the play as commentary on the next generation: "His life has no pattern . . . just traffic . . . and no hope—."[49] When the *flâneur* gets old, Ned continues, "he remembers . . . certain defunct cafes where he shared cups of coffee with . . . odd, scary strangers."[50] Ned's romanticized visions of the city are ironic when contrasted with Walker's specific encounters with coffee shops during his all-night wandering ("that was a bad idea") and his general desperation to find some pattern and purpose in his life. The failure of Ned's fantasy has less to do with Walker not living up to any ideal, though Walker probably believes this to be the case, than it does with the profound transformation (Jameson would say "mutation") of the urban environment between 1960 and 1995. Writing about the novels of Saul Bellow, Steven Marcuse defines the beginning of this transformation in *Seize the Day* (1956), where "the city is [already] ceasing to be readable," and argues that this illegibility comes to fruition in *Mr. Sammler's Planet* (1970).[51] This change from modernity to postmodernity was happening, at least in literary representation, during the time when Ned was becoming a well-known and successful architect, and this transformation drives the conflict between the acts of *Three Days of Rain*. The modern city presumed by Ned, which buoyed the existential freedom of the *flâneur,* has given away to the postmodern city, which perhaps has exceeded our capacity to understand the environment. Consequently the *flâneur* ideal, which Lechte describes as "an entity without a past or future, without identity," comes to ironic fruition in Walker's life.[52] Geographical, epistemological, and ontological indeterminacy produced by the urban landscape designed by Ned, then, becomes exigency of Walker's disorientation—of place, past, and identity—in the future already glimpsed.

Such juxtaposing of narratives across these acts certainly complicates antecedency for audiences. What comes first chronologically during the production—Walker's exegesis of the journal and the apartment—is (eventually) undermined by what comes after it. And what comes first chronologically in the dramatic world—Ned's fantasy of being "a wanderer through the city"—is (already) belied by what comes after (and before) it. This dramatic structure built upon unstable juxtaposition thrusts audiences into a conceptual terrain similar to that of postmodernity. It does so by challenging the horizon of expectations that follow from realism—coherent storylines, teleological plotting, and clear-cut denouement—that are seemingly endorsed by the mostly realistic first act of the play.[53] When audiences begin watching act two, they find themselves wandering, metaphorically of course, through the many slippages and elisions that begin to emerge from the competing and contradictory narratives derived from acts one and two: Walker's hope for continuity, and Ned's hope for patternless traffic. Many, no doubt, find themselves hoping for some landmark, some reference point that might help to resolve the dissonance between these acts, but to little avail since the acts militate against narrative closure. Consequently, audiences are, perhaps, made to experience some of the disorientation—more epistemological than existential—that bedevils Walker throughout the play.

The dramatic structure of *Three Days of Rain*, in effect, metonymically invokes the irreferentiality and attendant disorientation of postmodernity—of Janeway House specifically but also of the landscape where real and retro collide. Ultimately, audiences are invited toward—and frustrated by—the same exegesis that typifies Walker's efforts to decode his father's journal. They must read one text (or act) against another and try to find whatever meaning—tentative and idiosyncratic as it may be—they can out of this intertextuality.

A Place That Belongs to Me

Toward the end of *Three Days of Rain*, Lina asks the following of Ned while waiting out the rainstorm that provides the play's title: "What is it that some people in cities seem to know? What is this secret that is constantly eluding me?"[54] In this question, Lina reveals concerns about belonging, emplacement, and disorientation that she feels, as a southerner, living in New York City. In addition she foreshadows, or confirms (again, the inverted chronology of the play complicates antecedency), Walker's anxiety and her own institutionalization after her attempted suicide. "She flew out of the apartment," Walker says during act one, "and down the thousands of flights of stairs all the way to the lobby."[55] Overlapping with Walker's story of this night, Nan continues from what she imagines as Walker's perspective as he chased his mother down the stairs: "He arrived in time . . . to see her body pierce the glass façade of the building—." In act two, years before her Mary-Tyrone-like frenzy, Lina's question suggests that her unease or dis-ease (given her institutionalization, this word best describes her condition) with the city derives from some deficiency on her part. She believes that there is something wrong with her, that she is missing some integral information or experience or "secret" that would, ideally, help her to read and comprehend the nature of this city, or any city perhaps. Yet the play suggests that the opposite may be more likely: that she is sensitive enough to the urban environment of New York, perhaps because she is an outsider, to appreciate something of the transformation already under way in 1960. Set in the same year that Lynch's study of urbanism was published, the second act documents—through Lina—the increasing nervousness about the illegibility of cities: in how they were designed, constructed, and inhabited. More than that, she may actually anticipate something of the postmodern landscape that is so disorienting to Walker during the play's future, when the very buildings would become increasingly difficult to comprehend and change the relationships to the surrounding buildings and the environmental image of the city. Better than Ned, Lina sees the future of urbanism that Walker will know, and dreads it.

Three Days of Rain ultimately proposes a correlation of psychological or existential crisis with geographical or architectural postmodernity during both acts. When telling the story of Lina throwing herself through the building's façade—a remarkably dense image of violence, self-destruction, and architecture—Nan takes pains to stress the following: "We were living in a terrible skyscraper my father had designed, his first."[56] Although the point is subtle here, the suggestion is that something about the building, about the skyscrapers that were transforming the nature of New York was contributing to the psychosis that sent Lina running down those stairs beyond what familial problems were inferred by Walker and Nan decades later. Additionally, Walker confirms Lina's dis-ease with the city years later in his lifestyle. He has no connections, no ties to anything that provides any sense of place or purpose; his life has become, without any of the romanticism, his father's "no pattern . . . just traffic." This correlation among psychology, existentialism, and postmodernity is not just cause and effect in either case. But there is clearly a correlation between the transformation of the built environment represented in the play and the transformation of culture, family, and identity experienced by the Janeways that leaves Lina in a mental asylum and that turns Walker into a "nomad." Walker's remarks about himself could just as accurately describe his mother and others wandering the postmodern city in *Three Days of Rain*: "I love this city, but it's dangerous to me. It's let me . . . become nothing."[57] Without any place of belonging or belonging to place, those like Walker feel lost, emotionally as well as existentially. What Walker fears is what the city implicitly confirms: his dissolution into nothingness. And what he wants most is what this city, perhaps any postmodern city, can no longer supply: "I want to be sane. I want a place that belongs to me."[58]

Producing the Unproduceable

The next play considered in this chapter involves, like the dramatic structure of *Three Days of Rain*, moving backward chronologically. Sally Clark's *Lost Souls and Missing Persons* debuted in 1984, more than a decade before Greenberg's play and from a distinctly different cultural perspective. Not included among Clark's better plays like *Moo* (Belfry Theatre, 1988, for which she won Canadian theater's Chalmers Award) or *The Trial of Judith K.* (Tamahnous Theatre, 1985, for which she was nominated for the Governor General's Award), *Lost Souls and Missing Persons* has had only two full productions to date. The play had a reading at the Shaw Festival in Toronto, and then it was workshopped in 1983 by Banff's Playwright's Colony. The following year saw the debut at *Theatre Passe Muraille*, a noteworthy moment for Clark's career and for framing the concerns of *Lost Souls and Missing Persons* because this theater has come to be considered English Canada's national theater. Founded in 1968, *Theatre Passe Muraille* claims a double mandate: developing of "innovative and provocative Canadian theater" and creating a "distinctly Canadian voice."[59] While Clark's experimental play clearly falls in the former category, its inclusion in the latter proves intriguing with respect to the representation of urbanism and the framing of cultural reception. In 1989, this framing continued with a revival at Vancouver's Touchstone Theatre, another theater that insists on plays exploring or defining the Canadian perspective.[60] In stressing this stage history I am not suggesting that Clark's play is representative of *the* Canadian perspective any more than I was suggesting that Greenberg's was representative of *the* U.S. perspective. Nevertheless, it is true that *Lost Souls and Missing Persons* has been framed by such cultural nationalism for its original—and to date only—audiences, who would have watched and understood the play within this nexus of cultural self-definition, theatrical performance, and postmodern urbanism. Clark's play, then, considers the aforementioned interplay of (il)legibility and (dis)orientation in New York City from a distinctly different perspective than that behind Greenberg's *Three Days of Rain*.

Noteworthy for this consideration is the fact that *Lost Souls and Missing Persons* debuted the same year (1984) that Fredric Jameson published an article in the *New Left Review* that would become the introductory chapter of *Postmodernism, or The Cultural Logic of Late Capitalism*. In his well-known argument about the Westin Bonaventure Hotel's "mutation" of architectural space, which induces perceptual and cognitive uncertainty,[61] Jameson views this trend internationally. Not alone in producing "postmodern hyperspace," the Bonaventure Hotel instead echoes a number of buildings, including Eaton Centre in Toronto. Partially opened in 1977 and with final construction completed in 1979, Eaton Centre is an enormous shopping mall in downtown Toronto that displaced a number of older, more architecturally traditional buildings, with their relationship to the surrounding landscape, and pursued what Jameson calls a "total world" through its architecture and planning.[62] Without reference to each other, Jameson's criticism and Clark's play were responding to the same crisis in the urban environment, though Clark's concerns seem specifically linked to cultural apprehensions about changes to urban life in Toronto.[63] In this way, Clark's dramaturgy may have been more perceptive, or more attuned, to the changes in urbanism than Greenberg's: she anticipated many of the same concerns by more than a decade. In any event, Clark's play is less interested in describing the postmodern urban environment than exploring consequences of hyperspace, hyperreality, or postmodernity. Disorientation is the play's abiding theme: disorientation that is simultaneously psychological and cultural, empirical and geographical, epistemological and existential. *Lost Souls and Missing Persons* pursues this theme through the experiences of a Canadian housewife named Hannah Halstead, on vacation in New York with her husband, Lyle, when she disappears into the city, and, more significantly, through the episodic structure that produces something of the effects of Jameson's hyperspace. Unfolding without determining logic or recognizable segues—from New York streets to Canadian suburbs, from police stations to characters' minds—the play transforms the experience of urbanism into a free play of images, emotions, and sensations that taxes perceptual and cognitive capacity, like postmodernity itself.

In the "Playwright's Note" to the published text, Clark acknowledges the difficulty, for actor and audience alike, posed by this episodic structure when she half-jokingly describes *Lost Souls and Missing Persons* as "unproduceable."[64] Without diminishing the difficulty attendant with staging this play, this chapter considers how the episodic structure highlights and conveys sociospatial concerns about postmodern urbanism. While Greenberg's play depends chiefly on narrating effects of this postmodernity, Clark's play dramatizes its concerns with disorientation principally through its structure. Making none of the esoteric references[65] of *Three Days of Rain*, *Lost Souls and Missing Persons* confronts audiences with the postmodernity of urbanism directly, or as close as can be replicated through formal conventions. The play irreverently conflates time, place, and casual connections in ways that function, at least in part, expressionistically: these conflations reflect the breakdown of psychological stability in the mind of Hannah Halstead. In a way, then, the external city she wanders mirrors her internal instability. At the same time, though, the episodic structure functions, for want of a better word, analogically: it reflects an urban environment where buildings, streets, and neighborhoods have produced or succumbed to what Jameson calls "dissociation," the visual or conceptual detachment of buildings from their surroundings. In this way, Clark's play represents a city that has exceeded comprehension. Watching this play potentially induces something of Hannah's disorientation in audiences because it begins from the collapse of the traditional idea of perception, the "fixed point in space" that allows the viewer to comprehend the relationships among objects.[66] Without this point of reference—literal or figurative, geographical or epistemological—neither Hannah nor audiences find negotiating the urban environment pleasant or perhaps even plausible.

Magnificent in Her Madness

Summarizing the incidents of *Lost Souls and Missing Persons* in some coherent fashion is no less daunting. The central plot-point of the play is the disappearance of Hannah Halstead in New York City while vacationing with her husband, but the exigency, sequence, and reason for this disappearance are difficult to pinpoint with any accuracy. What little exposition audiences receive about this disappearance comes during the second scene when her husband, Lyle, appears at a police station and announces, "I—ah—seem to have misplaced my wife."[67] With echoes of vaudevillian comedy, the following scene unfolds through a series of double takes: by Lyle when confronted with the fact that "She's a missing person?"; then by the police officer following Lyle's remark that Hannah dyed her hair frequently, "Didn't that strike you as odd?"; and finally by audiences themselves when Lyle admits, "Well—she is sort of hard to describe." Details emerging from this encounter are few but significant: Hannah wanted to see the Cloisters and took the subway uptown while Lyle had a meeting, and Hannah's body is not in the morgue. When Hannah appears in act one, scene twelve—not her first appearance in the play but the one that *seems* to explicate this confusion—she is disheveled and disoriented in the Bowery. A couple of women stop to help Hannah, because they have mistaken her as a bag lady, and highlight her condition: Hannah's glasses are askew, one of her shoes is missing, and only the remnants of her camera strap hang around her neck. After offering her money, which Hannah confusedly crumbles up and forgets, they leave. Shortly thereafter, a man (identified as Mr. Cape in the stage directions) enters with a knife and a cartoonishly sinister intention. Before Mr. Cape can reach Hannah, however, yet another man—named Turner—appears and chases him away, but when he returns to Hannah, she responds to this gallantry only with gibberish: "Glimble nod bling" and "Heigh ho!" and the perplexing interrogatory "Zorn?"[68]

More questions than answers follow from this summary, most importantly, this: why is Hannah wandering the Bowery, the opposite direction from the Cloisters, muttering gibberish? By all appearances, she seems to have been the victim of street violence when she enters in act one, scene twelve, a conclusion that would resolve questions provoked during Lyle's visit to the police station. Furthermore, this conclusion seems to be corroborated in act one, scene seven, when Hannah is mugged by two bag ladies in the Bowery. But she is *already* disoriented during the mugging scene, even though her clothing and possessions are intact. In fact, when the bag ladies are robbing her, Hannah responds (casually?) with "Oooom bingle dee."[69] If anything, Hannah's disorientation provides the means and opportunity for this mugging instead of being a product of the event. Reading the aforementioned scenes alongside one another reveals little explanatory connection among them: they will not cohere in recognizable patterns any more than the walls of Janeway House. Clearly, the encounter with the bag ladies comes before Turner's rescuing Hannah from Mr. Cape, but constructing a chronology that leads to the incident with the bag ladies or from the bag ladies to Mr. Cape is made difficult by the intrusion of flashbacks in the play. In the scene immediately following Lyle's police report, for instance, Hannah and Turner are already together, somewhere in the city, even though he has not yet—at least in the chronology of the play's scenes—had opportunity to rescue her. Compounding this confusion are the many monologues that proliferate between scene two and scene twelve of the first act, monologues that comment not on the events unfolding in the present but rather on incidents from the past. These monologues function, initially, as digression, but digression becomes the defining element of *Lost Souls and Missing Persons.* Unfolding forward and backward in the lives of Lyle and Hannah—and seemingly sideways to introduce Mr. Cape's family—the play never addresses, much less answers, the initial question: what happened to Hannah on her way to the Cloisters that left her wandering the Bowery incoherently?

Underlying this confusion are tensions between the narrative(s) introduced in *Lost Souls and Missing Persons* and the play's rejection of narrative closure. When constructing a narrative, audiences attempt to resolve confusions like those in Clark's play by looking for causes, usually, by reading scenes against one another in order to derive a coherent picture of events, such as trying to understand the logical connections of scenes preceding and informing Hannah's disorientation. In most plays, this effort is rewarded with revelation and denouement. But not in *Lost Souls and Missing Persons,* where it is continually frustrated by the intrusion and proliferation of tangential narratives that lead away from the initial narrative thread. In act one, scene nine, for instance, the play leaves off Hannah's story to introduce the Cape family, which seems—and probably is—initially unrelated to Hannah's disappearance. The family includes Mr. Cape, his wife, and Nesbitt, their adult son who suffered a brain injury after attempting suicide and now speaks in fragments and repetitions. When Mrs. Cape tells a story about a woman who hears voices (not Hannah, but surely a reasonable guess at this point in the play), Nesbitt gets stuck on the source of the voices and repeats "chair" during the scene, thematically doubling Hannah's gibberish. When the play returns to the Cape family toward the end of act one, after the meeting of Hannah, Mr. Cape, and Turner, Mrs. Cape finds a note from her husband that she misinterprets as a suicide note and eventually holds his funeral—without his body, or even confirmed evidence of his death. Having disappeared from his family, Mr. Cape spends the rest of the play stalking Hannah through the Bowery: he appears in the background of the bag-lady-scene (1.7), in the scene when Turner rescues Hannah (1.12), and in the ending of the play, when he looms over her with a knife (2.20). But the introduction of this narrative only compounds the original problem of what happened to Hannah that left her wandering the Bowery with further questions—not resolved: was it Mr. Cape who induced her disorientation? What did he do? And of course, *why* is Mr. Cape stalking her?

What about Turner, the man who intervenes when Hannah stumbles confusedly in the Bowery with Mr. Cape lurking nearby? Just before this incident, Turner delivers a monologue that seemingly frames him as a *raisonneur*, or reflecting the author's opinion or understanding. "When did I first see her?" he begins, implying that he has knowledge of Hannah that will resolve the unanswered questions.[70] Adding to this authority is his familiarity with the Bowery, as he provides information for (Canadian) audiences unfamiliar with this region in 1980s New York City: "winos, bag ladies, the occasional crazed young man."[71] But Turner, too, does not know what caused Hannah's disorientation because she was already disoriented when he noticed her. "She was mad. Well, I suppose she was mad. Derailed might be a better way of putting it."[72] In fact, there is something about her madness that initially attracts Turner's attention: "She was gloriously derailed and she stood there, magnificent in her madness." Worse than his lack of explanatory information about her condition is his willingness to benefit from that condition. After rescuing her from Mr. Cape, he names her Zombie and takes her back to his apartment where he professes his love for her, "wrestles" with her, and apparently takes sexual advantage of her, though this, like so much in *Lost Souls and Missing Persons,* is never confirmed. While in his apartment, he enumerates the ways that she is "a perfect woman"—describing her eyes, a wrinkle, the folds of her neck—while she mutters more gibberish.[73] During the scene, trust in Turner's knowledge and intentions is soured, and audiences begin to suspect that he may be one of the "crazed young men" that he will describe in his monologue—but not until 20 pages later. Again, the chronology is fragmented and confused so that it becomes difficult to resolve the particular incidents or their causal relationships depicted in the play. The earlier scene concludes with Hannah leaving Turner's apartment, chronologically *after* the rescue, but dramaturgically *before* audiences witness the rescue. Even more confusingly, in act two, scene sixteen, Hannah and Turner are still together but now Hannah is coherent and asks, "Who is this man?"[74] As with Mr. Cape, Turner only complicates the questions of the play.

Embracing the Space Beyond

Lost Souls and Missing Persons, in other words, eschews the narrative structure described by Freytag's triangle: incident leads to outcome, crisis begins with cause and leads to resolution. Instead, the play unfolds through what might be described as concentric circles—Hannah's life in a Canadian suburb,

Mr. Cape's abandoning of his family to stalk her, Turner's wandering the Bowery for "love"—that intersect tangentially but nevertheless significantly. What brings these circles together is the urban landscape that they inhabit, permanently for Mr. Cape and Turner, and temporarily for Hannah. That is, New York City is more than just the setting of these overlapping narratives; it is the structuring principal behind *Lost Souls and Missing Persons*. Organized more spatially than narratively, Clark's play is more about moving through the streets and regions of the city, following the meandering of Hannah, than about answering the question of what initiated her meandering. In fact, each encounter of Hannah, Turner, and Mr. Cape widens the geography of the city imagined by the play: from the NYPD station where Hannah is reported missing, to the Cloisters where she intended to go, to the Bowery where she is found. The frustrated act of moving through the city "structures" the dramaturgy of *Lost Souls and Missing Persons*. A good comparison is with Gertrude Stein, who took "landscape"[75] as the defining principle of her plays. Of particular note is how illegible Clark's New York City is: rather than moving from point A to point B with a lucid "environmental image" that allows her to negotiate the environment, Hannah ends up disoriented, not just geographically but psychologically, incoherent and helpless as if suffering some trauma. This brings us back to the double representation of the city through the structure of *Lost Souls and Missing Persons*: first, expressionistic, as a reflection of Hannah's bewildered experience, and second, as analogy, as evidence of a city that becomes increasingly typified by Jameson's "dissociation," which is a *source* of disorientation, not a reflection. This link between city and psychological (in)coherence is established by Nesbitt, who once "said 'City, bad place' for an entire month."[76]

In examining what happened to Hannah that left her wandering this city, it becomes necessary to consider the nature of the city she is wandering and how it may influence or even produce Hannah's condition. Olalquiaga's *Megalopolis* offers a good beginning for theorizing what might be described as the pathology of postmodern urbanism. Beginning from the medical term "psychasthenia," which describes a "disturbance in the relation between self and surrounding territory," Olalquiaga defines a trope for the epistemological confusions that emerge from the urban culture of the 1980s.[77] This medical condition, which underlies autism and obsessive-compulsive disorder, characterizes those "incapable of demarcating the limits of [their] own body" from surrounding space, particularly regarding the (dis) order of that space. Consequently, the individual afflicted "proceeds to abandon its own identity to embrace the space beyond" the body, a space that can be ordered in ways that alleviate internal disorder. According to Olalquiaga, urban culture increasingly resembles or induces this condition by producing a dissociation of relationships through architecture and urban planning. Implicit in her argument is the traditional notion of perspective, or the fixed point from which one views the world and which endorses conceptual stability. This is undermined by the "quotation, recycling, pastiches, and simulation" of postmodern urbanism that produces more confusion than coherence—in ways that parallel psychasthenia.[78] Going beyond Jameson, Olalquiaga describes a correlation among the empirical world that exceeds comprehension, the epistemological process of comprehension, and most notably, the psychological or existential outcome of this incomprehension. This correlation proves menacing because "images are central to the shaping of identity: largely constituted by the perception of the self as a separate totality, identity must resort to an image to acquire a sense of wholeness."[79] When faced only with images of fragmentation or dissociation—hallmarks of postmodernity—the threat is that "self-perception remains fragmented exactly as if we had never seen our images in full."[80] Through its very constitution, the postmodern city can induce something like the crisis of perception, conception, and self-definition that defines "psychasthenia."

This argument goes a long way toward explaining Hannah's disorientation in *Lost Souls and Missing Persons*. This connection with Olalquiaga's theory is substantiated through specific references to New York City and representation of Hannah's disorientation. Like Olalquiaga, Clark demonstrates recognition that images pose a threat to psychological and epistemological integrity. One of the many flashback scenes locates Hannah, completely coherent if not terribly satisfied, in the Canadian suburb where she lives with her family of four. When trying to talk with Michael, her son, she finds herself competing with the television that absorbs his attention. Clark's stage directions call for the television to be "portrayed by an actor with a box around his head" rather than a stage property, an intriguing trope for the danger of images to identity: familial identity, with the breakdown of relations across generations evident here; to cultural identity, although Michael is watching hockey, the addiction to television suggests something about the intrusion of U.S. culture onto Canadian culture; and individual identity, with the combination of human body and technology.[81] Boundaries that define identity become porous, penetrable, by the profusion of images emerging from the television. This profusion of images would have been exaggerated exponentially during Hannah's visit to New York City in the 1980s. Beyond obvious changes of urban culture from the sleepy suburb to the metropolis, is the fact that the Times Square Redevelopment Project (beginning in 1981 and spanning the decade) was reconceiving the nature of buildings: images were overflowing the boundaries of television screens to fill—and paradoxically fragment—the landscape. Huge billboards, flashing lights, huge glassy buildings that reflected and refracted the surroundings are what would have greeted Hannah somewhere between her hotel (presumably in midtown) and the Bowery. In fact, the episodic structure of *Lost Souls and Missing Persons,* whether read expressionistically or analogically, reveals much about the landscape that Hannah perceived: fragmented and fragmenting images, undermining empirical and cognitive coherence.

Other than the Bowery, the most noteworthy place referenced in *Lost Souls and Missing Persons* is the Cloisters, the French monastery devoted to medieval art and architecture under the aegis of the Museum of Modern Art, in Fort Tryon Park in upper Manhattan. Much more than a throwaway reference about where Hannah was going when she disappeared, this line from Lyle further defines the nature of this city. The Cloisters includes and displays elements from five different French monastery sites drawn from twelfth to fifteenth centuries. Not a recreation, the Cloisters was uprooted from France—and from history and geography—and relocated in New York City during the 1930s. While encoded with the connotations of a museum, there is nevertheless something of a perceptual anomaly to look toward the Cloisters, a snapshot of medieval French countryside, from across the Hudson River, or, for that matter, to look west from the Cloisters toward New Jersey or south toward Manhattan. The Cloisters represents temporal and geographical fragmentation in ways that anticipate the ontological confusion of postmodernity. As Harvey argues, "With modern building materials it is possible to replicate ancient buildings with such exactitude that authenticity or origins can be put into doubt."[82] I am not sure that this experience of uncertainty applies to the Cloisters, but the point is that Clark chooses this reference point as the first—and perhaps defining—landmark for New York City. The reason is that it illustrates further fragmentation of anything like a coherent "image" of this city, suggesting why Hannah may succumb to disorientation. More than that, the Cloisters metonymically invokes many of the changes to New York during the Times Square Renovation Project, when many buildings were purposely designed to blur distinctions between ancient and modern[83] and confirmed Harvey's point about "images from the past or from other places" blended "eclectically" under postmodernity.[84] In making reference to the Cloisters, Clark reveals much about the nature of this city, where past and present, real and copy are becoming increasingly fragmented.

The urban environment that Hannah encounters during her vacation in New York City, then, offers anything but a coherent image, and if Olalquiaga is right regarding the interplay of perception, conception, and self-definition in urban culture, this explains much of Hannah's disorientation. She has suffered some sort of trauma or breakdown in her mind that leaves her at the mercy of whatever forces find her. She is verbally and cognitively incoherent. When she is lured into an alley by the bag ladies who mug her, she complies with an enthusiastic "Heigh ho."[85] When taken home by Turner and named Zombie, she responds to his condescending overtures—if "Snord" is a response—without resistance. Hannah is incapable of exerting control over the boundaries of her physical body (which is mugged and sexually violated) or her existential self (allowing herself to be renamed and treated like a pet) during the "third-person" scenes, or the scenes where she interacts, however passively, with others. During her "first-person" scenes or monologues, she is mentally and linguistically coherent, but without the ability to influence the actions of the play's present. In this division, of course, is another key point: her identity is fragmented between her mind and body, between past and present, between coherence and incoherence. More significantly, Hannah's fragmentation parallels or even derives from the fragmentation evident through the urban environment. Since *Lost Souls and Missing Persons* illustrates instead of describes this pathology of postmodernity, it never defines the triggering event that induces Hannah's disorientation. But the connection between her internal fragmentation and the external fragmentation of the city becomes undeniable. She cannot differentiate herself from the landscape in which she is lost, which is underscored by the episodic structure moving freely between third-person and first-person scenes. Moving from external to internal scenes without segues or logical connection, this structure suggests that the boundary between psychological and urban landscapes is porous at best. When Hannah looked into the landscape of New York City, she saw only fragmentation of buildings, of time, of geography and, thus, the territory of her mind became suffused with the territory of the city.

Without Reference Points

Already mentioned is what needs more consideration: how the structure of *Lost Souls and Missing Persons* communicates something of Hannah's disorientation—empirical and cognitive, if not existential—to audiences. In the play's opening scene, before Lyle makes his missing persons report, Clark deploys the following image: "*A MAN and a WOMAN in bed.*"[86] After a moment, long enough for audiences to register what looks like a traditional domestic scene, the woman sits up and screams "*long, loud, and bloodcurdling*" before a blackout.[87] However startling this is, it produces the distinctive image of a woman—as yet unknown—confused, distressed, or even terrified. The scene that follows sequentially *but not chronologically* is Lyle's account to the NYPD about his wife's disappearance, a scene that surely prompts some hypothesis building for audiences: what has this man done to his wife? If so, the play "begins" from and unfolds through incidents informed by this question. Conclusions reached during the opening scene, however, become increasingly untenable 16 scenes later when Hannah, by now known to audiences, wakes up next to a man whom she tells audiences—in a monologue—that she does not recognize. "I don't know how I got here, how long I've been here and I'm not sure I want to know."[88] At this point in the sequence of scenes, she has been mugged, confronted by Mr. Cape, rescued by Turner, and brought back to his apartment, but she does not seem to know where "here" is or how "long" she has been there. This time when she screams, in the same fashion as the earlier scene, it is when the unidentified man grabs her arm. Is this Turner, whose apartment she stays in briefly? Is this the same scene as the opening, just reenacted to supply more context? Is this another scene, as the additional details suggest? If so, what is its relation to the previous scene? Uncertainty replaces certainty as the original image becomes unstable through its inexact repetition in this new iteration. This uncertainty is compounded after intermission when, at the opening of act two, Hannah sits up in her own bed in Canada, next to Lyle, whom she fully recognizes, and unleashes the same long, loud scream.

Instead of supplying the stable image by which audiences can orient themselves within the narrative(s) about to unfold, *Lost Souls and Missing Persons* deliberately fragments the image, leaving audiences uncertain and uncomfortable with what they know or their ways of knowing. In this way, the play's structure anticipates and emulates the trope of psychasthenia: the failure of the image necessary to avoid epistemological, if not psychological, fragmentation. Without a coherent image from which to interpret the rest of the play, audiences find themselves in much the same condition as Hannah wandering the streets: confused, frustrated, and tentative. What Olalquiaga defines as the hallmark of the postmodern city, in fact, could just as easily describe the dramaturgy of Clark: it aggressively denies audiences any "fixed reference point" by which they could begin to comprehend an overall image or narrative and, instead, substitutes "an obsessive duplication of the same scenario" that goes on forever.[89] The aforementioned scene with the woman screaming in bed supplies the best instance of this denial of a "fixed reference point" in *Lost Souls and Missing Persons,* but more examples abound: the bag ladies mugging Hannah, Mr. Cape stalking Hannah, the possibility of Hannah having an affair.[90] Whatever audiences try to define as reference points for understanding Hannah's plight, those points never give answers to the questions confronting them. Instead, they confuse the referential relationships among incidents so that a coherent narrative becomes impossible, and confuse the epistemological assumptions between incidents and viewer. The episodic structure of *Lost Souls and Missing Persons,* then, indexes the postmodernity of the metropolis in which Hannah becomes disoriented and works against audiences' efforts to negotiate the landscape of the city or the play. In doing so, the play can perhaps foreclose engagement by frustrating audiences into indifference, or even departure at intermission. Nevertheless, in this structure Clark's play can reflect back something of the mutation of the postmodern environment described by Jameson, Harvey, Olalquiaga— through the difficulty, even impossibility, of comprehending the city.

City, Bad Place

Worth stressing before closing is that *Lost Souls and Missing Persons* is not merely about a Canadian woman who becomes disoriented and vanishes into New York City but instead about the postmodern city itself and its capacity for inducing disorientation. This distinction becomes evident with a return to the concentric circles in the play described previously, particularly, that of Turner. While Turner plays a significant, if morally suspect, role in the narrative of Hannah's disappearance, his life prior to their encounter supplies insights into the nature of the postmodern city represented in the play. During his penultimate scene with Hannah, who cheerfully mutters gibberish without regard for what he is saying, he describes himself as an "urban hermit."[91] This phrase warrants discussion in that it invokes but redefines many of the connotations that would normally apply. Most importantly, Turner uses the term "hermit" without reference to or perhaps knowledge of the traditional religious associations of the term: after all, we know he spends his time wandering the Bowery, looking for those who may be mentally disturbed. The term is used more secularly, with emphasis on the solitariness, or the withdrawal from society but still engaging with it tangentially. As Turner explains, "I'm out there mingling all the time" even though he rarely makes contact with those he encounters.[92] And, apparently, society's reaction is similar: "There are hundreds of us and yet, we don't exist." His terms suggest class consciousness as well as the legions of the poor in New York City in the 1980s, concerns echoed during flashback scenes between Hannah and Lyle with their concerns with workers' rights and strikes. But the play never develops such thematic concerns and instead focuses on the urban culture that has developed, in the United States at least, in the decades following the meeting of Lyle and Hannah. Unlike much of Turner's rambling, which usually feeds his narcissism, his comments on urban hermits extend toward an urban culture that complements concerns about disorientation pursued in relation to Hannah's vanishing. "Of course, I've met others of my kind but I wouldn't hang out with them. They're a bunch of assholes," Turner says. "That's the trouble with being an urban hermit. We don't form associations."[93]

In Turner's remarks emerge concerns about the postmodernity of Clark's New York City that extend the aforementioned interplay of empiricism, epistemology, and psychology toward larger conclusions about the city. Turner forms no associations, moral or civic, beyond what satisfies his ego or libido. Connected to nothing, he aspires to a life of dissociation, one of wandering, literally and metaphorically, through society. If Hannah's condition is mostly psychological, then Turner's is existential: a lifestyle predicated on irreferentiality that mirrors the urban culture theorized by Olalquiaga, Baudrillard, and Sorkin. Though Turner does not realize it, his definition of an urban hermit equally describes Mr. Cape: he has no meaningful associations with family or friends as demonstrated by his leaving his wife to stalk Hannah. Believing him dead, Mrs. Cape holds his funeral during which she learns that he had worked for years as a security guard and that he was deaf, when she had thought he was merely unresponsive during their marriage. She can be stunned by such discoveries because the language they used and experiences they shared were as fragmented and incomprehensible as Nesbitt's continuous stammering. And this final point, about language, connection, and meaning, is doubled by the introduction of Sweeny, an expert in missing persons hired by Lyle to find his wife (and another concentric circle). Describing the difficulty of finding missing persons at the end of the play, Sweeny shows Lyle two piles of names: the larger pile of those missing and the much smaller pile of those found. Sweeny then produces one more pile: "All these people. All suicides. Most of them match most of" those in the missing pile.[94] When Lyle asks why the "suicides" are not included in the "found" pile, Sweeny says, "Because they're not 'Found.' They're 'Dead.'"[95] Another clear breakdown of referentiality for this play: the language used to describe people, if not the conception of people, illustrates some lapse between reference and antecedent, between language and meaning. In this city, Hannah can exist *between* "Lost" and "Dead" or can be "Dead" without being "Found."

Brief and often bewildering, scenes like these complement the attention given to Hannah's disappearance and foreground the ultimate commentary of *Lost Souls and Missing Persons* about the postmodernity of contemporary urbanism. This city is without the "associations" of geography and ontology in architecture, or communality and civics in society necessary for sharing space with strangers without confusion or conflict. It is exactly the opposite, in fact, of both the "visibly organized and sharply defined" urban environment and the "clustering and organizations of . . . . meanings and *associations*" of culture defined by Lynch (emphasis added).[96] In many ways, the New York City of *Lost Souls and Missing Persons* demonstrates the mutation of urban culture that parallels the mutation in architecture defined by Jameson and others. In this new culture are considerable threats of becoming "lost," most notably the threats of violence, particularly against women. Noteworthy, too, are threats to psychological integrity induced by the fragmentation of image in the postmodern city, where dissociation may induce disorientation. And significantly, there is the threat of cultural loss—the loss of Canadian cultural identity—that corresponds with Hannah's vacation in New York and the play's debuting in the nexus of theatrical and cultural production at *Theatre Passe Muraille*. The city dramatized in Clark's play, specifically in Canadian theaters, confounds audiences with postmodern mutation of urban life just as desolate, baffling, and menacing as anything imagined by Kafka. Reinforcing the interplay of empiricism, epistemology, and psychology considered throughout the play is the aforementioned scene between Lyle and Sweeny, into which emerges Mrs. Cape and Nesbitt (she is his secretary, another crossing of concentric circles). During this scene, she explains Nesbitt's stuttering through the postmodern trope of inarticulateness: "He gets stuck on words. Repeats them endlessly."[97] Sweeny then provides the play's final commentary upon the urbanism that was becoming increasingly common during the 1980s and that has become almost the norm today: "Once he said 'City, bad place.' for an entire month."[98]

PART II

Iterations of Urbanism

CHAPTER 3

"Livin' in a Paradise": Suburbanism in Los Angeles

A growing disenchantment with urbanism emerged during the 1980s and 1990s from an improbable source. Unlike the 1950s and 1960s when riots and protests erupted among groups marginalized in urban life, this frustration came from the privileged and primarily white middle class of the United States. In *The Geography of Nowhere,* James Kunstler documents this disenchantment when he laments the "depressing, brutal, ugly, unhealthy, and spiritually degrading" reality of living in the metropolis.[1] More significantly, Kunstler locates the source of this problem in "the whole destructive, wasteful, toxic agoraphobia-inducing spectacle that politicians call 'growth.'"[2] Underlying this frustration, then, was a backlash against the utopian impulse behind the construction of cities following World War II.[3] After the war, Americans initially cheered the boom in urban growth meant, theoretically, to ameliorate social problems through a dubious equation: *bigger is better.* The answer to poverty and crime? More growth! The answer to overcrowding and unemployment? More growth! Half a century later many were rather dismayed at what this mandate had wrought. Troubled by skyscrapers towering over pedestrians and blocking out the skies, or freeways consuming vast stretches of landscape and pushing people farther and farther apart, those like Kunstler looked at what urbanism had become in New York City and Los Angeles and wept. They found themselves confronted by "all the terrors of giganticism and discontinuity" of the modern and postmodern metropolis, terrors that left them uncertain how to relate to one another in this environment, much less how to relate to the environment.[4] Lost in this metropolis was the feeling of "*connectedness*" that had been endorsed by the urbanism before such growth (original emphasis).[5] Because of this comes Kunstler's conclusion: "To me it is a landscape of scary places, the geography of nowhere, that has simply ceased to be a credible human habitat."[6]

Despite the *Sturm und Drang* of such lamentation, this eulogy for the metropolis did not correspond with blanket disillusionment with utopianism, or the impulse toward perfection in building cities. The indefatigability of Americans' faith in utopianism is among our leading and most endearing traits according to Baudrillard's *America.*[7] What followed from such lamenting, instead, was what had defined the urbanism of the West during much of the twentieth century: the search for utopian paradigms, only now reconceived toward the local and the nostalgic. Enter neotraditionalism, with flourish and trumpets. At once a cultural commentary on urbanism and an urban commentary on culture, neotraditionalism reimagined the urban environment from the perspective of Small Town America. "Conceived of in opposition to socially alienating, geographically dispersed, and environmentally harmful forms of urban development," neotraditional communities would be geographically small and socially self-contained in terms of housing, work, shopping, and social services.[8] Organized at what Kunstler describes as "the human scale," these communities boasted ample sidewalks for walking and streets "blessedly free of cars," all of which was a repudiation of the geography of nowhere.[9] Implicit in the geographical layout of neotraditionalism were social assumptions, or better yet, social ambitions: that is, the design of this environment endorsed a particular notion of community. The most laudable of these ambitions was the promotion of "a sense of social communitarianism based on local participation, self-governance, authenticity, and the equality of shared residence."[10] Because of this utopian impulse, neotraditionalism was "proclaimed as the solution to America's urban problems, from crime to community disintegration, from pollution to anomie."[11] To those troubled by what the metropolis had become, neotraditionalism promised a return to better times. Thornton Wilder's *Our Town*—without the irony.

But the irony proves as noteworthy to this representation of Small Town America as it did in Wilder's 1938 play. As James Duncan and David Lambert have demonstrated, not all of the ambitions behind the spatial organization of neotraditionalism were laudable. Considering three manifestations of neotraditionalism—New Bedford, New York; Seaside, Florida; and suburban enclaves in Los Angeles—they show that the communities provided escape not just from the *proportions* but further from the *demography* of the metropolis. Evidence emerged of what amounted to a correlation between exclusiveness—evident through the aesthetics of landscape and property ownership—and exclusion of "an increasingly multi-ethnic America."[12] In the suburbs of Los Angeles, the focus of this chapter, they documented "attempts at spatial manipulation" from zoning laws to homeowners' organizations to ordinances restricting access to public spaces, all serving to demarcate limits of admittance and belonging.[13] The "politico-legal suburban separatism of many

Los Angeles homeowners' associations," furthermore, was linked to the myth of "a 'lost Eden' of lily-white 1950s," an extension of the white flight from downtown Los Angeles in previous decades.[14] Neotraditionalism, in many cases in Los Angeles, amounted to another way of pursuing the ideological demarcation of space from Chapter 1. Noteworthy here is how suburbanism, as one branching of neotraditionalism, naturalized exclusionary politics in large part through the aesthetics of pastoralism (manicured lawns, landscaped yards, manor-type houses) and communitarianism (Small Town America) central to the American Dream. Under this mystified convergence of exclusive and exclusionary, the former was implicitly affirmed with the cultural pursuit of the latter. This mystification was one way of hiding the truth behind neotraditionalism according to Duncan and Lambert: "the notion of 'community' is always predicated on the expulsion of those not deemed to fit in."[15] Against this background of cultural, geographical, and class contestation, this chapter considers Sam Shepard's *True West* and Eduardo Machado's *Broken Eggs*. Distinctly dissimilar in exigency, these plays make for compelling contrast in their representation of suburbanism during the 1980s. Shepard, of course, is the quintessentially American dramatist,[16] whose plays reflect the myths, values, and culture of this country, however threadbare they may have become. By contrast, Machado was born in Cuba and now lives and works in the United States; his plays represent the cultural outsider, specifically, the Cuban exile trying to find a place in the United States. Nevertheless both playwrights represent suburbanism, in these plays, through the geographical as well as ideological struggle between insider and outsider: mostly in terms of class for Shepard, where the criminal confronts and finds himself confronted by his brother's apparently successful life in suburbia, and mostly ethnic for Machado, whose play represents the wedding reception of a Cuban girl who has married into a Jewish family in part to escape the constant familial struggle with exile. Complementing each other in surprising ways, *True West* and *Broken Eggs* expose the correlation between exclusive and exclusionary mystified in U.S. culture during the 1980s and, thereby, subject suburbanism to sociospatial criticism. Neither play considers suburbanism in isolation but rather locates and pursues the implications of suburbanism within national myths about freedom, individualism, and identity. In *True West*, Shepard contrasts suburban culture with the American West, a competing and yet similar mythology that shapes U.S. culture and leads the two brothers to mutually frustrated lives. In *Broken Eggs*, Machado locates the wedding within the context of the myths of America welcoming the immigrant into American society, and the family's nostalgia for the homeland lost in Cuba. From distinctly different but complementary perspectives of outsiders, then, the plays offer an indictment of the geography and ideology of neotraditionalism.

The plays of this chapter involve a significant shift of assumption and methodology in regard to the representation of the urban environment from those of the last chapter. While *Three Days of Rain* and *Lost Souls and Missing Persons* emphasize the incomprehensibility of the postmodern landscape, *True West* and *Broken Eggs* emphasize the semiotic apprehensibility of suburbanism. That is, they depict the landscapes of Los Angeles suburbs as fully legible texts that communicate simultaneously an aesthetic of place and a rhetoric of community. In truth, one informs the other through the signs of affluence that are easily readable for insiders and outsiders of suburban enclaves alike: the large homes that convey success and wealth; the manicured lawns that imply pastoralism; the clean streets that suggest security. Reading these signs for audiences, Austin reminds his brother, "We're livin' in a Paradise. We've forgotten that" in *True West*.[17] Of course, such enthusiasm is undermined by the fact that while describing the ideal neighborhood, Austin is thoroughly soused and stumbling toward a string of petty thefts to prove his mettle. But the significant point is that the landscape of *True West* and *Broken Eggs*, can be read and understood, including more subversive readings pursued by the plays. *True West* and *Broken Eggs* do not read *with* the texts of suburbanism, but instead *against* the aesthetic and rhetoric of "paradise" to expose the multiple layers of textuality therein: exclusivity *and* exclusionary, paradise *and* panopticism, affluence *and* authoritarianism. Working against the rhetoric of suburbanism, which makes an argument about the nature of suburbanism as a solution to the problems of Los Angeles, the plays of Shepard and Machado pursue a double ambition that contributes to the definition of sociospatial criticism. They read against hegemonic "readings" of suburbanism in order to reveal what would otherwise remain mystified in neotraditionalism. Secondarily, they invite audiences to become, in ways more skilled than Austin even while sober, readers and interpreters of the ideology of landscapes.

How Shepard and Machado pursue these ambitions corresponds with the ostensible realism of *True West* and *Broken Eggs*. In many ways, Shepard's and Machado's plays are the most realistic considered in this study: they both represent recognizable, real world locales (a suburban kitchen and a country club) and have scenography that insists, at least initially, on verisimilitude. But realism involves more than just *what* is represented; it additionally defines *how* the world will be represented and even how audiences will or will not *be engaged with* that world. Here, a return to W. B. Worthen's rhetoric of realism is in order. Worthen argues that drama includes particular conventions that invite or endorse particular modes of engagement. Realism, while only one example,[18] presents a world already complete and fully envisioned; in fact, realism works by obfuscating the process of representation before audiences and making the stage world as close as possible to the real world. Few demands, whether imaginative or critical, are put upon audiences: they become, in Worthen's argument, voyeuristic and even passive in their relation to the stage. If true, this obviously works against the aforementioned ambitions for *True West* and *Broken Eggs*. But I used the phrase "ostensible realism" because both plays draw upon realism in large part to critique its ways of representing the world: that is, both plays put pressure on the conventions of realism until neither play can be contained in this genre. As the realism breaks down, this puts pressure on audiences who are invited to question their modes of engagement with the play. This is certainly interesting unto itself, but beyond this is the link between Worthen's rhetoric of realism and the rhetoric of suburbanism that I have begun describing. In the following pages, I elaborate and pursue the implications of this link, but as a beginning to this argument, I suggest here that suburbanism, ideologically, makes an argument about itself that parallels the rhetoric of realism. It attempts to visually convince onlookers that the image of "paradise" is fully complete and not dependent upon any exclusionary politics. In interrogating the representation and engagement of realism, *True West* and *Broken Eggs* challenge suburbanism in much the same way they challenge realism.

Suburbanism and the Urban West

Sam Shepard's *True West* is, admittedly, an unlikely beginning to this argument about suburbanism. Overwhelming in its significance is the play's concern with the American West: the literal freedom of open territory far from an increasingly moribund society and the mythic premise of rebirth on the frontier first described by Frederick Jackson Turner.[19] Shepard's dramaturgy, *True West* included, demonstrates the inheritance of Turner's argument about national identity more than that of any U.S. dramatist. His characters cling to a symbolically sustaining, though tragically sterile, mythology of masculinity and Americanness grounded in the promise of the West. Because of this, no doubt, Bonnie Marranca has described the axes of Shepard's "poetics of space" as "East/West" and "North/South" and, more notably, distant from the subject of this book.[20] "Shepard's work should be vied in this context of a larger non-urban scale," she argues, because urbanism lacks the "feeling of space (and nature)" contained with the geographical scale of the continent: the "vastness that seems unfathomable, generous, still, triumphant, even religious [Shepard's] transcendental heritage."[21] Against this backdrop of the North American continent, the city seems "trivial" according to Marranca. If Shepard's plays have not been linked with urbanism, neither have they been linked with criticism. In *The Other American Drama*, Mark

Robinson argues, "Shepard has never pretended to more than a description of this image world. He unflinchingly has shown the lying and self-deception, the posing and posturing; but is always careful not to condemn them."[22] In this reading, Shepard's dramaturgy absorbs, internalizes, and mirrors— not without distortion—myths of America and Americanness central to our culture without serving any ideology.

In regard to Marranca's claims, this chapter offers the following emendation: *True West* demonstrates the swings between fascination and frustration in Shepard's dramaturgy for Los Angeles, the city in or near which many of his plays take place. This interest derives, in part, from the L.A. of the 1980s that probably represented the greatest threat to the vastness and significance of space defined by Marranca. But this interest, simultaneously, corresponds with what John Findlay defines as the mythology of the urban West of the 1940s and the 1950s: "People imagined the urban West (that is, the western metropolis with its central city, suburbs, and nearby countryside) offered Americans a unique opportunity to live according to their preferences."[23] In *Magic Lands,* Findlay contends that the mythology of the West was, quite purposely, turned into a marketing strategy for the American Dream, with Los Angeles of the early twentieth century promising much the same as the frontier promised in the nineteenth century: refuge against the problems of the East because the urban West was "more open to improvements in metropolitan design, social relations, and styles of living."[24] Concerns about the design of, relations in, and living style endorsed by the suburbs half a century later prove integral to the characterization, plotting, and conflicts of *True West.* In exploring such concerns, this chapter intends to suggest further axes of space in Shepard's dramaturgy—urban/frontier or desert/city—that complement those described by Marranca and better account for the "poetics of space" behind Shepard's plays. Of course, this marketing of the urban West cheapens the promise of the frontier, something that goes to the heart of Shepard's criticism of manifestations of the urban West like the suburbs of L.A. In regard to Robinson's argument, this chapter offers much the same emendation. While *True West* certainly does not emerge from the same sort of political consciousness as that behind *Angels in America* or *Marisol,* it still offers criticism of suburbanism: the actual landscape and the cultural promise of that landscape.

Making this argument means working more against, rather than with, the stage history of *True West,* which has not traditionally emphasized concerns with suburbanism in production or reviews. Debuting successfully in 1980 at the Magic Theatre in San Francisco, Shepard's play moved to the New York Shakespeare Festival later that year. Reviewing this production for *The Christian Science Monitor,* John Beaufort produces the reading of

True West that would dominate subsequent reviews and criticism: "The confrontation and its placid domestic setting seem to be ironically contrasting metaphors for the fragmenting of the American family and the emptiness of the American dream."[25] Family and the American Dream become paramount in part because they have long been the defining themes of American drama and in part because *True West* took its place among Shepard's "family" plays: *Buried Child* and *Curse of the Starving Class*. At best, suburbanism becomes a metaphor, rather subject in its own right, a conclusion that reflects the misnomer about space being an empty container. At worst, it perpetuates the superficial reading of the suburbs as "placid," which reinforces instead of interrogates myths of suburbanism. When revived in 1985 at the George Street Playhouse, *True West* garnered more consideration of the use of space in Alvin Klein's review for *The New York Times,* particularly the play's eruption in—if not of—space, with beer cans, toasters, and debris representing the "disintegration of the values, the past, the family."[26] Becoming more evident, the interest in suburbanism nevertheless remains secondary. In ways, it is easy to say that without the advances in cultural geography, there was no discourse for recognizing concerns with suburbanism, but this need not have been true. During the debut production, William Kleb stressed the tensions between the "rootless life" of Lee and the "West of the suburbs and freeways" of Austin, insights that would not be matched until the 1994 revival at the Cricket Theatre.[27] There, Peter Vaughn noted how Shepard "sets the play on the shifting suburban fault line that marks the end of one lifestyle and the beginning of another."[28]

Living in a Paradise

The "suburban fault line" defined by Vaughn informs the tensions between Shepard's brothers from the beginning of *True West*. While house-sitting for their mother in a suburban neighborhood some 40 miles east of Los Angeles, the college educated and middle-classed writer Austin is confronted by the unannounced arrival of Lee, his criminal brother. Confused but not yet threatened, Austin invites him to "stay here as long" as he likes.[29] Sensing insinuation, Lee growls, "I don't need your permission do I?" In Lee's comment, Shepard defines the opening conflict and something of the ultimate concerns of *True West*: the brothers are defined, culturally, as insider or outsider in this suburban community, probably Riverside.[30] When Lee talks about the community, in subsequent conversations, his concerns dwell on both what he can steal and what may impede his criminal endeavors: "Houses. Electronic devices" and the number of dogs.[31] To Lee, the neighborhood presents a prospective score that he needs after living for six months out on the desert. To Austin, on the other hand, the suburbs represent their mother's home, probably not that different from where he lives in Northern California with his family. Therefore, he suggests—to little avail—that Lee find another neighborhood from which to steal. He is trying to protect not just his mother's reputation in the community but further, the nature of suburbanism itself. The "here" that Lee ironically associates with permission is literally their mother's house and the suburbanism that welcomes Austin but excludes those like Lee. What lurks below the surface of this conversation between Austin and Lee becomes explicit during the argument that erupts in scene five. Angry at Austin, who gets "invited into prominent people's houses," Lee celebrates the freedom to "come in through the window" that comes from his being an outsider in this community.[32] Divided by class, education, and profession, the estranged brothers insult, aggravate, and eventually turn on each other *in* and *about* the suburbs of Los Angeles.

Despite these differences, the brothers share surprisingly similar attitudes about the suburban neighborhood at different times during the play and, when they convey them, supply the foundation for *True West's* interrogation of suburbanism. When Austin presses Lee about his wandering the neighborhood "with a purpose" between scenes one and two, Lee describes his reconnaissance in ways that stress his bravado: "One of [the houses] didn't even have a dog," he says, "Walked right up and stuck my head in the window" and took in the "suburban silence."[33] The tone and ambition of Lee's description, initially, emerge from his ongoing competition with Austin: he is attempting to prove that the world of the suburbs, Austin's world, is vulnerable to the likes of him. But the longer Lee describes the previous night, the more his description reveals enthusiasm for what he discovered while peering in the window: "Like a paradise. Kinda' place that sorta' kills ya' inside. Warm yellow lights. Mexican tile all around. Copper pots hangin' over the stove. Ya' know like they got in the magazines. Blonde people movin' in and outa' the rooms, talkin' to each other."[34] The short lines here suggest Lee's struggle to describe what he saw, or the longing he felt for it. After a pause long enough to suggest the latter, Lee adds, "Kinda' place you wish you sorta' grew up in." Remarkable not merely because it is one of the few times Lee talks without threatening or ranting, this short narrative is also noteworthy in that it thematizes the rhetoric of suburbanism. This image of "paradise" is what the suburbs, with its aesthetics of pastoralism and communalism, intend to communicate. So compelling is this rhetoric that Austin repeats Lee's conclusions later in the play: "The bushes. Orange blossoms. Dust in the driveway. Rainbird sprinklers. Everybody else is livin' the life. Indoors. Safe. This is a Paradise down here."[35] Where sincerity ends and irony begins in Austin's paean is difficult to ascertain since these remarks are preceded by drunken blustering and followed by his denuding the neighborhood of household appliances. Nevertheless both comments foreground the suburbanism interrogated by *True West.*

Like Lee, Austin understands the suburbs, implicitly, as a world defined and sustained by metonymy. This definition is integral to the rhetoric of suburbanism invoked and critiqued by *True West.* The bushes and blossoms mentioned by Austin designate—by standing in for—the blissful suburban life he praises. Likewise, the copper pots and Mexican tile described by Lee stand in for the blissful home inferred from his voyeurism, a home that metonymically doubles the neighborhood; the neighborhood, the community; the community, paradise. Underlying the beautiful landscapes of suburbanism represented in *True West* are a series of encoded messages about the lifestyles maintained therein, some of which are decoded and understood by Austin and Lee. The legibility of these messages derives from the messages' imbrication with notions of the American Dream: a happy family, owning property, living the "good life." In fact, the rhetoric of suburbanism depends on the propagation of indexicality, or the reassurance of an untroubled correlation between image and experience, between landscape and lifestyle. What onlookers see when looking at the suburban landscape—privilege, safety, wealth—is precisely what they will receive, according to this rhetoric. There is nothing in Lee's paean to "suburban silence" that suggests discord in the household that he watches through the window that night or, by extension, in this community in which Lee strolls (except, of course, for Lee himself). Nor is there anything in Austin's praise of the suburbs as "paradise" to remind anyone living in this or other such communities that Los Angeles, with its criminality, immigrant populations, and urban unrest is only a freeway away from this sanctuary. The reason Austin and Lee can look at the landscaped yards or well-furnished kitchens and reach basically the same conclusions—despite their differences—is because suburbanism advertises its paradisiacal nature visually and culturally. The home, the neighborhood, even the community are self-contained—but complementary—worlds isolated from problems of the metropolis by geography, socioeconomics, and the mystification of this isolation.

Suburban Fortification

If Austin and Lee introduce and succumb to this argument from metonymy, *True West* interrogates it by revealing what is necessary for maintaining this paradise. During scene two, for instance, Lee remarks bemusedly, "I never knew the old lady was so security minded," as he wanders around their mother's house, trying to open the cabinets and drawers: "She's got locks on everything. Locks and double-locks and chain locks and—What's she got that so valuable?"[36] Importantly, this scene comes *before* Lee's account of the house that defines the suburban neighborhood as paradise and, therefore, frames this description of paradise. The answer to Lee's question, of course, emerges from his voyeurism. Their mother has precisely what the blonde people with the Mexican tile seemingly have: a lifestyle that corresponds with the beauty of the landscape, a community founded on utopianism far away from the turbulence of Los Angeles. When put in terms of the lamentations about the metropolis in *The Geography of Nowhere,* the "suburban silence" of this community is considerably more valuable—for those living there—than the television that Lee steals during act three, or the toasters with which Austin absconds during scene seven. Implicit in Lee's inquiry about their mother followed by the "answer" suggested by his paean to suburbanism, then, is the imbrication of exclusive and exclusionary found in studies of suburbanism mentioned in the opening of this chapter. The locks and double-locks convey another level of textuality about suburbanism, this one not as readable for Lee and, at times, for Austin in part because it is usually mystified by the aesthetics of pastoralism in the landscape. Part of the pleasure of inhabiting, if only briefly, this suburban paradise is the obfuscation of the problems of the metropolis. During this scene, then, *True West* introduces something paradoxically dissonant to the ideal but fundamental to the reality of suburbanism: the need to defend this paradise against threats of the metropolis.

In this conflict of ideal and reality, *True West* confronts the rhetoric of suburbanism with what Duncan and Lambert describe as the "suburban fortification" of 1980s Los Angeles.[37] This "fortification" involved defending the suburbs against threats—to property, lifestyles, and diversity—and included[38] installing surveillance, restricting admittance to public parks, and hiring private security firms.[39] Much of this is suggested in *True West.* During the opening scene, when the tensions emerge around definitions of belonging and trespassing, the language used by Austin in his warning stresses this fortification: "You're going to get picked up if you start walking around here at night."[40] Suggested here are both the community's mandate of defending the dichotomy of insider and outsider, and the means employed toward protecting that dichotomy, in this case, the unseen presence of security patrolling the area. This reference to patrols becomes more explicit, even nightmarish, during Austin's drunken taunting during scene seven: "The sounds of the Police Helicopters prowling above the neighborhood. Slashing their searchlights down through the streets. Hunting for the likes of you."[41] In the tensions between the brothers during these scenes, *True West* interrogates the panopticism and security patrols subsidizing this paradise of suburbanism. If this community is a paradise, then it is a paradise thanks to its own cherubs—with nightsticks and side-arms instead of flaming swords—who vigilantly safeguard (the fantasy of) this paradise. Exactly what suburbanism wants to mystify through its rhetoric of privilege or exclusivity, this reality emerges from the arguments between Austin and Lee throughout the play: the suburban community defines insiders and outsiders through rhetoric, ideology, or if necessary, through intervention. More significant is how *True West* works against the rhetoric of suburbanism by situating a comment, by Austin or Lee, which stresses the Edenic quality of the suburbs, against details like the locks and double-locks that make public the surveillance of terrain and the policing of borders.

Necessary for maintaining the "paradise" of suburbanism described by Austin and Lee are any number of "fortification" strategies that would normally be obfuscated by the rhetoric of suburbanism. *True West*, in effect, offers a double reading of these suburbs: the first carried out by the brothers, which serves to thematize the play's sociospatial concerns, and the second carried out by the play, which reads against the visual and cultural beliefs behind suburbanism. Not built upon a conversion narrative, involving the discovery of truths by one or more characters, *True West* instead continually interweaves the two readings in ways that develop an increasingly complex and critical conclusion on suburbanism. Defined through metonymy, once more, *True West* reveals the panopticism and patrolling underlying but simultaneously obfuscated in Austin's comment of "Orange blossoms" and his conclusion "Safe." Once revealed, this subtext of suburbanism suggests the less appealing reality behind the community of "blonde people" living at some remove from Los Angeles and whose definition of "paradise" is predicated upon the exclusion of immigrants and minorities, which are both conspicuously absent from the suburban landscape. In this way, the play implicitly corroborates conclusions by Duncan and Lambert, though *True West's* concerns seem more relevant to what Mike Davis argues about greater Los Angeles in the 1980s: that the (sub)urban landscape was becoming increasingly divided into communities of "affluence" and "the criminalized poor."[42] *True West* is not concerned with the efficacy of panopticism and patrols in suburbanism as demonstrated by the inability of the community's security services described by Austin to stop Lee from walking up to windows and peering inside. Even Austin, soused and unproven in breaking-and-entering, has little difficulty pillaging community toasters. Instead, *True West* exposes the hypocrisy *upon which* suburbanism is predicated: the paradise of these suburbs is no more "real" than the adventure of the Old West in Lee's screenplay.[43]

In *True West*, this hypocrisy is worthy of condemnation not merely because of duplicity but instead because of its inherent futility that always borders upon the absurd. The trouble with suburbanism is not just that it fulfills its promise of paradise through the dissonant means of fortification but that what this fortification intends to defend is diminished, if not moribund as demonstrated by Austin's increasing dissatisfaction with his life. Not surprisingly, Shepard makes something of a joke of the exclusionary ethos that proves so integral to the paradise of suburbanism through the reversal of roles by Austin and Lee. After Lee supplants Austin's period piece with his hackneyed western, for example, Austin turns to criminality: drinking until he finds enough courage to carry out his criminal enterprise of petty thefts in his mother's neighborhood. Become a screenwriter, at least in name after selling his "true to life" western, Lee finds himself struggling to navigate the intricacies of the typewriter and threatens to kick Austin out when he refuses to help him. Just before Lee begins attacking the typewriter with his golf clubs, Austin describes their reversal of fortunes: "Oh, so now you're gonna kick me out! Now I'm the intruder. I'm the one who's invading your precious privacy," he mocks from the floor, surrounded by empty beer cans.[44] This scene, of course, perfectly inverts the opening scene with Lee intruding on Austin's privacy, and conveys the existential transposition of the brothers that has so frequently been subject of scholarship on *True West*.[45] At the same time, this inversion corresponds with their changes in relation to the suburban backdrop of the play: Austin now the maudlin outsider, drinking and plotting his crimes, and Lee the feckless insider attempting to fulfill his responsibilities as a screenwriter. Reduced here to parody, the division between insider and outsiders becomes something that deserves ridicule, especially since it was induced by a wager between Lee and Saul on a golf course. And I am willing to generalize briefly and contend that this is the effect—a joke—for middle-class audiences who watch *True West*, especially when Lee exclaims, "I'm a screenwriter now! I'm legitimate!"[46]

Despite the laughter induced by this scene, *True West* dramatizes increasingly serious concerns about geography, culture, and ideology in ways that offer criticism of the nature of suburbanism in the 1980s. Few dramatists would be described as *less* Brechtian than Shepard,[47] but in *True West* Shepard's iconoclasm, when directed toward the play's locale, serves quasi-Brechtian ends. The depiction of suburbanism encourages what Brecht describes as "the social laws under which [the characters] are acting" to "spring into sight," that is, they become defamiliarized in ways that encourage consideration.[48] This outcome is evident in Austin's mentioning of the surveillance and security patrols of the community, however feeble they may be. This outcome is additionally evident in Shepard's making Lee the "insider" during the transposition of the brothers, however much it may be a joke. In fact, the laughter that follows from Lee's adamancy about being "legitimate" becomes a way of "making strange" the process of exclusion/inclusion since audiences are left with the incongruity of what they are watching and what they know. They must reconcile Lee's claims with the nature of suburbanism in ways that allow them to question this. *True West* is certainly no epic play, and I do not want to put too much emphasis on relations with Brecht, but instead, to I want to underscore how Shepard's dramatization of suburbanism involves criticism of culture and urbanism. This interest may not rise to the level of interest in the mythology of the American West, but it certainly suggests further axes in the paradigm of Marranca: suburban/frontier or city/desert. Beyond this *True West's* representation of the suburbs of Los Angeles corresponds with Pierce Lewis's argument that landscapes are an "unwitting autobiography" inscribed in geography, of the cultures that inhabit those landscapes.[49] How suburbanism is designed, geographically or ideologically tells us much about the people—notably blonde—inhabiting them. One thing learned through reading *True West* as "autobiography" is what Duncan and Lambert concluded: "the notion of 'community' is always predicated on the expulsion of those not deemed to fit in."[50] Another is that the rhetoric of suburbanism continually works to obfuscate this fact.

Distort Its Dimensions

Importantly, *True West* invites reading *against* not only the geography of suburbanism, but further, against the rhetoric of suburbanism defining this geography. Toward this second and perhaps more challenging endeavor, the play enlists the realist stage. In the "Note on Set and Costume" that accompanies the published play, Shepard consciously stresses the realism of the scenography and, by extension, the nature of the reception that follows: "the stage should be constructed realistically with no attempt to distort its dimensions, shapes, objects, or colors."[51] This is a distinct break from earlier plays like *Chicago*, which opens with a policeman assaulting a chair and Stu lounging in a bathtub, or *The Unseen Hand*, which opens with a 1951 Chevy with "Kill Azusa" painted on the side and Blue talking to an imaginary driver. Just two instances of Shepard's plays' flaunting their incongruity, these plays intend to challenge assumptions about empiricism and interpretation. Not so with *True West*, which led reviewers during the debut season to stress the play's accessibility.[52] Implicit in Shepard's "Note" is reassurance that the staging, at least initially, will not make excessive demands on audiences. Instead, Shepard suggests something close to the "contract of total visibility, total knowledge" described by Chaudhuri.[53] Starting from the "well-stocked stage of naturalism"—telephone, refrigerator, chair, any number of stage properties that mystify their theatricality by erasing any distinction between symbol and object—this theater invites audiences toward comprehensibility.[54] The world represented on the stage through the metonymic reasoning of such objects promises indexicality or a one-to-one relationship of sign/signified: the chair is always a chair, not a symbolic throne as the couch becomes in *Buried Child*. Making sense of the scenography involves little cognitive or imaginative engagement from audiences, particularly when compared to works like *Chicago* and *The Unseen Hand* and their overt incongruity.

This initial emphasis on realism, intriguingly, puts audiences of *True West* in much the same epistemological relationship to the stage as Lee is to the interior of the house with copper pots and Mexican tile. Sitting in a darkened theater (much like Lee hiding in the shadows) and anonymously gazing through an imaginary fourth wall (the window), audiences observe what proclaims itself to be a hermetically sealed and fully transparent world. In this juxtaposition, the rhetoric of realism overlaps and converges with the rhetoric of suburbanism. This proves integral to *True West's* interrogation of the latter, which begins from Lee's observation through the window. If this world is truly enclosed, then there is nothing beyond what can be seen: for Lee nothing like the problems of crime or poverty, which he embodies, of the metropolis, and for audiences, none of the work unfolding in the wings of the theater necessary for scene and costume changes. If truly transparent, then meaning is easily discerned and always stable: for Lee, the signs read—pots, tiles, conversation—correspond directly with the conclusion that he reaches, "like a paradise"; for audiences, stage properties and the stage itself put no pressure upon phenomenology, that is, they never challenge the definition of a chair or table or locale. More than merely looking at suburbanism—literally for Lee, thematically for audiences—this convergence implies much about *ways of looking*, or how particular landscapes can condition audiences toward specific assumptions. In both cases, after all, we are discussing rhetoric, or the effort to make an argument about *how* and *what* to observe. During Lee's reconnaissance between acts one and two, he observes several details about his mother's neighbors, details that result in flawed conclusions about this "suburban silence" because he never questions what he sees, or the promise of suburbanism: the paradise that is enclosed (distant from Los Angeles) and transparent (telling the whole truth). Likewise, audiences of realism are invited toward voyeurism and passivity: they are tacitly "told" they should accept what they are being shown without questioning the manner or the nature of the representation. The rhetorics of realism and suburbanism, in other words, use many of the methods and endorse the same ends.

But *True West* cannot be constrained by the realism introduced during the initial scene any more than the brothers can be contained by the suburban kitchen. Moving forward from Lee's voyeurism, the play increasingly gestures toward the frequent elisions in the dramatized world—Austin's observations about security patrols and Saul's and Austin's references to Los Angeles freeways—and thereby reveal the limits of the promise of realism and suburbanism. Although evidence abounds, one of the best instances comes during scene eight, which begins with scenographic corroboration of Austin's turning to a life of crime. When the scene opens, Austin is polishing a long line of toasters that he has stolen during the night and that will facilitate his absurd Eucharist later in the scene. The toasters are something of an interruption, or perhaps irruption, between mimesis and diegesis, or what is represented visually and what is represented narratologically. Until this moment, the suburban neighborhood has been limited (except for Lee's stolen television set) to descriptions from the characters; but now, audiences are confronted with an abundance of toasters that, implicitly, comprises one of the defining elements of realism: Chaudhuri's "contract of total visibility." Where did the toasters come from? How were they assembled so quickly? Could the described security forces of the community burst into the house? Bringing these toasters into the ostensibly closed stage of realism puts pressure on the concept of enclosure, on being able to segregate one space successfully from another. Additionally, it encourages audiences toward consideration of what they cannot see, what is left out of or obfuscated in the realistic stage and, by extension, the suburban neighborhood. The toasters become a comical rejoinder to the promise of the rhetorics of realism and suburbanism: however complete or transparent the worlds represented under these rhetorics may be, they produce completeness or transparency through omitting anything that might disrupt this world (in terms of realism, the stagehands necessary for moving properties; in terms of suburbanism, the conspicuous consumption and external criminality). Revealing this definition-through-omission serves the condemnation of hypocrisy driving *True West*, hypocrisy that may be harmless with realism, though debate continues about this point,[55] but that is undoubtedly harmful with suburbanism.

Quite deliberately, then, *True West* fragments the coherence of the realistic stage, which invokes suburbanism mimetically and metonymically, introduced at the beginning and moves steadily toward the incoherence of surrealism. The ambition being, sociospatially, to expose the hypocrisy upon which suburbanism is built. If considered through a chronological progression of production photos, this ambition becomes evident in the destruction of the suburban kitchen. The first scene of *True West* reveals a slightly tacky but nevertheless well-kept and middle-class home with hints of bushes and citrus trees outside the windows, glimpses of pastoralism in the midst of the California desert. The third scene shows basically the same detail at the beginning, with Saul and Austin discussing the latter's screenplay but concludes with the anomaly of the stolen television in the kitchen. The seventh scene reveals Austin, drunk and sprawled among beer bottles, empty and overturned, on the kitchen floor. The ninth scene opens with even more debris, so much that Lee has to kick his way through it as he paces back and forth, dictating his western to Austin, with the visual effect being that of a "desert junkyard."[56] More than just fragmenting this metonymic location of suburbanism, the kitchen that is the source of nostalgic values and definitions of family, *True West* fragments the rhetoric of suburbanism in ways that parallel its subversion of the rhetoric of realism. During the play's early scenes, Lee's account of the neighborhood as being "like a paradise" accurately registers the cultural understanding of suburbanism, in the 1980s, produced by this rhetoric. It is presented as overwhelmingly true, so much so, that it wins over the sensibilities of the outlaw brother who, subsequently, struggles to become "legitimate." But this understanding of suburbanism is complicated, first by Austin's revelations about the panopticism and patrolling of the area, and second by those irruptions in the theatrical production considered above. All this undermines not just the conclusion reached by Lee but also the naïve reading of suburbanism that he uses to reach his conclusion. This double reading encourages audiences toward questions about the hypocrisy of suburbanism.

Streets Misremembered

Toward this end, audiences of *True West* can follow Austin's growing disillusionment with suburbanism. At the beginning of the play, Austin takes suburban life for granted and his only concern about suburbanism is protecting it, or perhaps their mother's reputation therein, from Lee's criminal wrongdoing. Hence his urging Lee to find a different neighborhood from which to steal. During his argument with Saul about Lee's western, later in the play, emerges something of Austin's disenchantment with Los Angeles in references to smog, freeways, and strip malls—but these implicitly reinforce the attraction of suburbanism, which was marketed as ways of escaping troubles of the metropolis. But Austin never really feels comfortable in his mother's neighborhood and not merely because of the aforementioned panopticism necessary to fulfilling the promise of living in a paradise; in this, he epitomizes much about the suburban inhabitant during this period of fortification in Los Angeles. Instead, there is something within Austin that remains dubious about the very promise of paradise. During the penultimate scene, Austin reveals what has been troubling him for years: "There's nothin' down here for me," he tells Lee, a conclusion that stands in obvious contrast to what is promised by suburbanism.[57] "But now—I keep comin' down here thinkin' it's the fifties or somethin'. I keep finding myself getting off the freeways at familiar landmarks that turnout to be unfamiliar." Coming near the end of the play, long after the existential reversal of the two brothers, Austin's laments have certainly been exaggerated by losing his movie deal with Saul. In many ways, what Austin says about the neighborhood could be a byproduct of the collapse of career and life that correspond with Lee's ascendance, something that invites contrast of the promise of the American West—freedom, fulfillment, and renewal—with the reality of suburbanism—domestication and diminution. But Austin's discomfort with suburbanism precedes this existential crisis that leads to his Faustian bargain.[58] In this preexisting anxiety, emerges much of the criticism of suburbanism, specifically as nested in the cultural project of neotraditionalism.

Neotraditionalism, if we return momentarily to the opening of this chapter, promised a life away from "the terrors of giganticism and discontinuity" that were making the metropolis increasingly "uninhabitable." In particular to Los Angeles, this meant escape from both the growing urban unrest that would eventually lead to rioting in 1992 (not included in *True West* but still central to the cultural phenomenon of neotraditionalism) and the endless sprawl (mentioned by Austin and Saul). Away from this conglomeration of freeways, people would find a renewed sense of "*connectedness*" at the social—the homogenous populations of suburbs in L.A.—and spatial—the roadways, yards, and buildings—levels. But this is precisely what Austin does *not* experience during his frequent visits to his mother's neighborhood; in fact, the more visits made correlates with increasingly *less* connectedness. During these visits, he finds himself "wandering down streets I thought I recognized that turn out to be replicas of streets I remember," he tells Lee, "Streets I misremember. Streets I can't tell if I lived on or saw in a postcard."[59] Troubled by the cognitive dissonance between what is promised, even if only implicitly, by the nature of his mother's neighborhood and the reality of what he finds there, Austin struggles to make sense of locations that he might have "lived or" or, as likely, only ever experienced as simulacra. Evident in Austin's confusion are, paradoxically, the promise and problem underlying neotraditionalism. Neotraditionalism emerged from the amalgamation of nostalgia and geography: the effort to recreate Small Town America based on mythical models of the 1950s. But this precisely what troubles Austin: the uncertain conflation of geography, history, even ontology. Rather than producing any sense of connection to the suburban neighborhood, this conflation induces his feeling of geographical and ontological confusion: what is real about this neighborhood? And what is imagined? How does one *misremember* something, especially that which one may have never seen or known?

So troubling is this experience that it leaves Austin uncertain about not just *where* or *when* but also *who* he is: "There's nothin' real down here, Lee!" he shouts, "Least of all me!"[60]

Intentionally or not, Shepard locates suburbanism and neotraditionalism in the crisis of meaning derived from simulation described by Baudrillard, Jameson, and Soja among others. Defined in Baudrillard's *Simulacra and Simulation,* the term describes the production of a "copy" without an "original"; or, the subverting of referentiality (historical or ontological) between this "copy" and its "original" attendant with postmodern culture.[61] This subverting collapses distinctions, argues Baudrillard, between real and imaginary, true and false. This collapse describes Austin's epistemological struggle to distinguish replica from remembering, as well as his ontological struggle to differentiate streets "lived on" from those "in a postcard." He cannot tell what is actually from the 1950s in the neighborhood where his mother now lives from the replication of the 1950s—in architecture, streets, or businesses—distributed throughout the landscape. The reason for Austin's difficulty hearkens back to the premise of neotraditionalism, which was to reimagine urbanism from the perspective of Small Town America, an ambition that begins from idealized assumptions about the nature of 1950s small towns, and from the belief that recreating the geography of this town will translate to the recreation of the sociality of this town—without producing any dissonance of modern life. In this, *True West* foregrounds the underlying flaw—another hypocrisy—of neotraditionalism as it was manifested through suburbanism. Although it can distinguish itself from the metropolis of Los Angeles through replicating Small Town America, it can never completely mystify its own simulacral ontology. There will always be that nagging sense that Austin, as someone used to living in the suburbs, experiences that leads to his conclusion that "There's nothing real down here!" This compounds the hypocrisy of suburbanism: what those like the blonde people watched by Lee are defending is not truly paradise or it would it ever be. Instead, it is the simulation of paradise. This explains something of Austin's desire to leave his family and career behind him for the desert; but here, Shepard piles irony upon irony here since Austin was the one who argued, rightly, that there is little "real" about the West of Lee's screenplay or the desert.

Generalizing conclusions about suburbanism based entirely on Austin's experience or perspective is not necessary in *True West.* During the closing scene Shepard produces further evidence of the play's attitude toward suburbanism, beginning with the unexpected arrival of Austin's and Lee's mother, back from her cruise to Alaska. When not lamenting the condition of her kitchen—dead plants, beer bottles everywhere—she is full of enthusiasm regarding her latest news. Picasso is at the museum! When Austin explains that Pablo Picasso died nearly a decade earlier, she will hear none of it because she saw an advertisement on a bus on her way home. Surely, this is part of the conclusion on suburbanism in *True West*: to live happily in the "paradise" of the suburbs, people must have little awareness of either historical or ontological dissonance; or worse, perhaps living in the suburbs induces this unawareness. In either event, Austin's and Lee's mother would seem to epitomize those who have bought into the rhetoric of suburbanism, at least in *True West*. Against this background, Austin's eulogy for the suburbs—"There's nothing real down here!"—sounds less maudlin than truthful. Though it almost certainly means reading more into his words than he intended, Lee's explanation about why he has to go back out on the desert, likewise, contribute to the play's conclusions on suburbanism: "All this town does it drive a man insane."[62] In the movement from the "paradise" of Lee's account of the neighborhood, doubled in the kitchen where all the action occurs, to the "desert junkyard" of empty beer bottles and open flames in trash bins, to the final tableau where Lee and Austin, in silhouette, are frozen in an eternal death struggle, the structure and setting of *True West* convey its commentary on suburbanism. Without suggesting that Baudrillard was making reference to this play, his remarks in *America* supply an apt epilogue to *True West*: "But is this really what an achieved utopia looks like? Is this a successful revolution? Yes indeed! What do you expect a 'successful' revolution to look like? It is a paradise . . . Mournful, monotonous, and superficial though it may be, it is a paradise. There is no other."[63]

Those Who Get Picked Up

With only few exceptions, thus far, racial and ethnical difference have been conspicuous in their absence from this consideration of suburbanism. However critical Shepard's play is of suburbanism, its criticism centers on the failed mythology of place and not the segregated demography of this place. This is noteworthy since neotraditionalism, suburbanism included, correlated with efforts to shut out "an increasingly multi-ethnic America" in the 1980s.[64] *True West* merely hints at this through Lee's description of the "blonde people" living in suburbia before exploring the hypocrisy of this paradise. This downplays crucial concerns of racial or ethnic exclusion in suburbanism. Worse, *True West* may, frankly, perpetuate at least the rhetoric of exclusion by ignoring the corollary between racial and spatial difference in suburban fortification in greater Los Angeles. It is not just the likes of Lee, after all, who gets "picked up" for trespassing upon serenity of suburbia. It is those who stand out visibly, culturally, and linguistically, those who cannot easily be assimilated into the homogeneity of Small Town America, those whose very presence threatens the promise of paradise underlying suburbanism. If anything, the rhetoric of suburbanism is distinctly visual and works to naturalize differences in place not merely by linking exclusive and exclusionary but additionally, white and welcome, and minority and menace. In many ways, including this element of suburbanism in the discussion only adds to *True West's* criticism of the hypocrisy of this paradise: a paradise founded upon, at least in part, excluding those who are most plainly outsiders. But this chapter now goes beyond *True West* to consider these questions that underlie sociospatial drama about suburbanism: is it enough to foster awareness of hypocrisy without reference to effects beyond this community? Or is it necessary to confront audiences, in particular white middle-class audiences, with this racialized problem and their accountability in any interrogation of suburbanism?

This chapter turns now to Eduardo Machado's *Broken Eggs* to address these questions. The final play in *The Floating Island Plays,* a quartet of works that dramatize the struggles of three generations of the Marquez family and their efforts to navigate the tumultuous history of Cuba during the twentieth century, *Broken Eggs* debuted in 1984. These plays reflect a number of Cuban *(The Modern Ladies of Guanabacoa, Fabiola,* and *In the Eye of the Hurricane)* and Cuban American *(Broken Eggs)* concerns, most significantly exile from Cuba; nostalgia for lost homeland; and discrimination in their new home of Woodland Hills, L.A. Appropriately, *Broken Eggs* debuted at International Arts Relations, Inc. (INTAR), which was founded in 1966 with the following mandate: "1) to nurture the development of Latino artists; 2) to produce bold and innovate plays that reflect diverse perspectives; and 3) to make accessible the diversity inherent in America's cultural heritage."[65] Obviously, any play that pursues this mandate, like *Broken Eggs,* poses an intriguing challenge to the philosophy and rhetoric of suburbanism as discussed so far. A Cuban exile,[66] Machado writes from a different perspective about U.S. culture than Shepard, which was nurtured by INTAR. In fact, Machado began writing *The Modern Ladies of Guanabacoa* while working as an actor for the company, before taking the playwriting lab from Maria Irene Fornes, another Cuban dramatist, who would shift his focus from acting to writing.[67] During the following years, Machado maintained his affiliation with INTAR, producing plays there and becoming the artistic director in 2004. Interviewed by Liesl Schillinger not long after assuming the leadership of INTAR, Machado defines some of his ambitions in terms of the interplay of culture, geography, and identity: "A Latino who lives in Latin America knows that he has a culture, that he belongs in the country where he lives. But us, living here, we are still looking for a culture, and for a place to belong."[68] This search for belonging, literal and figurative, proves central to the sociospatial ambitions of *Broken Eggs*.

In production and reviews of *Broken Eggs*, this search for belonging has been principally considered at the global scale, that is, about the exile from Cuba. Gilberto Zaldívar's New York-based *Repertorio Español*, which took *Broken Eggs* on a touring production in Cuba in 1998, nicely demonstrates these concerns. Met with enthusiasm by small Cuban audiences who "applauded each time a familiar face came on stage" and which "shrieked with laughter at lines like 'Do you remember when we used to think Fidel was sexy?'" observes Mireya Navarro, the play engaged audiences in terms of a shared, scarred past.[69] And, most significantly, the play may have prompted or eased the process of healing cultural wounds. Alongside this global scale, however, is the local (suburban) setting and storyline, which has received little discussion thus far. The story takes place backstage during the wedding reception for Lizette Marquez, the eldest daughter of the Cuban family, who has wed a Jewish boy who is never named but whose family, the Rifkins, apparently have money and privilege in the Woodland Hills community. In the anteroom to the reception hall—the entire play unfolds in this marginal and marginalizing space—Lizette's estranged parents and rebellious siblings relive generations of problems that arise during the reception and constantly remind the Marquez family that they are outsiders in this suburban community. Ranging from teenage pregnancy to addiction, from generational antagonism to name calling between Osvaldo's children and his second wife, these problems stress the psychological and existential burdens of always being in search of a place, not just in terms of exile from homeland but also in terms of exclusion from suburbanism. The argument that follows does not intend to replace one reading of this search for "a place to belong" with another, but instead to consider the dialectical interplay of geographical scales in *Broken Eggs*. In fact, concerns about exile prove integral to the play's criticism of suburbanism. Concerned with how communities influence each another, including the ways they define themselves at the expense of the "Other," Machado's play interrogates the philosophy and politics behind suburbanism in Los Angeles in ways that prove particularly revealing—and troubling.

Sorting Out Race

The geography of *Broken Eggs* is defined, from the beginning, through the contrast of downtown Los Angeles and the suburbs of Woodland Hills. When the lights come up, Sonia and Manuela, the mother and grandmother of Lizette, enter arguing about why the cake has arrived in the middle of the reception rather than before the ceremony. Determined to blame Osvaldo, Sonia's ex-husband for anything amiss, Manuela maintains that this embarrassment must be because of his stinginess. But Sonia corrects her by explaining, "Because the Cuban bakery only delivers in downtown L.A. They don't come out this far."[70] Sonia's intent in this explanation is to defend Osvaldo, with whom she still hopes to reconcile despite the fact that he has remarried, but her remark additionally suggests much about Los Angeles in 1979, when the play takes place. In downtown L.A., there are several Cuban bakeries because that is where populations of Cubans—like other immigrants—are located. Implicitly, there are very few Cubans, certainly not enough to support a bakery, living in Woodland Hills, a community 25 miles west of Los Angeles. Of course, the distance from downtown to "this far out" is more than simply geographical; it is also cultural and ideological, the distance between the nostalgic promise of suburbanism and the "multi-ethnic America" against which suburbanism defined itself. Though it does not become evident until later in the play, inherent in Sonia's remark is the boundary, at once geographical and ideological, which defines the limits of access and acceptability for immigrants, Cubans in this case, in suburban communities like Woodlands Hills. Today, Woodland Hills has little in common with the smaller scale of neotraditionalism; it is defined by the same endlessly sprawling streets and neighborhoods of Southern California. But originally, it was another attempt at paradise, and even today has a population of only 7–8 percent Latinos (over 80 percent white), numbers that are striking when contrasted with the San Fernando Valley, which has a population of about 40 percent Latinos.[71] In Sonia's remark, Machado defines the geographically "local" poles of belonging in *Broken Eggs*: the downtown of diversity and the "out this far" of homogeneity.

As much as any considered in this book, Machado's play demonstrates the argument made by Pierce Lewis about landscapes serving as "unwitting autobiography" of culture. This is true whether this landscape of Southern California is read diachronically or synchronically. Evident in the urban/suburban landscape defined by Sonia's remark and supported by the storyline that follows is what Mike Davis describes as the "racial sorting out process" that Los Angeles was undergoing from 1972 until 1989.[72] It was then that L.A. experienced "white flight," the relocation of wealthy middle-class whites away from the downtown core, which was triggered originally by the Watts Riots in the 1960s and the considerable property damage left in its wake.[73] During this period, Los Angeles "sort[ed]" itself into communities which were defined, ostensibly, by socioeconomics but that reinforced what amounted to racialized segregation between inner-city and "edge cities" surrounding the derelict core—which is basically what remains today in Los

Angeles. This "sorting" of race was in all probability simultaneously geographical and ideological, or if not *simultaneously,* then certainly *sequentially.* As Davis contends, this sorting of race conflated "the semantic identity of race and urbanity" in the United States imagination so that "big-city" became synonymous with or euphemism for the "Black-Latino 'underclass.' "[74] Noteworthy, here, is how this history of "sorting" race corresponds with the argument for neotraditionalism: how much of the anxiety about the metropolis, with its "terrors," was coded anxiety about race, ethnicity, and diversity? Admittedly the community of Woodland Hills predated the period considered by Davis (the area was occupied as early as 1922 and was named Woodland Hills in 1941), but it did not grow to its current population and demography until the 1970s, during this period of "sorting" the landscape. It became one of the suburban communities that defined itself against the problems of the metropolis, one of which Machado highlights from the beginning of *Broken Eggs* being racial and ethnic difference, neither of which are not welcome "out this far."

While Machado includes few references to this *history* of "sorting out" race, much of it is nevertheless evident in the synchronic reading of Woodland Hills during the play. In 1979, this sorting out has become so thoroughly naturalized in this community that is it taken for granted not merely by members of the community—represented by the Rifkins[75]—but additionally by those sorted *out* of the community. The Marquez family fully understands that Cubans, like other immigrants, do not "belong" in suburban communities. This is evident, first of all, in how matter-of-factly Sonia explains the cake's late arrival: it apparently makes sense to her that there would not be Cuban bakeries in Woodland Hills or anywhere other than downtown L.A. This notbelonging becomes more evident during the reception. While the Rifkins sit comfortably in the ballroom offstage, Sonia and Manuela, the matriarchs of the family, spend most of their time trying to please or impress the Rifkins; their relationship to their new in-laws is closer to that of servants to their employers, which metonymically reproduces the fundamental relationship of Latinos and Caucasians throughout suburbanism. Worse, when it becomes clear that there will not be enough cake for all the guests, Sonia is humiliated: "I can't embarrass the groom's family again," she tells Osvaldo.[76] Not really worried about ruining her daughter's wedding, her thoughts focus on appeasing the Rifkins. Osvaldo's remedy unintentionally confirms the social hierarchy implicit in Sonia's anxiety: "go up to the Cubans we know and ask them not to eat the cake. Then serve it to the Jews."[77] It hardly matters that the Rifkins, it turns out, do not want the cake, perhaps because it is too "ethnic." What matters is that Cubans, even wedding guests, are trespassing on this community, and it is expected that they will go without. Like the bakery dismissed from Sonia's thoughts, they do not belong in suburbanism; in fact, they are a reminder of precisely what suburbanism defined itself against during the "sorting out" of race in the years when the play is set. Aware that they are trespassing, the older generation of the family acquiesces to the social hierarchy of suburbanism rather than upsets it. In fact, Lizette's regular pleading, "No Cuba today," can be interpreted as warning about publically displaying their ethnicity as much as avoiding arguments between her parents and grandparents.

No Cuba Today

In Lizette's plea, comes the initial conflating of the geographical scales of belonging/not belonging in *Broken Eggs*. Beyond implying that they must conceal their ethnicity from Lizette's new family, this appeal thematically links the condition of exile from homeland (the global) and exclusion from suburbanism (the local) for the Marquez family. Not to suggest that they are the same, but instead, that one conflict informs the other. However much Lizette's parents and grandparents want to make her happy on her wedding day, they have considerable difficulty not talking—or arguing—about Cuba "today." They reminisce about, fight with each other over, and express their longing for their lost homeland throughout the reception. Reasons for this may be simply because they are gathered together and their thoughts naturally return to Cuba. But another reason is that their awareness of one exclusion triggers painful memories of another, which is supported by the storyline of *Broken Eggs*. Within five pages of the reference to the Cuban bakery, their thoughts turn to the food and lifestyle they had known, as a wealthy family, in Cuba. A favorite memory includes the maid[78] crossing the yard to put "two pieces of hot buttered bread" bought fresh every day, in Sonia's hands.[79] Surely, there is something in this memory that is soothing to the family that has to struggle to get the cake to the reception in Woodland Hills. But not all memories of Cuba are as soothing. Soon after this memory comes Sonia's story of leaving Cuba and finding themselves living "behind a hamburger stand between two furniture stores" in L.A., suddenly "three thousand miles away from" everything they had known.[80] This memory conveys their feeling of dislocation and uncertainty, again linked with food, which approximates the feeling they have during the reception. Whenever something goes wrong, their memories go back to either the life they had in Cuba or what they lost in leaving Cuba. The details of these stories, like the one where Sonia gets lost and cannot find "the right words" to ask for help, suggest much about the interplay of exile and exclusion felt by this generation of the Marquez family while in Woodland Hills.

Underlying such memories about Cuba or leaving Cuba is their knowledge that they are outsiders in this country, much as Machado describes in the interview with Schillinger, a condition that is exaggerated by the ethos of suburbanism. Informed that they do not belong, by methods implicit and explicit, they turn toward memories of both belonging and belonging lost. Significantly, the younger generation of Lizette's siblings knows much the same feeling of being outsiders and react in dissimilar, though complementary ways. They actively devalue their Cuban heritage as something that marks them as outsiders and define themselves through U.S. culture or against Cuban culture. Lizette's sister Mimi, the youngest of the family, goes out of her way to mock her mother's nostalgia for Cuba: "It was and is a myth. Your life there is mythical."[81] In the jokes made about Cuba as paradise with her brother Oscar, it is obvious that they do this often enough, but they feel especially hostile toward Cuba while in Woodland Hills, probably because they know better than their parents how and why they are outsiders. Evidence for this comes with the next geographic reference to the landscape of Southern California made by Mimi: "I'm Manuela Sonia Marquez, better known as Mimi Mar-kwez. I was born in Canoga Park. I'm a first generation white Hispanic American."[82] Another suburb of Los Angeles, Canoga Park proves noteworthy because it illustrates the "sorting out" of racial division during the 1970s and 1980s. Originally founded in 1912, the city was subdivided during white flight into three communities: a portion of the western region was renamed West Hills, a portion of the eastern region was renamed Winnetka, both of which had noticeably higher socioeconomic status than the remaining portions of Canoga Park. Growing up in this city, Mimi may have witnessed the increasing segregation in the landscape between privileged ("white" Americans) and underprivileged (minorities) and consequently she disavows her Cuban heritage. Although Oscar, the oldest, has memories of leaving Cuba, they are blended with the same experience of suburbanization and this most likely contributes to his determination to humiliate and torment his father, and with him, Cuban patriarchy.[83]

But it is through Lizette and her wedding that *Broken Eggs* best dramatizes the struggle across geographical scales of belonging/not belonging in this Cuban family. Certainly more stable than Mimi (who is pregnant as a teen and on drugs), Oscar (who is on drugs and in therapy), or her mother and aunt Miriam (who turn to valium to dull the ache of exile), Lizette nevertheless struggles with her Cuban heritage. Marrying into the Jewish family of the Rifkins, which may certainly be motivated by love—the play never explores her reasons directly—simultaneously suggests one way of resolving this struggle. In communities like Woodland Hills, it is Rifkins and *those who look like them* who are welcomed into suburbanism because this homogeneity is necessary for maintaining the (hypocritical) myth of Small Town America. (Worth mentioning here is that *Broken Eggs* considers questions of insiders and outsiders for suburbanism entirely based on skin color and offers no suggestion of anti-Semitism in Southern California. The reasoning behind this derives from the play's critique of the visual rhetoric of homogeneity that provides the most obvious bulwark against ethnic difference.) Marrying into the Rifkin family, just as significantly, means to some degree marrying *out of her Cuban family.* That is, through her marriage, Lizette finds an escape from the suffering of exile, if only experienced vicariously through her parents; and implicitly from the exclusion of the Other, if only through association. Not that Lizette consciously thinks of her family or her marriage in such terms: during the opening scene, she tells Mimi how much she wants her siblings to "pretend you come from a happy home."[84] The key word here, of course, is "pretend" they come from a happy home, a happy home defined perhaps through the Rifkins. More than Mimi and Oscar, Lizette has internalized what it means to be an "outsider" in Los Angeles. Her "No Cuba today," which is repeated throughout the play, suggests her awareness of her Cuban heritage as something that will only burden her life in Southern California. More significantly, it suggests the promise of acceptance, if not assimilation, in the otherwise antagonistic landscape of suburbanism.

The Politics of (In)Visibility

If the story of the Marquez family demonstrates the problems that follow from or are at least exaggerated by the ethos of suburbanism, the structure of *Broken Eggs* interrogates these problems. This interrogation begins from the visual and cultural premise behind suburbanism: omission of anything aberrant, especially ethnic difference, from the landscape. Like *True West*, *Broken Eggs* thematizes and problematizes these omissions, though in ways distinctly different than those of Shepard's play. Instead of addressing the *means* of exclusion, like panopticism or patrols, Machado's play addresses the *subject* of exclusion. Normally, it is the Marquez family and those who look like them, who are erased from the suburban landscape through a variety of fortification strategies discussed already. This reality is conveyed in the dramatic world of *Broken Eggs* through the Cuban family spending most of their time in the backroom—really an anteroom—to the country club where the wedding reception is occurring. Although they may be hiding from the Rifkins, given the embarrassments that happen during the reception—their running out of cake, the catcalls between Oscar, Mimi, and their father's wife—they are at the same time hidden from the Rifkins. In this staging, Machado thematizes the omissions evident in the landscape beyond the country club. Simultaneously, however, he problematizes these omissions in the dramatic and theatrical text of *Broken Eggs* by situating the Rifkins, throughout the play, offstage. The Rifkins spend the reception in the ballroom and "enter" the play only in the reports by members of the Marquez family who hurry back and forth between "privileged" and "marginal" spaces. The terms "privileged" and "marginal" are intriguing when considered here since the Marquez family enjoys more freedom of movement across the boundaries of such spaces than the Rifkins, and more than immigrants in suburban communities. Visually, at least, Machado reverses the hierarchy of ethnicity, though this does not minimize the authority of the Rifkins. As Worthen notes, anonymity sustains privilege.[85] Instead, Machado's reversing this hierarchy becomes a means of exposing the "social laws" underlying suburbanism.

Defined from the dramatization of suburbanism in *Broken Eggs,* these laws correspond with what I have called the politics of (in)visibility. This phrase describes, first of all, the power attendant with concerns of visibility and invisibility that puts immigrants in a double bind in relation to suburbanism. On the one hand, immigrants have been regularly rendered invisible in the landscape of suburban communities, literally (the lack of Cuban bakeries in Woodland Hills) or figuratively (Mimi's and Lizette's impulse toward renouncing their Cuban heritage). As landscape and lifestyle, suburbanism tends to naturalize such invisibility through elision: because the suburban community excludes multiethnic America, because of property values and housing ordinances or geographical removal, it becomes necessary that immigrants of any heritage be omitted. Their presence represents an anomaly to the nature of the community. On the other hand, immigrants become completely "visible" and thus subject to the panopticism underlying the fortification defined by Duncan, Lambert, and Davis whenever they enter the suburbs. While *Broken Eggs* does not highlight this fortification directly, it is nevertheless evident in internalized anxiety felt by Sonia during the reception as well as Osvaldo during his shopping in Canoga Park, another of the stories recounted within the play.[86] Noteworthy is that whichever condition prevails, the difficulty experienced by the immigrant serves the interests of the privileged group: paradoxically, whether by keeping immigrants from being acknowledged, or by keeping them continually under scrutiny. This is just one of the ways that "place" becomes a creator "of difference" between "outsiders" and "insiders," as theorized by Cresswell: "An outsider is not just someone literally from another location but someone who is existentially removed from the milieu of 'our' place."[87] All this informs the politics of (in)visibility, which governs suburbanism through a distinctly visual rhetoric of belonging/not belonging for those living there or just passing through the community. Implicit in this rhetoric is a hierarchy of social relations that has become naturalized, in the cultural imagination, as an ethos of place.

It is this politics of (in)visibility that Machado thematizes in *Broken Eggs*. This ethos becomes evident *in the play* after Oscar and Mimi have done what Lizette asked they not do: misbehave in front of the Rifkins by exchanging cat-calls with their father's second wife. Overcome with anxiety Lizette says, "Oh God, Mama. Everybody's looking at us. They are so embarrassed."[88] In Lizette's complaint emerges evidence of suburbanism's ethos of place. In order to blend into the community of Woodland Hills, represented metonymically through the country club where the wedding reception is taking place, the Cuban family must try to make themselves as "invisible" as possible by not drawing undue attention to their ethnic difference. They must try to mediate the distinction between "outsider" (immigrant, minority, Other) and "insider" within suburbanism if the day is to be successful. What upsets Lizette so thoroughly is that Oscar and Mimi make their difference from the Rifkins—familial, cultural, and even ethnic[89]—public in ways that probably confirm the worst assumptions about Cubans or any immigrant group. In this same remark, Machado thematizes the ethos of place underlying suburbanism *through the play's form*. In Lizette's lament, Machado metatheatrically involves audiences of potential productions by signaling their absent presence: "Everybody's looking at us." On the surface, Machado's play is the most realistic of any in this study. Unlike Shepard's play, where the realism frays diachronically, *Broken Eggs* never overtly diverges from this realism on the stage. But it does challenge the rhetoric that follows from realism: the passivity and anonymity that situate audiences as voyeurs instead of critical participants in the dramatic world on stage. Through this gesture and others like it, *Broken Eggs* accomplishes complementary ambitions in regard to concerns with suburbanism. The first involves defining the Rifkins, metonymically, as those complicit in and benefiting from, even if only implicitly, the politics of (in)invisibility governing suburbanism. The second involves linking, thematically and epistemologically, non-Cuban audiences with the Rifkins within *Broken Eggs*.

Layers of performance, privilege, and reception intersect politically and theatrically in Machado's representation of suburbanism. Working entirely "inside" the play, momentarily, this intersection illustrates the exclusionary ethos of suburbanism and the consequences with which immigrants, like the Marquez family must endure in communities like Woodland Hills. Most evident in Lizette, though including other members of the family like Sonia and Osvaldo and perhaps even Mimi and Oscar (who act out through rebellion), is the awareness that they are performing their worthiness to become part of the Rifkin family and to belong in suburbanism. As audiences, the

Rifkins and those like them can sit back and enjoy themselves because of the double bind in which immigrants find themselves: that they are an intrusion into the idealized and homogeneous world of suburbanism. Though the play never reveals how the Rifkins are behaving or reacting to the reception, except through the perspectives of the frantic Marquez family, one point remains clear. The privilege granted the Rifkins in Woodland Hills or other such suburbs depends on the symbolic erasure and literal omission of those like the Marquez family from the landscape. Because the Rifkins offer nothing beyond their absent presence in the play, they sabotage the family's best endeavor to perform their belonging. Normally, this interplay of performance, privilege, and reception is what is hidden through naturalization or mystification in suburbanism: it is taken for granted that the social hierarchy currently in place was always in place, or should be in place. By inverting this hierarchy as the premise behind the play's representation of suburbanism, Machado demonstrates how the "social laws" and of this place are culturally and politically conceived to buttress the privilege of those represented by the Rifkins. Audiences of the play, then, have their perspective inverted, visually if not epistemologically, toward this ethos of place. Even as members of the family, Lizette and Sonia most notably, try to keep from making public any ethnic difference from the inhabitants of Woodland Hills, Machado's play works against this premise by foregrounding the inequity inherent in this landscape defined and defended according to the politics of (in)visibility.

Additionally, Machado develops an intriguing corollary throughout *Broken Eggs*: the reception, with the Marquez family performing before and for the Rifkins, doubles the realist production of Machado's play. When Lizette talks about pretending that she is from a happy family near the opening, she describes both the ambition of the character (who wants to have a happy wedding day) and the activity of the actress (who is playing Lizette). When she laments everyone "looking at" the Cuban family, she describes the Rifkins in the play and the audience watching the play. This latter conflation is particularly noteworthy for Machado's sociospatial ambitions, particularly how it situates audiences toward the politics of (in)visibility in suburbia. First of all, the Rifkins sitting anonymously in the wings and "watching" the family become a surrogate for audiences in the auditorium—or the portion of that is white and middle classed—watching the play (Audience diversity for *Broken Eggs* provides a particularly interesting challenge and opportunity for considering how themes and concerns are received in ways that anticipate the plays considered in Chapter 5.) More than that, because the Rifkins become at least complicit in the politics of (in)visibility, this doubling with audiences of the play serves an interrogatory end. During the second act, when the surrogacy of the Rifkins becomes evident, Machado's audiences "become" those who will judge the Marquez family not only regarding the behavior of Mimi and Oscar but regarding questions of belonging/not belonging. Machado does more than just dramatize the conditions of exclusion experienced by the immigrant in the suburbs; he metatheatrically exposes audiences to and even implicates them in the visual and epistemological process of exclusion. In this way, his play exceeds the rhetoric of realism and comes closer to Worthen's rhetoric of political drama which, broadly defined, dramatizes the "working ideology in the making of meaning."[90] Clearly, audiences of any background remain free to ignore the implications of comparison with the Rifkins, either because they are invested in the politics of (in)visibility or are indifferent to them. But Machado's *Broken Eggs* makes this decision an informed decision, so that our response to suburbanism as depicted in the play becomes some marker of our complicity in and responsibility for such politics.

Getting Kicked Out

This rhetoric of political drama frames reception toward an indictment of suburbanism in *Broken Eggs*, which comes through the increasingly explicit conflation of geographical scales: exile from homeland and exclusion from suburbs. The second act of *Broken Eggs*, in fact, is book-ended by comments from Sonia that emphasize this conflation. After the intermission Lizette's parents, Sonia and Osvaldo, share the stage and dance to "Snow," an Argentine folk song playing in the offstage reception hall. This moment of renewed intimacy between the estranged couple is undermined by the fact that it was Osvaldo's new Argentine wife who requested the song, and by its lyrics. Not the sort of music usually played at weddings, "Snow" describes a forced march into exile that includes confronting winter and wolves and all manner of imagery suggesting death and displacement. Beyond making Sonia angry at the audacity of her ex-husband's wife requesting the song during her daughter's wedding, the song prompts Sonia's memories of leaving Cuba. "Remember when we thought Fidel was going to send us to Russia, to Moscow?" she asks Osvaldo.[91] Her intention here, as elsewhere, may be to reestablish the bonds that they had as a married couple. But her next remark stresses not just the commonality of shared experience but the commonality of that experience of the United States with the following remarks about Woodland Hills and other such communities: "Siberia, Siberia, this place is like Siberia!"[92] Much later in the play, when Lizette and her husband have left the reception, Sonia and her sister-in-law Miriam begin taking valium in part to deal with the stress of the wedding but additionally in part to assuage the feelings of exile that have become almost unbearable during this day spent in suburban Los Angeles. They return, at least through their imaginations, to

Varadero Beach in Cuba, far away from Woodland Hills until Mimi enters and reminds Sonia that they only rented the reception hall for half a day: "They're going to kick us out."[93] Her phrasing metonymically conflates the country club, Woodland Hills, and even Cuba—as Sonia's response makes clear: "I've been kicked out of better places."[94]

In the first comment, Sonia links Cuba and Los Angeles through causation: because the Marquez family was driven from their lives in Cuba during Fidel Castro's revolution, they found themselves trapped in a place that feels like Siberia. It hardly matters that they did not walk "a thousand miles to their exile" but instead "took a plane ninety-nine miles," as Sonia acknowledges.[95] What matters is that she and her family ended up as existentially removed from the only world they had known as Siberia would be for Machado's audiences. Invoking punishment and isolation, this reference to Siberia suggests a distinctly different experience of "this place," whether Woodland Hills or Los Angeles, than which dominates the cultural imaginary of the United States.[96] Additionally, this remark, which is intended for audiences as much as Osvaldo, is framed by the metatheatrical referencing of audiences in Lizette's apprehension about being looked at, which follows a few pages thereafter and is distinctly involved in representation of "this place." Contained in Lizette's apprehension and furthered by Sonia's second remark is how "this place" is not just consequence of exclusion from Cuba but reenacts this exclusion. Sonia's "I've been kicked out of better places" draws direct parallel between Cuba after the revolution and suburbanism of 1979 United States: they both involve and perhaps depend on exclusion, political and cultural, as part of their very definition. With this second remark, *Broken Eggs* conflates not merely geographical scales of local and global but further the political and ideological mandates defining these scales: that is, Machado's play draws parallels between suburbanism and communism or, even more polemically, between suburbanism and totalitarianism. Though Sonia is well on her way toward her valium-induced return to Varadero Beach when she says this, her comment proves revealing about suburbanism in that she senses something of the fortification that was underway. Almost paradoxically, suburbanism becomes *cause* and *consequence* of the feeling of being an "outsider" for this woman and this Cuba family.

Machado's *Broken Eggs*, then, may offer a more polemical reading of suburbanism than *True West*. Conflating the geography, politics, and ideology of Cuba and suburbanism during the early 1980s had significant potential of shocking and even offending segments of audiences (again, the diversity of audiences for this play proves crucial to its sociospatial ambitions). This polemicism was probably intended, though not necessarily with the ambition of holding members of the audiences accountable for the problems dramatized in the play. More likely, the ambition was to demonstrate some of the same conclusions—through his characters—as those that would be documented by Duncan, Lambert, Davis and others: that suburbanism is predicated upon exclusion of anything that might interfere with the nostalgia for 1950s Small Town America, especially ethnic difference. By reading *against* the neotraditional promise of paradise, *Broken Eggs* intended to question and make questionable the politics of (in)visibility underlying suburbanism; in other words, this subversive reading could include audiences, in ways that precisely parallel metatheatrical invoking of audiences. They can do more than the Rifkins, their dramatic surrogates; they can recognize the "social laws" at work in "this place" and begin to resist them. Such possible praxis goes beyond the purview of this argument, but it is worth mentioning that Machado's play is important—if for nothing else—because it stages the immigrant's experience of Woodland Hills—the segregated geography, the knowledge of being outsiders, the continued feeling of exile—and thereby offers audiences, however briefly, another perspective on suburbanism, a glimpse from the outside that reveals much about the nature of what is inside. While this perspective can be just as unsettling and offensive as the connection to communist Cuba, there is almost the invitation toward white, middle-classed audiences toward a shared, communal experience—a chance to see from another's eyes what they thought they know: Sonia's resentment and resignation at being an "outsider"; Lizette's desire for acceptance, if not assimilation; Mimi's frustration with her heritage. But the most important experience may come through the words of Oscar, which involve pronouns which invite audiences toward instead of away from the play's reading: "Despair, that's always the story of a people that gets kicked out, that have to find a refuge, you and me . . . us."[97]

CHAPTER 4

"Does it Explode?": Ghettoization and Rioting in New York City and Los Angeles

The rioting that threw into startling relief the economic disparity and racial tensions in cities during the late 1980s and early 1990s had an almost comical beginning. In 1988 NYPD personnel, trying to enforce a 1:00 A.M. curfew in the East Village's Tompkins Square Park, found themselves besieged by a motley crowd "of antigentrification protestors, punks, housing activists, park inhabitants, artists, Saturday-night revelers, and Lower East Side residents."[1] Lasting about three hours, when the police withdrew,[2] this melee was grounded in the simmering antagonism about living conditions for lower-income residents and the "rampant gentrification of the Lower East Side."[3] Three years later, the outrage, recrimination, and violence that embroiled the NYPD and African Americans and Lubavitchers (Hasidic Jews) in Brooklyn's Crown Heights was anything but humorous. Gavin Cato, a seven-year-old immigrant from Guyana, was killed when the "three-car procession carrying the Lubavitchers Hasidic rebbe (spiritual leader) ran a red light, hit another car, and swerved onto the sidewalk."[4] Later that night came the presumably retributive stabbing of Yankel Rosenbaum, a Hasidic scholar from Australia who had not been involved in Cato's death but who nevertheless died from the wounds. The NYPD was blamed by the African American community for letting the rebbe's motorcade drive recklessly and censured by the Jewish community when the African American accused of Rosenbaum's death was acquitted. Unfortunately, the tragic incidents of Crown Heights of 1991 proved to be prologue to the "explosion of interracial violence which during three days of burning, looting, and killing laid waste to parts of South-Central Los Angeles" in April of 1992.[5] Triggered by the acquittal of four Los Angeles Police Department (LAPD) officers caught beating Rodney King on videotape by George Holliday, the rioting had a complex exigency located in the history of racism in Los Angeles. Notably, many incidents of the rioting played out—live—on nightly newscasts, like an epilogue for urbanism.

This chapter begins with a recounting of the incidents that beleaguered New York City and Los Angeles in the last decades of the century not because they have already slipped from memory, though the terrorist attacks of September 11, 2001, have, no doubt, supplanted rioting in thoughts about urban tragedy in the United States. Rather, the chapter begins from this history because the rioting produced a moment of rupture in the history of urbanism. The rioting thrust words like "ghetto" and "slum" and phrases like "South Central" and "inner-city" into the national vocabulary in ways that nothing had previously. Prompted by televised images of buildings on fire and looters hauling plunder through streets and the LAPD assaulting an African American, Americans everywhere found themselves talking about what the inequities revealed by the riots meant for the future. Writing about the 1993 riots in Bombay, India, Jim Masselos, offers language that just as effectively describes what happened across the United States: "the riots revealed as particularly fragile . . . all those tacit assumptions, those accepted and unarticulated norms about the nature of urban living, which enable a city to function."[6] This anxious introspection about urbanism played out in New York City and Los Angles and elsewhere as arguments emerged about how to describe what occurred—rioting or uprising?—and how to go forward. Not surprisingly, a number of playwrights found themselves confronting the same question, including Djanet Sears in *Harlem Duet* and Anna Deavere Smith in *Twilight Los Angeles, 1992*. Demystifying the long, tangled history of racism and urbanism these plays stage the exigency and the legacy of the demands for social justice and racial equality that were, in the estimation of many, behind the rioting. Among the questions posed by the plays are these: what does it mean psychologically to live in the most inhospitable corners of the metropolis? And what sustains the racial divisions evident in urbanism that are tantamount to segregation?

In asking these questions, *Harlem Duet* and *Twilight Los Angeles, 1992* stand on the considerable shoulders of Lorraine Hansberry's *A Raisin in the Sun*, which debuted in 1959. The Younger family's tenement apartment in Chicago's Southside, in fact, becomes an illustration of the urban enclaves—defined here as communities sharing, or trapped within, the same space and same socioeconomic horizons—considered in this chapter. When Ruth announces her farewell to the apartment, she captures the humiliation and demoralization felt by the family: "If this is my time in life—MY TIME—to say good-bye—to these goddamned cracking walls!—and these marching roaches!—and this cramped little closet which ain't now or never was no kitchen!...then I say it loud and good, HALLELUJAH!"[7] The Youngers' efforts to leave the tenement for Clybourne Park spoke to a generation of African Americans reaching toward the American Dream after segregation. Although the play ends with the hope of inaugurating a new period of, at least, racial tolerance, much the same discriminatory impulse shaped urbanism well into the 1990s. Thanks to means like "block-busting," in which African Americans entered formerly all-white neighborhoods and triggered white flight, or the Federal Housing Administration's segregationist practices,[8] racial divisions not only continued in the metropolis but become naturalized. Without overt authority advocating the practice, it came to look like a "natural" distribution of racial groups. But the reality is more cynical. More than three decades after *A Raisin in the Sun* debuted, "a substantial number of African-American children continue to grow up in urban environments as highly segregated," notes M. Patricia Kelly, "as those that existed...before the beginning of the Civil Rights Movement."[9] The hugely successful revival of *A Raisin in the Sun* during the 2003–2004 Broadway season was hailed by many,[10] but its success may be more deflating when considered against the history of racism and urbanism.

Ruth's discontent with the Southside tenement, of course, speaks to the hostility toward the urban environment evident among those living in the enclaves represented in *Harlem Duet* and *Twilight Los Angeles, 1992*, especially those without the windfall of an insurance check. Feeling trapped in and forgotten by the city, many paraded their antipathy, like when women gathered on windowsills in L.A. during the chaos and shouted, "Let the motherfuckers burn" to the Los Angeles Fire Department (LAFD)—as depicted in *Twilight Los Angeles*.[11] More violent than anything expressed by Ruth but still of a kind, this outrage turned against the city: they were willing the destruction of what had become de facto segregation.[12] Yet any blanket denunciation of the enclaves ignores how other enclaves, like Harlem, functioned, at times, as refuges for African Americans against the antagonism and acrimony of racism. *Harlem Duet*, in fact, begins from this premise by having SHE, an African American woman living in Harlem in 1928 and allegorically doubling the protagonist of the play, proclaiming in all sincerity in the prologue: "Harlem's the place to be now. Everyone who's anyone is here now. It's our time. In our place."[13] More than just invoking the Harlem Renaissance as touchstone for African American culture, this prologue shows what *Harlem Duet's* characters most obviously lack and most desperately want: a sense of belonging—within a community and to a place. Harlem may nurture the emotional and existential well-being of African Americans by providing security and a shared lifestyle as well as the opportunity to develop socioeconomic networks.[14] The intent here is not to romanticize the difficult lives that often go along with living in enclaves like South Central or Harlem. Instead, it is to consider tensions surrounding the ways that urban enclaves are organized and inhabited, how they simultaneously become—in the words of *Harlem Duet's* Othello—homeland and reservation, or refuges against racism and contributors to segregation.

Equal parts theater and ethnography, these plays are the most overtly political and, by extension, Brechtian of any in this book. In invoking Brecht as a way of talking about *Harlem Duet* and *Twilight Los Angeles,* I do not mean to undertake an inventory of the techniques described by Brecht, though the staging and acting required by both corresponds with much of epic theater. Instead, I invoke Brecht because epic theater and the plays discussed in this chapter share this fundamental ambition: to foreground the "social laws" governing how individuals and groups interact.[15] Like Brecht, Sears and Smith locate events in sociohistorical and sociospatial circumstance that inform behaviors. The ambition of *Harlem Duet* and *Twilight Los Angeles* is to demystify these "social laws" by representing the rioting within the long history of racism and urbanism[16] and thereby demonstrating how the incidents were the products of a particular time and place: the unemployment and poverty, the racial profiling and police harassment, the disillusionment and despair of having no hopeful future, only an unbearable past. Neither play proposes or pursues the exoneration of those involved in the rioting, looting, and violence during the early 1990s. Instead, they attempt to stage the interplay of place and perspective beleaguering those like the protagonist of *Harlem Duet,* who succumbs to madness against the backdrop of urban riots and the women in *Twilight Los Angeles* who applaud the immolation of their neighborhood. When framed by this historicizing and spatializing rhetoric, the rioting of this period becomes *about* the circumstances that prompted it. If attention shifts from event to causes of event, there may come the recognition—deeply Brechtian—that the circumstances themselves, the ghettos and slums in the metropolis, *can* and *should b*e changed.

Worth noting is how *Harlem Duet* and *Twilight Los Angeles* reject anything resembling the rhetoric of realism discussed during the last chapter. Going further than Machado in *Broken Eggs,* Sears and Smith foreground an interrogatory relation among audience, place, and play that corresponds with Worthen's rhetoric of political theater. In a striking shift already begun by *Broken Eggs,* the emphasis of this interrogation falls as much on audience, a part of which is usually implicated in the flawed perspective of place questioned by the play. That is, the plays begin from rather conservative knowledge of South Central or Harlem that represents how this locale was "known" to the majority of U.S. citizens before, during, and perhaps after the rioting. While the techniques for questioning this knowledge differ with each playwright, they involve, foremost, putting the present crisis in the context of the history of racism and urbanism and/or putting that crisis within the larger mosaic of urban geography. *Harlem Duet's* story of African American families being torn apart in the 1990s, for instance, is told through the intrusion and interpolation of scenes of the 1860s and 1920s—which suggests how the present can and should be read through the past. *Twilight Los Angeles*, Smith's one-woman show, unfolds through Smith's embodying one character—one perspective about L.A. and the rioting—after another so that her performance involves the uncomfortable coalescence of competing voices in one body. In both plays there are distinct elements that echo Brecht's epic theater that the following pages consider. But it is also worth mentioning that these plays emerge from a long lineage of political writing about racism and urbanism that goes back through Lorraine Hansberry, Langston Hughes, Martin Luther King Jr. and others. Like these works, *Harlem Duet* and *Twilight Los Angeles* depict what Benjamin Forest defines, in terms that echo the sociospatial concerns of this study, as "the tension between a universalistic ideal of American citizenship . . . and the particular experience of socioeconomic disparities faced by racial and ethnic minorities."[17]

Something About Harlem

In 1997, Djanet Sears's *Harlem Duet* debuted at Tarragon's Extra Space in Toronto and, following this successful debut, was remounted at the Canadian Stage's larger theater later that year. During this first year of productions, the play earned both audience approval and critical acclaim, winning the Governor-General's Award, the Chalmers Canadian Play Award, and the Dora Mavor Moore Award.[18] Despite the many awards for Canadian drama, *Harlem Duet* focuses more on racial—instead of cultural—identity that emerges from history and place. Suggested in the name of the male protagonist, Othello, that history begins from Shakespeare's tragedy; in fact, many reviewers describe the play as a prequel to the story of the Moor: the marriage to an African American woman named Billie before finding his Desdemona. When revived as part of the Stratford Festival in 2006, in a flawed production,[19] *Harlem Duet* was contrasted with Shakespeare's tragedy and, at least for one reviewer,[20] hoped to be paired with *Othello* in the future. More noteworthy is how Sears envisions her characters negotiating their identity at the geographical nexus of racism and urbanism. "There's something about Harlem," Sears said when interviewed in 2006, "The place of [the] Harlem Renaissance, the place of extraordinary poverty, of riots . . . It feels like an axis, a central point, a hot spot."[21] While more attention has gone to the play's exploration of gender, *Harlem Duet* depicts the complexity of Sears's description of Harlem: being a place to celebrate African American culture and history while still supplying evidence of the continued secondary status of African Americans. And while her perspective is undoubtedly informed by her living in Canada, she wrote one draft of the play during a three-month residency at the Public Theatre, and when it was produced in New York in 2002, it fulfilled Sears's hopes: "It's a play about Harlem . . . I want to see it [and, no doubt, have it seen] in New York."[22]

Demanding much from directors, actors, and audiences, *Harlem Duet* blurs customary demarcations among story, history, and allegory toward a sociospatial reading of Harlem. The storyline begins from and repeatedly returns to the failed marriage and difficult divorce of Billie and Othello, two well-educated African Americans who sought out Harlem, not long after they were married as a refuge against discrimination. Though the reference to Shakespeare comes in the husband's name, it is Billie, the woman without antecedent in Shakespeare's tragedy, who is driven toward her and Othello's demise by trying to poison him with a strawberry handkerchief. As the play unfolds, Billie moves from depression toward a mental breakdown, but her motives have as much to do with the history of racism in the metropolis as they do with Othello divorcing her. This bridge between story and history emerges from the allegorical scenes set during the Harlem Renaissance and the Civil War that interpolate the play's present. During such scenes, Billie is doubled by SHE and HER, African American women who feel they have no choice but violence when their husbands—HE and HIM, doubles for Othello—leave them for white women. In both allegorical scenes as well as the play's present, the woman kills or attempts to kill—it is unclear if Othello dies during the present—the man over and over again, seemingly with much the same tragic inevitability that underlies tragedy. What brings these moments in history together, beyond the shared domestic situation, is the centrality of Harlem: in the Civil War scene, as the place that the former slaves look toward with hope, and in the other scenes as an enclave where African Americans are living. "I call it a blues tragedy," Sears explained in a 2002 interview, "so I deliberately fragmented time and place to give a sense of the blues aesthetic."[23] Beyond illustrating this aesthetic, the allegorical intrusions frame Billie's transgression within this history of African American men leaving African American women because of racialized assumptions of normalcy. In this confluence of story, history, allegory, race and racism, love and jealousy, transgression and tragedy are grounded in Harlem.

Most noteworthy for discussion of sociospatial drama is how the allegorical intrusions endorse an interrogatory engagement with the interplay of racism and urbanism. Sears's stage directions indicate that the actress and actor playing Billie and Othello should play their allegorical doubles: SHE and HER, HE and HIM. This tripling of performative roles extricates actors and audiences from the simple one-to-one relationship of actor/character rather like Brecht's strategy of having actors "quote" characters.[24] Watching an actor/actress playing multiple roles not only tends to mediate realism's invitation to audiences to become emotionally caught up *in the story* instead of intellectually engaging in the critique undertaken *by the story*. Additionally, watching this tripling of roles urges audiences to consider each character—and perhaps each scene—alongside one another so that individual scenes (like Othello explaining his need to be accepted by his white colleagues or Billie's disillusionment with Harlem) is framed within the historical context of race and place. In this way, the play attempts to acculturate audiences to an interrogatory ethos that encourages them to question why this same history plays out again and again—especially, why and how this history is located in Harlem. This ambition is further augmented by the narrative voice-overs, ranging from Malcolm X to Martin Luther King Jr., from Marcus Garvey to Paul Robeson, which highlight the sociospatial context against which the scene plays out. Allegory always begins with the engagement of audiences, who ultimately make explicit whatever commentary may be implied. Unfortunately, allegory cannot presume such engagement even when techniques for encouraging it have been written into the text. In some productions of *Harlem Duet*, the transitions "between periods and places" have been "too rough," unnecessarily drawing attention to themselves as stagecraft instead of depicting Harlem as the nexus of racism and urbanism.[25] Nevertheless, Sears finds an intriguing way of highlighting the questions posed by Othello during an argument with Billie through the allegorical staging that this chapter will consider: Is Harlem homeland or reservation?

Our Time, Our Place

Opening on an actor's dressing room and to the accompaniment of cello-and-bass blues in 1920s Harlem, the prologue commemorates the African American music and art, culture and community that were the Harlem Renaissance. In this dressing room are SHE and HE, one of the allegorical incarnations of Billie and Othello, talking about what Harlem means to them and, presumably, to African Americans more generally. "It's our time. In our place," SHE insists, not acknowledging the irony of HE applying burnt-cork for blackface performance.[26] Like most prologues, this one works to introduce the major concerns of the play and how it will consider those concerns: here, that Harlem was conceived of as a refuge against discrimination and disillusionment, which plagued the children and grandchildren of slaves even though this enclave was certainly not without its dangers. Concerns like these are unmistakable during performance, as Donna Bailey Nurse reveals while reviewing the original production of *Harlem Duet*. "The location proves symbolic of the play's dynamics . . . *Harlem Duet* explores the historical conflict over which ideology best sustains black emotional health: integration or separation."[27] Clearly, SHE believes that the enclave of Harlem, where African Americans gathered at the beginning of the twentieth century, displacing white residents who moved elsewhere in New York City,[28] will nurture them despite the emotional, psychological, or existential costs therein—costs suggested in the reference to minstrel shows. So powerful is this hope imagined in *Harlem Duet* that is extends into SHE's future. During a flashback set toward the end of the play but remembering a time nine years before Billie and Othello divorce, Billie expresses similar sentiments to SHE when talking about the black boutiques, bookstores, and groceries of the neighborhood: "I've longed for this sanctuary," she tells Othello as they look at the apartment.[29] Surrounded by black businesses, this younger Billie believes that they can insulate themselves against the racial antagonisms of the 1980s and 1990s, even though this belief is made suspect by dramatic irony.[30]

However naïve this belief may become for these women during the play, it underscores the significance of what Lynch defines as the "social role" of urban landscapes.[31] Not limited to enclaves like Harlem landscape informs a communal identity by "furnish[ing] material for common memories and symbols which bind the group together."[32] Full of connotations and associations distinctly felt by those living in this enclave, Harlem's landscape links those like Billie and Othello through shared memories as illustrated when they come together to divide their possessions after divorce proceedings have begun—back in the play's present—and find themselves staring out the apartment window and telling each other stories that emerge from the observed landscape. They talk about the Apollo Theater, visible from the fire escape, where "almost every notable black singer, dancer, and comedian in America, and virtually all the major jazz bands" got started in the 1930s and 1940s—notably, during the period when the theater opened its doors to African Americans.[33] They talk about the Hotel Theresa, the "Waldorf Astoria of Harlem," located at the intersection of Adam Clayton Powell Jr. Blvd and Martin Luther King Jr. Blvd—streets renamed in ways that memorialize African American struggle and experience. Like the Apollo Theater, the Hotel Theresa was originally open only to whites, but in the 1930s opened its doors to African Americans, and so in both buildings Billie and Othello can witness the history of segregation and that history overcome. This explains why they are overwhelmed with nostalgia that becomes a sexual need that temporarily mediates the growing emotional distance between them. Looking at the landscape of Harlem, reinforces their bond in ways that leads to their lovemaking *and* excludes the white woman Othello will marry. They feel, intensely and instinctively, what the mercurial Magi, Billie's landlady, says: "When I go out my door, I see all the beauty of my Blackness reflected in the world around me."[34]

The Soweto of America

Shortly after the prologue and long before the intimate encounter between Billie and Othello, however, *Harlem Duet* deploys a distinctly different way of considering Harlem. When Amah, Billie's sister-in-law, mentions Magi's professed enthusiasm for the Harlem community, Magi replies dismissively: "Nothing but weeds growing in the Soweto of America, honey."[35] More than merely evidence of Magi's swings of mood, this reference to South Africa's infamous township serves as the play's rejoinder to naïve enthusiasm for Harlem as refuge. An acronym for "South Western Townships," Soweto was created in 1954 after the government's bulldozing of Sophiatown, where blacks, whites, and Indians lived alongside one another. Consigning blacks to Soweto and other such townships, where they suffered deprivations ranging from housing to human rights, was more than merely means of marginalizing populations of blacks. Townships were official repudiations of the multiculturalism that had existed in Sophiatown and perhaps elsewhere—apartheid inscribed onto the landscape of South Africa. When *Harlem Duet* invokes Soweto in its ethnography of Harlem, the play intends to foreground the former as a "frame" for reading the latter: that is, audiences are encouraged to recognize the difficult living conditions and disregard for racial equality that are the legacy of the interplay between racism and urbanism in the reference to Soweto. Forest defines the history of U.S. ghettoization in terms that support the comparison with Soweto: "the difference in social and legal status between freemen and slaves established during the nineteenth century became geographically inscribed as racial difference during the twentieth century" following "the creation of black urban ghettos during the 'Great Migration' of African Americans" which, of course, would have brought SHE and HE of the prologue to Harlem, where they would become trapped in the racially inscribed demarcations.[36] In effect *Harlem Duet* superimposes Soweto over Harlem, however briefly, to reveal the same process of ghettoization in the United States as South Africa.

Magi's cynicism about Harlem passes without comment from Amah in the play. Much the same possibility of dismissing the implications of this reference to Soweto exists for audiences, except that the contrast proves central to the conflicts between Billie and Othello. Unlike Billie, Othello was more suspect about living in Harlem, while pursuing his academic career, from the beginning. During the flashback scene when Billie expresses her "longing" for this "sanctuary," Othello foregrounds the danger of embracing Harlem, or any urban enclave, as refuge. "Think Chris Yago and Mona and the other faculty will feel comfortable coming here . . . for meetings and the like?"[37] Giving him pause about taking the apartment that looks out on the history of Harlem is not the geographical distance from Columbia, where he is the only African American faculty in his department. Instead, what troubles Othello here and throughout their marriage is the cultural distance between the white faculty and the African American enclave. He knows full well that the connotations of Harlem, historically, involve criminality, violence, poverty because of gentrification of other neighborhoods in New York during the 1980s and 1990s that had displaced more and more lower-income families and because of the criminalization of race media reporting—all of which his colleagues at Columbia and audiences of the New York production of the play would certainly recognize. And for the Toronto productions, Sears included a summary of these connotations through Canada, Billie's father, and his memory of Harlem years before when he was afraid to walk the streets because "everything I'd ever learned told me that I wasn't safe in this part of town."[38] Interestingly, Othello feels vulnerable not to the violence or criminality that Canada describes but instead to being associated with—and, perhaps, circumscribed by—these connotations of Harlem by his white colleagues. Harlem may only be a subway ride away from Columbia geographically, but it is a world away, culturally, from white middle-class American life to which his education and career have granted him access, despite his African Americanness.

What Othello fears, though he does not fully articulate these fears until years later, is the possibility that by moving into enclaves like Harlem, African Americans like Billie and himself are enabling their own marginalization. This fear derives from Othello's understanding that New York City, like most cities with large minority populations, is composed of "walls" that serve, as Peter Marcuse has theorized, as "both a reflection and reinforcement of divisions" across socioeconomic as well as racial lines.[39] Describing the urban environment as increasingly partitioned into clearly defined "quarters" ranging from wealthy, privileged neighborhoods through the gentrified and suburban "city," down to the tenement and abandoned city, Marcuse argues that such division is defended through any number of figurative "walls" that prove just as efficacious as literal enclosure. Harlem, which plainly falls in the latter categories in Othello's estimation, certainly does not insulate those living there from racism. If anything this enclave, socially and spatially marginalized from the centers of power and privilege, may reify racial difference between residents of different "quarters." For those like Magi, not fortune enough to work at the university, being consigned to the periphery may reinforce generations of a culture of poverty by denying access to meaningful education and good jobs. For those like Othello, who enjoy greater opportunity, it means still feeling that this part of the metropolis determines "the position of its residents within the hierarchy of quarters."[40] Living in Harlem, in other words, reminds Othello of his difference. This conclusion comes during an argument with Billie when Othello describes the taint of affirmative action that he feels: "No one at school tells me I don't know how to do my job," he says bitterly, "It's implied."[41] Because he felt trapped, he believed that he had to escape from Harlem and Billie, so he leaves her for a white colleague. More notably, during this argument he links their divorce to Harlem's walls when he condemns the enclave in language that echoes Magi's remark; he calls his "Africantown, USA."[42]

Though *Harlem Duet* does not endorse Othello's condemnation of Harlem directly, the play is certainly sympathetic to what motivates that condemnation. More than that, the play is determined to foreground what leads Othello to his conclusions about Harlem. Interviewed in 2006, when *Harlem Duet* was being mounted at the Stratford Festival, Sears set about correcting the general assumption that the play functioned as indictment of Othello's view: "I'm Billie and I'm Othello. That's the conflict. This is the effect of 400 years of white supremacy [and] what that has done to the psyche of black people."[43] Dramatizing Harlem as the nexus of history, psychology, and discrimination, Sears's play stages the ways that African Americans, turning to Harlem to insulate themselves from discrimination elsewhere in the metropolis, can become disillusioned by the reality of this urban enclave. Knowing how Harlem is defined by his colleagues, Othello comes to believe that his only choice is to exonerate himself from racial difference by leaving Harlem and his African American wife—even though he still finds himself drawn to it during the scene when they recall stories about the landscape. Even though Billie is victimized by Othello's anxiety about Harlem, she, too, comes to doubt Harlem's promise. When she describes the enclave as a sanctuary during the flashback scene, this remark is made ironic by her confession to Magi—nearly an act earlier in the play—that "I don't believe in Harlem" anymore and her calling it "an illusion."[44] Describing her failed marriage most directly, her remark suggests that she conceived of Harlem as community: at first, her marriage; beyond that, a communal sense of who she was as an African American woman, which has been threatened by Othello's leaving and which pushes her toward madness. *Harlem Duet,* then, complicates the portrait of Harlem—as homeland or reservation—by demonstrating how African American women have struggled with disillusionment without external outlets. During the same argument in which Othello refers to apartheid,

Billie highlights the internalized racism with which Othello is struggling: "Our success is Whiteness. We religiously seek to have what they have. Access to the White man's world."[45] Simultaneously, though, she acknowledges the reality of the walls of racism that she, like so many, feels closing in around her in Harlem.

Trapped in History, History Trapped in Me

Considering Harlem as the Soweto of America means describing a complex psychology of doubt, denial, and displacement in Billie and Othello, and therein lies one obstacle to the sociospatial ambitions underlying *Harlem Duet*. Audiences could easily conclude that Billie and Othello represent anomalous responses, rooted in psychology, not ethnography. Worse, if conceived in relation to urbanism, their responses could be seen as potential problems *for the city* instead of problems *of the city*. The challenge for Sears is to demonstrate how her characters' reactions are governed by the "social laws" of ghettos, not the idiosyncrasy of psychology. This problem is intriguingly met in *Harlem Duet* by the allegorical interpolations of the central story, all of which locate present in the past. Othello's frustration at having to endure the demeaning implications of affirmative action, at least in his mind, become much more than self-hatred when contrasted with HE of the 1920s who knows the nightly indignity of performing the worst cultural stereotypes to appease white audiences in minstrel shows. Told that he is tolerable in society through the paradoxical obfuscation and exaggeration of his blackness, HE knows the difficulty of race and acceptance. Though unaware of this past incarnation, Othello becomes framed—allegorized—by HE, with whom he has little in common other than where he lives and to what he aspires, and the compromises necessary because of both. Similarly, Billie's effort to poison Othello for divorcing her for his white colleague becomes more than just the psychosis of one African American woman when read against the same violence in the vignettes: SHE stabbing HE in the throat, HER strangling HIM with a rope. Like her allegorical incarnations, Billie feels that she "has nothing more to lose" despite her education.[46] What stays the same across the vignettes? The hope represented in Harlem and the walls of race and racism that suffocate the hopes of each character despite what Harlem may promise. Or, as Billie says of herself ominously: "Trapped in history. A history trapped in me."[47]

　　The juxtaposing of Harlem during the 1860s, 1920s, and 1990s no doubt confuses many audiences during the first half, or more, of the play because they have few means—other than foreknowledge of the play—for resolving this dissonance. But that confusion, which would probably induce any number of questions or, in Bennett's terms, hypotheses, can become the means for developing the interrogatory reception necessary to consider the history of racism and urbanism that entraps Billie. Why, audiences might ask, would Othello, who is faculty at Columbia University, feel essentially the same shame about his blackness as HIM, not even considered a "person" during the Civil War vignette? Why does Othello, more than a century removed from the end of slavery and half a century from the end of segregation, need a white woman to "feel like . . . a man"?[48] Why does Billie, a woman of considerable intelligence and ability, feel that she cannot escape the hopeless violence of her antecedents? Why does this marriage, again and again, turn to tragedy? Worth noting here is that *Harlem Duet* demands an engagement from audiences distinctly different from the modes of reception suggested through reference to HE acting in blackface. Unlike minstrel shows, which reinforce discriminatory assumptions of white audiences, Sears's play invites audiences to question those assumptions by reading past and present, story and allegory alongside each other. Rather than reinforcing racial privilege, *Harlem Duet* encourages audiences to consider how this history of racism manifests itself through the geography of urbanism: specifically in Harlem. Most noteworthy about the questions posed by the play's juxtaposing different periods is that foreground the "social laws" governing racial relations, laws made explicit by Billie: "Did you ever consider what hundreds of years of slavery did to the African American psyche?" she asks Magi.[49] *Harlem Duet* poses a corollary question to contemporary audiences: Did you ever consider what decades of ghettoization and segregation continue to do to the African American psyche?

Complementing these allegorical vignettes are the narrative voice-overs, recorded from archived material and played during performance, preceding the play's scenes. Ranging from Malcolm X to Martin Luther King Jr. to sound bites from the 1992 L.A. rioting, the voice-overs "introduce" each scene in ways similar to Brecht's use of titles and screens.[50] That is, they stress the "historical quality" by contrasting them with recognizable moments from the history of U.S. race relations. Thereby, Sears suggests a double interpretive gesture: the voice-over provides what might be described as conceptual "frame" for understanding the implications of that scene and, simultaneously, suggests that the play's scene offers ways of reading these trends or trajectories of history. The voice-overs do this, first of all, by urging audiences to use the voice-over to distill the core of the scene, a strategy evident from the opening scene of *Harlem Duet*. When the lights come up on Billie's apartment, Malcolm X is heard "speaking about the nightmares of race in America and the need to build strong Black communities."[51] Suggested here is the equation that community can serve as the bulwark against racism, one of the central connotations attached to historical enclaves like Harlem. Noteworthy too, though, is that racism threatens not just the individual but the community itself, which must be "strong" to survive the nightmare of racism. Hearing these words prepares audiences for the all-female scene, which is what remains of African American community in *Harlem Duet*: with husbands or fathers absent from the family, it proves anything but a sanctuary from racism. Therefore the failed marriage of Billie becomes simultaneously cause and casualty of the nightmare of racism according to Sears's argument. Also worth noting is that the female community metonymically doubles the female households of African Americans communities that often served as prime indicator of poverty.[52] Thanks to the voice-over, then, the personal becomes the political.

Elsewhere, the voice-overs function ironically in contrast to what plays out in the scenes, a different strategy that serves the same prompting of audiences to read the scenes dialectically. Set during the 1860s, scene two opens with recitation of the Declaration of Independence, and although the stage directions are ambiguous about which parts should be heard in the theater, it is not difficult to imagine most directors choosing "life, liberty, and the pursuit of happiness" because of its iconicity. But the words of Thomas Jefferson surely ring hollow when followed by the conversation between HIM and HER about the patrons of a hardware store who "gawk as [a black man's] shriveled, pickled penis" kept in a jar.[53] This violence and objectification of African American bodies is doubled by HER's story about the Hottentot Venus, whose vagina is "entombed for scientific research." Contrasted with the Enlightenment philosophy behind the Declaration of Independence is violence inflicted on African Americans as slaves, which was so common that HER jokes, "Must be a lot of us there walking around in purgatory without genitals."[54] Certainly the ambition here involves dissonance: the dissonance of what is heard during the voice-over and the scene and, more significantly, that of universal, unalienable human rights, and the maltreatment of African Americans. Scene four, which is set in the play's present, begins from much the same premise, with Martin Luther King Jr. asserting "his dream, its relationship to the American Constitution, and the Declaration of Independence."[55] Starting optimistically, the next scene centers on Billie and Othello dividing belongings, including books that have advocated racial difference as scientific truth, like *The Great Chain of Being*, which includes "the scientific foundation for why we're not human."[56] Again, audiences are urged to recognize dissonance between what is ideal and the reality of how racial difference has been reified. To make this unmistakable, Billie and Othello take turns reciting King's speech, which suggests the promise in this vision and the frustration of it still not having become reality.

The many voices—Martin Luther King's hopefulness, Paul Robeson's disappointment, Malcolm X's outrage—reflect the multitude of African American reactions to the long-standing antagonism toward racial difference in the United States. They reflect a community trapped in enclaves but rebelling against walls—socioeconomic, cultural, or geographical—working to delimit who they are and what they can become. It is certainly not incidental that Billie poisons the handkerchief that she will give Othello, against the auditory background of "*a cacophony of strings* [which] *grooves and collides as the sound bites from the Anita Hill and Clarence Thomas hearings, the L.A. riots, the O.J. Simpson trial, Malcolm X and Martin Luther King loop and repeat . . . over and over.*"[57] The voice-overs thematize the allegory of urbanism and racism at the heart of *Harlem Duet*: it illustrates the history trapped in Billie and her trapped in history, a history of discontent and disillusionment with the lives that African Americans have led in the Soweto of America, a history that turned some African Americans against their communities in Los Angeles during those three, long days in 1992, a history that drives Billie, like SHE and HER, toward attempted homicide. In effect, the widening gyre of this multitude of voices becomes chorus to Billie's (urban) tragedy, suggesting the worst possible answers to her question about the burdens heaped on African American psyches. Nor is it incidental that the voice-overs become increasingly chaotic during this scene when Billie becomes caught up in the hopelessness beleaguering African Americans. Become frenetic, almost frantic when Billie poisons the handkerchief, the voice-overs suggest much more than the despair of one African American woman who lost her husband, or the discontent of any community that has grown weary of living behind walls, however figurative they may be. The implications are much more serious, the play suggests: they call into question all the "tacit assumptions" about urban life described by Masselos in regard to rioting, assumptions necessary for living in the city.

Dreams Deferred

Harlem Duet concludes with an intriguing relocation, thematically and geographically, during the play's present. Following Billie's attempted poisoning of Othello and her becoming delusional, the play moves from the Harlem apartment to the visitor's lounge of the psychiatric hospital where Billie has been committed. Making such a transition—in which mental hospital literally and figuratively replaces the urban enclave on stage—suggests much about the notions of how particular spaces within society determine the limits of acceptability. In fact, Sears's final scene invokes Foucault's "heterotopias of deviation"—including rest homes, prisons, and mental hospitals—those places "in which individuals whose behavior is deviant in relation to the required mean or norm are placed."[58] Though routinely invoked toward explaining any number of literal and figurative spaces,[59] Foucault's concept of heterotopia, or counters-sites that invoke, contest, and invert all the other sites in society, proves helpful for consideration of this conclusion. Mental hospitals culturally and geographically define the limits of who or what is acceptable in society, or, stated through the corollary, who or what is aberrant. They lock away those who do not conform to social or legal norms, with the implicit goal of protecting society. By superimposing mental hospital over Harlem, the play makes explicit what was implicit in Othello's distaste for and Billie's growing disillusionment with Harlem: this enclave defines the limits of who/what is *racially* acceptable or *racially* aberrant. Whether in Chicago's Southside or L.A.'s South Central, or New York's Harlem, these enclaves are constructed on the margins of society to exclude African Americans from the rest of the city. Like Foucault's counter-sites, the enclave-become-mental-hospital reflects back the antagonism toward racial difference and, in the process, suggests a number of questions. Can the hospital, predicated on the exclusion of aberrance, allay the burdens of racism that lead to Billie's breakdown? Can a white doctor—all her doctors are white—answer Billie's question about African American psyches?

More noteworthy in terms of sociospatial criticism than questions like these, perhaps, are the conclusions regarding racism and urbanism reached in *Harlem Duet.* The reality that Lucinda, Billie's doctor in the mental ward, cannot (yet?) comprehend Billie's dreams suggests more than the inefficacy of psychotherapy. The distance between doctor and patient, between white and black women, instead, thematizes the profound chasm of experiences and emotions, perspective and place that divides minorities from white society. In this way, Billie's dream of a sanctuary against discrimination in Harlem and a place to call her own—"It's our time. In our place," says SHE during the play's prologue—becomes as much ethnographic as psychological. In *Harlem Duet,* in other words, this dream echoes the hopeful possibility of Martin Luther King Jr.'s dream of "a nation where [his children] will not be judged by the color of their skin but by the contents of their character."[60] Three decades after this speech, however, Billie and Othello represent and recognize how little race relations in the United States have changed as Sears underscores during scene four when they recite fragments of the speech. "America has given its colored people a . . . " Othello begins, and then the two of them continue, "bad cheque . . . ." Then Billie: " . . . a cheque that has come back marked . . . " and then, once more, the two together: " . . . 'insufficient funds.' "[61] Noteworthy, here, are two things. First, that King's speech enters the play as fragments of the hope that African Americans were holding onto, something that they have memorized and repeat to themselves but something that has, nonetheless, become frayed thanks to ongoing discrimination. During the concluding scene of the play emerges the second conclusion about this dream. While talking with Amah, Billie says, "I have a dream" but then corrects herself: "I had a dream."[62] Disillusioned with much of what Harlem promised, Billie's experience speaks to the Youngers in *A Raisin in the Sun* and to those who turned against the city during the rioting that beleaguered New York City and Los Angeles in the 1990s.

Recited at the beginning of this final scene and furthering the allegorization of Billie in African American urban life is Langston Hughes's "Harlem," which has been published under the title of "A Dream Deferred." The same poem that gave Hansberry the title *A Raisin in the Sun*, then, frames the conclusion of Sears's play, suggesting the literary lineage of *Harlem Duet*. Drawing on Hansberry and Hughes, Sears depicts a further snapshot of the African American family living in troubled corners of the metropolis and struggling against the walls of racism that keep them trapped in history. In fact, the dates of *Harlem Duet* (1997), *A Raisin in the Sun* (1959) and "Harlem" (1926) suggest three generations of African Americans struggling against problems of racism and urbanism that remain fundamentally unchanged despite differences in the characters or narrators of each. Although published in the 1920s, Hughes's poem asked the question—"What happens to a dream deferred?"— that speaks to the conclusions about racism and urbanism during the 1990s in *Harlem Duet*. Just as significantly, Hughes's poem predicted with remarkable foresight the many reactions by African Americans throughout the twentieth century to having their dreams continually deferred by the walls keeping them trapped within lives marked by deprivation and despair. For those like Ruth Younger, that dream begins to "dry up/ like a raisin in the sun," only to be temporarily revived with the determination of the family to move to Clybourne Park. For those like Billie, who seemingly had every opportunity to live the American Dream, that dream "just sags/Like a heavy load" that she cannot endure, emotionally or psychologically. Her shift of tense from "have" to "had" during this final scene undoubtedly speaks to the sense of disillusionment felt by many African Americans. But for some African Americans trapped in enclaves like Harlem or South Central, where the ongoing legacy of segregation is most intensely felt, the dreams deferred resulted in the most fearsome possibility envisioned by Hughes and included in *Harlem Duet*'s narrative voice-overs as the L.A. rioting, a social corollary to Billie's psychological breakdown: *Or does it explode?*

Street Scene, L.A.

Anna Deavere Smith's *Twilight Los Angeles, 1992* begins where *Harlem Duet* leaves off: with the rioting that followed the acquittal of four police officers caught beating Rodney King on videotape and the indignation for many in the African American community in Los Angeles. Commissioned by Gordon Davidson, the artistic director of the Mark Taper Forum, Smith's one-woman show combined ethnography and performance. Smith interviewed around two hundred participants in, victims of, and commentators on the "civil disturbance" that made Americans hold their collectively breath for three days in April 1992, though only about 25 are performed any night.[63] Smith's "characters" range from anonymous gang members to frightened University of Southern California (USC) students; from Daryl Gates, police commissioner when the first windows were shattered, to Reginald Deny, the truck driver attacked by young African Americans at the intersection of Florence and Normandie. Because the characters performed change from one production to another, they suggest what Patti Hartigan observed while reviewing the 1996 revival at New Haven's Long Wharf Theater: " '*Twilight*' gives us a panoramic view of a city at war with itself."[64] Instead of addressing any one production, however, the following argument works with the published text of *Twilight Los Angeles* and augments this discussion with reference to productions when doing so helps explicate issues of performance, staging, or reception. Any conclusions reached here about sociospatial concerns, then, are mediated by the changes made for productions, but the argument describes the guiding ethos of Smith's documentary theater. Worth noting here is that Smith falls within a tradition of documentary theater that extends back at least a century instead of invents one, as many reviews incorrectly claimed.[65] Like Smith's earlier work, *Fires in the Mirror: Crown Heights, Brooklyn, and Other Identities, Twilight Los Angeles, 1992* is part of *On the Road: A Search for the American Character*, which, after April 1992, includes the story of Los Angeles slowly imploding years before the rioting shattered assumptions of urban life.

In 1993 *Twilight Los Angeles* debuted at the Mark Taper Forum to ample enthusiasm from theatergoers and reviewers alike. Writing for *The New York Times*, Bernard Weinraub highlights proof of Smith's triumph by describing the "standing ovation and more flowers than she could carry" that followed the first performance.[66] Christopher Meeks of *Daily Variety* provides further details of this triumph, stressing how "astoundingly [she] captures multiple true life personalities" and remarks on how "Deavere [Smith's] delivery is sensitive and often touching" and specifically notes that "impressively, Smith gives one portrayal speaking entirely in Korean and another in Spanish."[67] Meeks does include a note of concern that would become a hallmark of reviews of *Twilight Los Angeles* when he worries about "characters" becoming "caricature."[68] Despite this general enthusiasm, the Los Angeles production was not the success Smith had hoped for since "not a lot of people came from South Central."[69] In 1994 *Twilight Los Angeles* moved to Joe Papp's Public Theater, where it was met with more enthusiasm. Michael Kuchwara described the production as being "ambitious" in scope while stressing how "memorable" Smith's portrait of "a pregnant Panamanian woman wounded in the rioting and whose fetus caught the bullet"; or how "hilariously [Smith] impersonates real estate superagent Elaine Young describing how she took refuge in a Beverly Hills hotel when the riots broke out."[70] Again much of the interest in *Twilight Los Angeles* focused on Smith's ability as performer and less on the exploration of the conflicts in Los Angeles. Intriguingly, when the play moved to Broadway's Cort Theater later that year, these concerns came to the foreground and, in part, derailed the production. As David Patrick Stearns observed about the Broadway show, Smith's play "has been losing money ever since it moved from off-Broadway" because "Broadway escapists perceive [*Twilight*] as 'cough syrup' theater."[71] Following this run on Broadway, *Twilight Los Angeles* moved into regional productions during the next decade.

During much of this stage history, tensions between performative success and sociospatial concerns inform consideration of *Twilight Los Angeles*. The focus on Smith's acting ability is unsurprising given that she performs—through slight changes in posture, movement, or intonation—the people interviewed while researching the riots. She becomes the conduit for their outrage, frustration, and grief about what occurred in Los Angeles in 1992.[72] Nevertheless, much about the dramatic and performative texts indicates that Smith's ambitions have as much to do—if not more—with tracing the rioting not simply to proximate causes like the exoneration of the police officers or the beating of Rodney King but further to the racialized antagonism—cutting across numerous ethnicities but rooted in the discrepancy of institutional power and daily freedoms enjoyed by whites and denied minorities—in Los Angeles. *Twilight Los Angeles* tries to recast the rioting as manifestation of the contestation in the city: particularly, patterns of spatial manipulation defined by Mike Davis and others as de facto segregation.[73] During many productions, like that at the Cort Theater in 1994, *Twilight Los Angeles* begins "with the pocky black-and-white video of Rodney King being pummeled and kicked by the police" but then the dramatic script turns not to King but rather to those who describe the history of hostility between the LAPD and minorities. This opening locates the King beating in the context of this hostility, to show the history of antagonism in L.A. In other productions, like that at the Long Wharf Theater in 1996, the video works to contextualize *Twilight Los Angeles's* representation of the riots in geography of LA. "At first, we see the snaky maze of highways that weave together like a Mobius strip and isolate the residents in their fancy or not-so-fancy cars," writes Hartigan, "then the camera moves to the barrio of East LA, to the streets of Koreatown, to the swanky streets of Beverly Hills."[74] In short, *Twilight Los Angeles* offers a spatializing corollary for Brecht's dramatic use of history in epic plays like *Mother Courage* and *Galileo*.[75]

Carl Weber has already described the affinity between Smith and Brecht, in particular Smith's acting in *Twilight Los Angeles* and Brecht's enumeration of epic acting in "Street Scene" and thereby suggests a way of bringing together performance and ambition. The title for this section then, refers to Smith's subject matter and her performative mode. In defining that mode, Brecht turned to analogy to explicate the means and ends of epic theater in "Street Scene": the untrained demonstrator's reenactment of a traffic accident. "The event has already taken place," says Brecht, and therefore the reenactment never intends to "transport people from normality to 'higher realms'" by trying to make onlookers believe that the scene is happening again.[76] Instead, the demonstrator foregrounds the "socially practical significance" of the driver's attitude toward or responsibility for the accident. Did the driver ignore traffic signals? Was the driver drunk? Never attempting the ontological gymnastics of trying to "become" the driver, "the street demonstrator's performance is essentially repetitive" and intends to teach a lesson about the social implications of what occurred.[77] As Weber notes, Smith's performance works in much the same way. She quotes her characters, speaking their words but hardly making any changes to her wardrobe and not changing scenes and thereby never fully foreclosing the distance between performer and performed despite her talent for mimicry.[78] Though reviewers of *Twilight Los Angeles* often become mired in the technique, there is much potential—according to Brecht—for showing what these characters have in common, in particular, what "social laws" inform their actions. Repeated before audiences as social and spatial phenomenon, the rioting becomes—if Smith's production is successful—explication of the divided geography of Los Angeles. Invoking spaces ranging from Beverly Hills to Pasadena, from the USC campus to South Central neighborhoods through dialogue, video projections, or photographic blowups, Smith foregrounds the frustration, despair, and apathy borne of the worst enclaves of L.A. and invites audiences toward recognizing the sociospatial laws informing these spaces.

Hatred of Place

Long before Rodney King's beating made it visible, there was animosity between the LAPD and minorities living in Los Angeles. This fact is stressed through Smith's first character in the section entitled, "The Territory." Speaking in his Brentwood home, Stanley K. Sheinbaum, former president of the L.A. Police Commission, talks about attending a gang meeting with Congresswoman Maxine Waters, the subject of which was creating a truce. More noteworthy, to Sheinbaum, than what he learned about gangs during the meeting are the reactions that followed from his LAPD colleagues: "Two days I got a letter" that read simply, "You went in and talked to our enemy."[79] Here, the title of this section becomes evident: much of the geography of Los Angeles is viewed in terms of territory, whether controlled or contested. To the note-writer, Sheinbaum sinned because he communicated with the enemy with whom the LAPD was frequently—if not daily—having clashes over certain regions of L.A. "Gangs are the enemy here," he says, though with the intent of explaining and mediating the letter: "The city has abused both sides," he insists, the cops and the gangs.[80] Much has been made, positively and negatively,[81] of Smith performing the roles of *Twilight Los Angeles* without judgment. According to this premise, Smith brings to the stage conflicting voices about the rioting but never intervenes in the conflict. Beginning with Sheinbaum's story of gangs and police may, initially, seem like evidence of such withholding of judgment, especially with the conclusions reached by Sheinbaum. "So which side are you on?" his LAPD colleagues ask of him, and he responds, "Why do I have to be on a side?"[82] Nevertheless the way that the scenes have been organized into juxtapositions in the text, in this case in "The Territory," demonstrates how each section of *Twilight Los Angeles* derives from and pursues rhetorical ambitions.

Immediately after Sheinbaum's question is the story of Michael Zinzun, representative for the Coalition Against Police Abuse. He describes being awakened along with his neighbors by "this guy calling out for help."[83] When he went to investigate, he recognized that another African American who, while being arrested by the police, was getting "the shit" beaten "out of him." When he and others confronted the police, according to Zinzun, the police "began Macing the crowd" and handcuffed Zinzun before hustling him down an alley.[84] Blinded by the Mace, Zinzun could only "feel all these police stompin' on my back" and then the flashlight that struck him above the eye and left him permanently blinded. Suggested here is more than Sheinbaum will admit or perhaps can conceive: that the animosity by the LAPD is not limited to gangs but extends to the African American community whether because of guilt-by-association or perhaps because of the racism of individual officers. In any event, it becomes plain that taking sides, at least in 1990s Los Angeles, is not a matter of choice but a reality that leaves those like Zinzun and ultimately Rodney King—victimized by the police. Worse still is the story told by Theresa Allison, founder of Mothers Reclaiming Our Children, elsewhere in "The Territory." Her nephew, Tiny, was killed by the police in a way that left her believing that young African American men were being targeted.

"They shot forty-three times./Five bullets went into Tiny./No bullets went into nobody else's body."[85] What does it mean to Allison? "I think what they do, they want to make it look like a drive-by/shooting."[86] Not an isolated incident, the death of Tiny contributes to history of abuse by the police. "They used to take our kids/from one project and drop 'em in another area where the young man would be assaulted or worse by rival gangs "and then say it's a gang-related thing."[87] Emerging from this narrative, which adds to the necessity of taking sides, is the idea that animosity between the LAPD and African Americans has been playing out in and about Los Angeles for generations.

Rather than simply presenting the conflicting perspectives of those inter-viewed, Smith makes an argument—in the same way epic theater makes an argument—regarding the rioting through her dramaturgy. The three days of looting and violence that followed the acquittal of the four police officers who allegedly beat Rodney King was not merely response to the verdict or even response to the beating itself; instead, it had deeper roots that derive from the "social laws" that inform living in enclaves like South Central and Compton. During the third section of the play, entitled "War Zone," Smith makes this plain in Allen Cooper, ex-gang member and activist in the national truce movement. "What Rodney King . . . /It been—/it's been twenty, thirty years,/and people suffered beatings from law enforcement./It ain't nothin' new."[88] Like Zinzun and Allison, Cooper views King's beating as just another incident in a long line of African Americans being abused by the LAPD. "If you put twenty hidden cameras/in the country jail system," insists Cooper, "you got people beat worse than that/point blank." In fact, every time Cooper says the name, his incredulity becomes glaringly evident: "Rotney King, Rotney King, Rotney King./It's not Rotney King./It's the ghetto."[89] Here Cooper makes the link that is central to *Twilight Los Angeles* and its sociospatial ambitions. In shifting attention from one person's public victimization—which was the touchstone for media accounts of the rioting—toward the conditions that informed this event, Smith's dramaturgy redefines the exigency of the rioting and the responsibility of the audience. More than outrage at King's beating or the acquittal of the police officers involved, what sparked the rioting according to *Twilight Los Angeles* was grounded in the living conditions and maltreatment endured for years, if not generations of African Americans in the ghetto. Because of this, Cooper—and *Twilight Los Angeles*—contend that "You gotta look at history, baby,/you gotta look at history."[90]

In an unlikely alliance of voices, Cooper's insistence on historicism is complemented, at least thematically, with the speech by Congresswoman Maxine Waters—whose district includes South Central—at the First African

Methodist Episcopal Church shortly after the riots subsided. Importantly, Waters admits transgressions during the rioting by many, who would not usually have committed the sorts of crimes that were often televised on the nightly news. But then she immediately locates those transgressions in the living conditions endured in the worst enclaves of L.A.: "the times are such,/the environment is such, that good people reacted in strange ways. They are not all crooks and/criminals."[91] Like Cooper, Waters conceives of the rioting as emerging from the history of racism, not the least of is the fact of all the "young men who have been dropped off of/America's agenda."[92] "They don't show up on anybody's statistics./They're not in school,/they have never been employed,/they don't really live anywhere." Implicit in Waters's description is the notion of a social contract that has been broken by the government and therefore strikes young African Americans as nothing more than empty rhetoric. Her reasoning begins with history of the ghettos of Los Angeles. "There was an insurrection in this city before," she says, invoking the 1965 Watts Riots at the opening of the speech, "and if I remember correctly/it was sparked by police brutality."[93] After the riots came the Kerner Commission report, which was the government's investigation of root causes behind the rioting that left many in Los Angeles stunned and uncertain. "It talked about what was wrong with our society./It talked about institutionalized racism./It talked about a lack of services,/lack of government responsive to the people."[94] Two key points emerge from Waters's framing of the 1992 riots against the 1965 riots. First is the continued stress on historicism that reveals little having changed in Waters's estimation: "Today . . . it seems as though we are talking about what that report cited/some twenty years ago still exists today." Second is how Waters links the "social laws" attendant with the local living conditions in the ghettos of L.A. to national policies that (indifferently? deliberately?) ignored the needs of this community.

Intended for the president, governor, or "anybody else who wants to listen," Waters's words, reenacted through *Twilight Los Angeles,* further Cooper's insistence that "you gotta look at history" to understand anything of the rioting.[95] Cooper's adamancy about historicism, paradoxically, demands that we recognize the limits of what can—and cannot—be understood about the rioting, or what can or cannot be expressed through performance: "You got to live here to express this point, you got to live/here to see what's goin' on."[96] Like any other text, *Twilight Los Angeles* can never fully communicate the everyday reality or experience of the people who witnessed, participated in, or were victimized by the rioting—no matter how well Smith may capture their habits of speech or mannerisms. The staging of *Twilight Los Angeles,* in fact, suggests Smith's implicit acknowledgement of this. Smith usually performs on a relatively bare stage, with only a few props (chair, table, et cetera) and blow-ups of photographs or projections of images from the rioting in reference to the event. (Images in the published text include buildings burning, looters pushing shopping carts of stolen goods, and bloodied or fighting people). Never attempting to create realistic representation of the rioting or ghettos on stage, Smith instead performs outside the images, visually suggesting the experiential and existential distance between herself—not to mention audiences—from those interviewed for *Twilight Los Angeles.* Certainly Smith intends, like Brecht, for audiences to make critical connections between characters/interviews performed and the contextualizing properties brought to the stage. But simultaneously this critical engagement becomes a gesture toward the limits of knowledge, which perhaps undermines the universalizing tendency of reading the outraged, frustrated reactions of rioters against audience's assumptions of how they relate to urban locales. And this gesture toward limitations perhaps highlights the ways that urban geography is continually contested—not just physically or legally but further experientially or existentially.

Whereas many Americans no doubt understood the rioting as a problem for the city of Los Angeles, and perhaps cities everywhere, *Twilight Los Angeles* demonstrates how the rioting was a problem *of the city*—in particular, of the long history of discrimination, ill-treatment, and impoverishment attending life in the ghettos. The "characters" performed by Smith frequently reference the buildings, streets, and neighborhoods of L.A. as well as their difficult interactions with the police but almost never with the naïve idealism evident during the flashback scenes of *Harlem Duet.* There seems to be little hope left in Smith's L.A. that could at least be imagined in Sears's Harlem. Many during the rioting paraded their antipathy toward Los Angeles without qualms, like the women gathered on windowsills, shouting, "Let the motherfuckers burn" to Captain Haywood of the LAFD, a reaction that he finds shocking. Others flaunt their outrage in ways that surely make middle-class white Americans uncomfortable, as when Paul Parker, Chairperson of Free the LA Four,[97] cautions the wider audience imagined when interviewed by Smith: "We didn't get to Beverly Hills, but/that doesn't mean we won't get there,/you keep it up."[98] Made evident through these "characters" is what ethnographer Delmos Jones describes as "a deep hatred of place and all its elements: location, landscape, life experiences in the setting"—all of which contrasts markedly with more privileged perspectives included in *Twilight Los Angeles.*[99] Instead of trying to bring audiences together, the dramaturgy of *Twilight Los Angeles* explored what about the geography of L.A. has driven them apart—experientially as much as spatially, as Smith has remarked elsewhere[100]—so that so many could take to the streets with such disillusionment that they can only strike back at the city they hated. Waters defines "riot" as "the voice of the unheard."[101]

Similarly, Gladis Sibrian of the Farabundo Marti National Liberation Front highlights the social implications in the penultimate vignette of *Twilight Los Angeles*: "What happened here in LA, I/call it a social explosion," what happens "when people can no longer take it—/ the status quo."[102]

Delusion to the Problem

Borne of history, in particular the antagonisms among minority communities, municipal authority, and urban environment, the rioting nevertheless proves vulnerable to historiography. How the rioting is defined, in other words, can prompt dialogue about what induced the hatred of place, or can just as easily foreclose discussion through expedient conclusions. One example of this occurred during the rioting—and continued after—as the media and politicians defined the looting and violence as reaction by the African American community to the verdict exonerating the four LAPD accused of beating King. Defining the rioting this way downplays the diverse demography of those involved in or victimized by the riots and ignores the historical conditions of Los Angeles that nurtured frustration and outrage. In *Latino Metropolis*, Victor Valle and Rodolfo Torres reveal that "Latinos made up at least 49 percent of the population residing in the most damaged areas of the rioting" and that "nearly 51 percent" of those arrested were Latino.[103] According to this analysis, participants and victims of the riots alike were "united more by levels of joblessness, homelessness, and educational failure"—all of which are problems *of the city* endured by minorities—"than by race."[104] The problem, say Valle and Torres, is that Hispanics, Latinos, Koreans or other ethnic groups that constitute much of the demography of Los Angeles put pressure on traditional ideas of "race," centered on black/white antagonism, and therefore were left out of the discussion. In *Dead Cities and Other Tales*, Mike Davis extends this argument toward the Korean community, which was perhaps targeted by many African Americans during the rioting. "By Friday morning 90 percent of the myriad Korean-owned liquor stores, markets, and swapmeets in South Central LA had been wiped out," notes Davis, "Deserted by the LAPD, which made no attempt to defend small businesses, the Koreans suffered damage or destruction to almost 2,000 stores from Compton to the heart of Koreatown itself."[105] He locates this animosity in the killing of an African American girl named Latasha Harlins by a Korean grocer.[106] The historiography of the rioting, then, is fraught with questions of authority and authenticity: Whose story do we tell? And notably, who does the telling?

Certainly sensitive to questions like these, Smith makes gestures toward the limitations of the black/white framing of the riots through her dramaturgy. Included in prominent locales in *Twilight Los Angeles* are interviews of members of communities left out of this binary. In fact, the story of Rudy Salas Sr., a sculptor and painter of Mexican ancestry, serves as the prologue to *Twilight Los Angeles*. Sitting in his home, he talks about years earlier when he was arrested by the LAPD: "they took me to a room/and they locked the door behind me/and there was four guys, four cops there/kicking me in the head."[107] The legacy of this is a double consciousness about the police: he insists that "it's not a hate thing/the insanity that I carried with me when I took the beating" but then moments later admits the "insane hatred" he feels for his "enemy." His struggle with this legacy frames "The Territory" and its history of the antagonism between ethnic communities and the LAPD.[108] Toward the end of *Twilight Los Angeles,* similarly, comes the voice of Mrs. Young-Soon Han, who owned a liquor store before the riots, whose epiphany and questions powerfully interject another perspective in the struggle for equality in LA. "I really realized that/Korean immigrants were left out/from this/society and we were nothing . . . Why?/Why do we have to be left out?"[109] Including perspectives like these militates against the historiography defined by Valle, Torres, and Davis and, more importantly, makes the contested landscapes of L.A. subject to interrogation, though it can be argued that these voices are drowned out by the number and volume of those considering the rioting in *Twilight Los Angeles* in terms of the black/white binary. The majority of the characters in the published text (as well as those performed) talk of race in terms of African Americans and whites. But Smith mediates, to some extent, this disproportional depiction by thematizing—in order to problematize—the lessons potentially learned from the rioting. She does so by putting into conversation two racialized conclusions about what the riot meant from this perspective.

The first of these belongs to Reginald Denny, the truck driver who was pulled from his truck—on live television—and assaulted by a group of African American men the morning that the verdict exonerating the LAPD was handed down. Denny talks initially of the incident itself or at least what little he remembered of it and the details that followed when he was visited in the hospital by four bystanders "Titus and Bobby and Terry and Lee" who came to his rescue.[110] In describing meeting them[111] he is fascinated with what binds them together when everything in L.A. seems to be spiraling apart: "There was a weird common thread in our lives."[112] Determined to make something of that "thread," Denny turns the discussion to what he hopes will transpire through the rebuilding of L.A. "Someday, when I,/uh,/get a house,/I'm gonna have one of the rooms/and it's gonna be/of all the riot stuff," he says, "and it won't be a/blood-and-guts/memorial,/it's not gonna be sad,/it's gonna be a happy room."[113] This memorial will become a testament not merely to the four African Americans who rescued him from the street but to racial acceptance, more of the "common thread" that crosses racial lines. "There won't be/a color problem," he adds, "in this room."[114] This sentiment makes for excellent contrast with the second of the memorials, this one belonging to Paul Parker, of Free the LA Four Plus Defense Committee. Initially, Parker talks about the incident with Denny in tones that are openly hostile to the assumptions about race: "If Denny was Latino,/Indian, or black,/they wouldn't give a damn . . . Because many people got beat,/but you didn't hear about the Lopezes or the Vaccas."[115] Though Parker's tone is more strident than Denny, his words become intriguingly similar to Denny's as he talks about the lessons learned. "When I finally get my house I'm gonna have just one room sent aside./It's gonna be my No Justice No Peace room./Gonna have up on the wall No Justice,/over here No Peace."[116] Intended as testament to racial injustice in L.A., this room will be where Parker's children "can just see what it takes/to be a strong black man": "You either be black,/or you die."[117]

Interviewed during the 1996 revival in Boston, Smith ascribed considerable importance to this contrast in terms of the play's ambitions. "The tenuous line between hope and despair echoes in '*Twilight*,' most notably in the conflicting views of a bitter black man and Reginald Denny," Smith tells Hartigan.[118] In Denny's room "there's no race problem there" while in Parker's room there is nothing but race. "So there are two rooms," says Smith, "And we have a choice." It is unclear from her remarks if Smith is being disingenuous, but *Twilight Los Angeles* suggests that the rooms of Denny and Parker—one hopelessly utopian and the other openly militant—serve not so much as choices for audiences but rather to demonstrate the limitations of either choice as memorial to the rioting. Denny's naivety, after all, will not only be considered alongside Parker's cynicism. Simultaneously, it will be read alongside the characters performed before and after it, like that of Allen Cooper, which immediately precedes Denny in the published text. Cooper's refrain—"You gotta look at history, baby"—highlights the banality of Denny's presumption that he can somehow cordon off the historic animosities between minority groups and municipal authority. Noteworthy is how the room described by Cooper, where the LAPD beat minorities—and have for decades—echoes throughout Denny's imagining of his room where there is no "color problem." And Cooper's final words, which still linger in the theater even as Smith segues to Denny, put audiences in the position of questioning Denny's proposal about how to memorialize the riots well before it is made. "This Reginald Denny thing is a joke./It's a joke./That's just a delusion to the real problem."[119] In effect, audiences are asked—thanks to the juxtaposition of Denny and Cooper—to read one vignette in contrast to another, which further problematizes conclusions reached therein. The same is true with Denny's remarks about this room being "a wild place" where there is no race, words that linger when Captain Haywood—during the next vignette—describes the women shouting "Let the motherfuckers burn" as LAFD personnel try to dowse flaming buildings, another possible memorial.

Likewise is Parker's argument about African American identity defined—not merely for him but for generations—through militancy problematized by *Twilight Los Angeles's* syntax. His "room" is preceded in the published text by two vignettes by Maxine Waters, during the first of which she admits wrongdoing by members of the African American community in breaking—momentarily—the social contract uniting members of the city and the nation. In the following vignette, Waters describes her determined efforts to get federal attention and aid with "dealing with this joblessness" plaguing many lower-income communities in Los Angeles as well as for better intervention by the government "in these cities when these/police departments are out of control."[120] Waters, then, enters *Twilight Los Angeles* as representation of another kind of African American identity, one that begins not from closing herself off—like Parker—from the rest of the city or nation and nurturing animosity toward white society. Instead, she demands acknowledgement and assistance from the government for the problems besetting the worst corners of L.A. Importantly, Parker's "No Justice No Peace" room, which draws defining lines between black and white, between oppressed and oppressor, is followed by one of the vignettes about Daryl Gates. Gates laments openly that he has become, for many, "the symbol" of police brutality and apartheid politics in Los Angeles but he comes across as more deluded rather than racist, something that should be questioned rather than condemned.[121] In this, *Twilight Los Angeles* interrogates Parker's claims about African American identity made necessary by the rioting as flawed since the antagonism he would pass on to his children would only compound the problem. Parker's memorial to the rioting may be flawed because it metonymically reproduces the ethnic enclaves—divided and divisive—that were underlying the exigency of the rioting as well as the ongoing problems of L.A. Like Denny, Parker begins from totalizing conclusions about race, place, and identity that serve, intentionally or not, to reinforce the worst racial fault lines of Los Angeles—another strategy that, borrowing from Cooper, may prove further delusion to the problem of L.A. The syntax of *Twilight Los Angeles,* then, thrusts competing conclusions about the rioting into juxtaposition to question choices (to be) made.

This is not to say that Smith's emphasis on making choices is misplaced, only too easily misunderstood. In fact, the juxtapositional syntax of *Twilight Los Angeles* self-consciously[122] invites audiences toward making choices—not to endorse one particular choice over another but to demonstrate what we reject or ignore in making that choice. If audiences choose Denny's "happy room" as the best way of making sense of and memorializing the rioting, that means rejecting Cooper's adamancy about looking the history of the ghettos, and essentially the same is true about choosing Cooper's frustrated acceptance of that history of African American abuse by the LAPD. What future can there be in Los Angeles without concerted efforts toward reconciliation? In this way the dramatic structure of *Twilight Los Angeles*—episodes juxtaposed with one another, demanding interpretation—produces something similar to Brecht's theory of the "not-but." "There is not just one possibility but two" whenever any action is taken on the stage or any choice made in the auditorium, insists Brecht: "both are introduced, then the second one is alienated, then the first as well."[123] The point here was to problematize actions or choices by showing audiences that they were *not this, but that*—not inevitable but instead willingly chosen. Informed by this knowledge of choices not made, we are, the theory goes, empowered toward more critical engagement with the play unfolding before us and with the world beyond the theater, where our more complex form of seeing[124] will be most valuable for addressing social or, in this case, sociospatial concerns. In highlighting the choices made and the consequences of those choices—by characters during the riots and by audiences during the production—*Twilight Los Angeles* militates against our taking epistemological refuge (like Denny and Parker especially) in shortsighted and ultimately dangerous historiography. In effect, Smith thematizes the problematic interplay of audience, performance, and place—like Brecht, in ways that never work to make the events depicted more easily comprehended—that is central to her sociospatial ambitions in the juxtaposing of Denny's and Parker's rooms.

Part of the Act

Twilight Los Angeles and Smith herself, interestingly enough, have been criticized for not trying to convince audiences of particular conclusions. Smith generally dismisses this criticism as rather myopic in the first place: *Twilight Los Angeles* or any literary work cannot resolve long-standing problems of racial antagonisms, police misconduct, and apartheid politics. More notably, Smith has described this criticism about clear-cut conclusions as misguided, perhaps dangerously so: "I don't think my job is to give the conclusion because the complexity of our culture, the damage that's been done is because people did come to conclusions," she explains when interviewed during the writing of this book: "For all those years we had one conclusion—the white man's conclusion. And now we finally have a series of conclusions."[125] Not surprisingly, Smith's postmodern fragmenting of epistemology is reflected in the dramatic structure of *Twilight Los Angeles,* which endeavors to prevent audiences from becoming mired in any conclusions that can be reached during the two and a half hours of the performance. The juxtaposing of perspectives evident in the published text (and, presumably, the performances) is especially noteworthy given the selectivity demonstrated by Smith in choosing 25 "characters" out of nearly 200 interviews: her process of organizing the characters, even though invisible in either published text or theatrical performance, suggests much about her ambitions. And these ambitions are deeply invested in influencing audience reception, more than most of the plays discussed in this study with the exception of Rivera's *Marisol* and Kushner's *Angels in America.* In fact, *Twilight Los Angeles* best demonstrates Worthen's argument that what defines political theater is "the formation of the audience's experience" and by extension, "the formation of the audience itself."[126] Instead of leaving audiences with a particular conclusion about the causes or consequences of the riots in L.A., Smith's dramaturgy poses and prompts questions that may be more radical in influencing the experience and composition of audiences: in particular, asking what responsibility audiences, simultaneously citizens, have in confronting the discrimination that led to the rioting in L.A.

Twilight Los Angeles's ethnography of the rioting and of L.A.—the inseparability of the two being one "conclusion" advocated by the play—is always incomplete, always implicitly gesturing toward the necessity of audience engagement. During the penultimate section, entitled "Twilight," this responsibility of audiences becomes explicit through the remarks of Homi Bhabha, which further link the events of the rioting and the dramaturgy of *Twilight Los Angeles.* "The inclarity,/the enigma,/the ambivalences/ in what happened in the L.A./uprisings/are precisely what we want to get hold of."[127] If anything, the riots threw into abeyance what assumptions we shared about living in cities since the riots revealed markedly conflicting experiences and understandings of the same urban geography. Like Bhabha, Smith suggests "that the hard outlines of what we see in daylight . . . disappear[ed]" when the rioting erupted and clear-cut conclusions only further obfuscate the underlying problems in L.A.[128] In language that further describes Smith's play, Bhabha notes, "That fuzziness of twilight/allows us to see the intersections/of the event with a number of other things that daylight obscures for/us." The reason? "We have to interpret more in/twilight" because what we are looking at is suddenly not (if it ever was) well defined or clearly understandable. When this happens, "we have to make ourselves/part of the act." This language speaks to *Twilight Los Angeles's* sociospatial ambitions, in particular the demands upon audiences to recognize and judge the experiences before, during, and after the rioting alongside one another. This dramaturgy can potentially foreclose audience engagement because it proves too demanding or it implies sentimentalizing, the intellectual equivalent of King's "Why can't we all just get along?" More than any other play considered here, *Twilight Los Angeles* depends on the subjunctive "what if" possibility that defers and determines the efficacy of political theater.[129] The sociospatial ambitions of *Twilight Los Angeles*, then, depend on making audiences from different backgrounds "part of the act."

But the question remains, what kind of engagement—if not rallying around particular conclusions—does *Twilight Los Angeles* demand? Robin Bernstein suggests an answer when he contends that *Twilight Los Angeles* "call[s] for people to witness."[130] Writing about the 1997 Berkeley Repertory production and its rebuttal to the ways the video of Rodney King's beating was mediated by defense attorneys during the trial of the four officers, Bernstein's definition of "witness" highlights the epistemological. "Witnessing means honoring individual, subjective, human perspective. Witnessing implies responsibility; this responsibility precludes viewers being severed from their vision—from each other."[131] More noteworthy through much of *Twilight Los Angeles*, though, may be the moral responsibility among one another thematized through the story of Josie Morales. Ignoring her husband's insistence that she come inside the apartment during the King beating, Morales recalls, "I said 'No.'/I said, 'we have to stay here/ and watch/because this is wrong.'"[132] Her witnessing of the beating epitomizes the ethical obligation between those living in neighborhoods, communities, and cities—exactly what was missing from L.A. as depicted during "The Territory" where police misconduct and racialized antagonisms had turned the city into a powder keg. However implicitly, Morales understood her responsibility during such an event—the beating of one African American, the beating of a white truck driver, the looting of businesses across L.A.—toward more than just herself, toward that silent reciprocity that makes living in cities and among strangers possible. Much later in the play, at the beginning of "Twilight," Smith complements Morales's insistence on moral obligation with the remarks of theatrical director Peter Sellars: "We all live in the same house," he says, invoking a trope that speaks to the different quarters[133] of the city: "Start a fire in the basement/and . . . nobody's gonna be left on the top floor./It's one house./And shutting the door in you room doesn't matter."[134] Conservatism that advocates closing the door to the riot-ravaged areas of L.A., in other words, is merely adding fuel of indifference to the still-simmering embers of the riots. What is needed for the future of Los Angeles are audiences willing to say, "No . . . we have to stay here/and watch/because this is wrong."

The concluding vignette of *Twilight Los Angeles* extends the motif of witnessing beyond the infamous incidents of the rioting and toward the urban environment through Twilight Bey, who gives Smith's play its title. Growing up surrounded by gangs but eventually organizing a gang truce in his neighborhood, Bey epitomizes the kind of engagement advocated by *Twilight Los Angeles*. His story begins with description of his community: "I'm up twenty-four hours, it feels like,/and, you know,/what I see at nighttime" includes preteen children "beatin' up a old man on the bus stop,/a homeless man."[135] "When I'm in my own neighborhood, I'm driving/through and I/see the living dead, as we call them, the base heads" stumbling down the streets and toward oblivion. During these vigils, which began when Bey was 12 or 13, Bey becomes increasingly troubled by what he sees: evidence of people grown away from one another, of individuals disillusioned and drugged, not really part of the city, not part of the United States. Moved by what he witnesses, Bey intercedes when the young boys—perhaps those described by Maxine Waters who have no jobs, no homes, or no hope—assault the homeless man, and his melancholy tone when describing the drug addicts evidences his sympathy for another's suffering. Because he spends so much time in twilight, Bey finds himself more willing to confront connotations of discourse and definition, race and place, often used to underscore racialized difference that has become synonymous with Los Angeles or Harlem or any city that has endured rioting borne from the twin pressures of racial discrimination and communal disintegration. "Light" may be "a word that symbolizes knowledge, knowing,/wisdom," says Bey, but he rejects the dichotomy that frequently follows: "I don't affiliate/darkness with anything negative."[136] Instead of conceiving of this discourse in binary he redefines differences as complementary in his ongoing self-definition. "I see darkness as myself./I see the light as knowledge and the wisdom of the world/and/understanding others."[137]

In many ways, Twilight Bey becomes a model and mentor for audiences of *Twilight Los Angeles* when it comes to understanding something of the rioting that left parts of Los Angeles in ruins and left many of our assumptions on urbanism in tatters. For Bey, this understanding begins with the recognition that "I can't forever dwell in darkness/I can't forever dwell in the idea,/of just identifying with people like me and understanding me and mine."[138] Implicit here is the knowledge of how limiting this self-definition exclusively through one's community can be, and, when contrasted with the reactions of others in *Twilight Los Angeles,* how this may have originally contributed to the crisis. Those like Elaine Young who took refuge during the Beverly Hills Hotel during the rioting or Paul Parker who turns to militancy following the riots both epitomize those who identify only with their own and thereby reinforce the fault lines of race, place, and difference dividing Los Angeles.

Merely closely the doors to the house on fire just ignores, instead of dealing with, the problems of the city. Much of Smith's dramaturgy in *Twilight Los Angeles* encourages audiences toward a similar recognition as Bey's by confronting them with multiple voices and conflicting experiences of the city, few of which will correspond with those of any one community. The goal is fundamentally pedagogical: to challenge how we know the city. Importantly, however, the last section of *Twilight Los Angeles* is entitled "Justice" and not "Twilight," suggesting the need to move beyond self-discovery and toward communal regeneration. Precisely what audiences are supposed to do, beyond witnessing the stories that emerge from the rioting, remains ambiguous, suggesting the limitations of *Twilight Los Angeles* as epic theater that intends to induce social or political change. Nevertheless, Smith makes clear the stakes for confronting the problems of the city in Los Angeles during the 1990s through Maxine Waters's words that echo long after they are spoken: "Los Angeles burned . . . but Los Angeles is but one/city/experiencing/this kind of hopelessness and despair."[139]

CHAPTER 5

"Part of the City": Enclaves and Exiles in Los Angeles

Evident in chapters 3 and 4 are tensions defining the final theme considered in this book: the steadily increasing multiculturalism of cities like New York and Los Angeles. Though most large cities (and many smaller ones) have long-standing immigrant communities, the number of immigrants from particular regions like Asia, Mexico, and Latin America grew significantly in the 1980s. According to Chalsa Loo's *Chinatown: Most Time, Hard Time,* the "newcomers from these countries" constituted around 30 percent of immigrants in the United States; but from 1981 to 1985 the numbers ballooned to 83 percent of immigrants, vastly changing the face of cities.[1] Changing the ethnic make-up of urbanism, however, was just the beginning for immigrants bringing their traditions, languages, and customs. In *Megalopolis,* Celeste Olalquiaga describes changes corresponding with immigration from Latin America: "cityspeak," which blends Spanish and English toward new kinds of discourse, and "casitas," which "install a piece of Puerto Rico in the middle of New York City."[2] What changes like these represent is the "Latinization of urban culture in the United States, the formulation of hybrid cultures such as the Chicano and the Nuyorican."[3] Celebrating this transformation is performance artist Guillermo Gomez-Pena, who contends that cities like New York and Paris "increasingly resemble Mexico City and Sao Paolo" and that Tijuana and Los Angeles "are becoming models of a new hybrid culture."[4] Unlike Gomez-Pena, however, many living in New York City and Los Angeles in the 1980s met these changes with anxiety and antagonism. Underlying the neotraditional movement discussed in Chapter 3 was the goal of returning to a "lily-white" Small Town America, an effort to preserve urban living from immigrants who are defined as intruders. Hostility toward immigrants is implicit in the processes of suburbanism and ghettoization, and that hostility became explicit in acts of violence or intimidation[5] against immigrants who, through their very presence, were at the center of sociospatial crisis.

Told symbolically and literally that they were unwelcome in many neighborhoods or cities, immigrants from Asia, Mexico, and Latin America were confronted with this dilemma. Geographically removed from their homelands—for any number of reasons[6]—they are at the same time epistemologically distanced from the cities where they found themselves in the United States. Dramatist Dolores Prida, born in Cuba but living in New York at the time of this interview, describes how this quandary influences her writing: "Most of my plays have been about the experience of being a Hispanic in the United States, about people trying to reconcile two cultures and two languages and two visions of the world into a particular whole."[7] Normally, consideration of this dilemma takes place on the global scale, with emphasis placed on international displacement, but this dilemma can be compounded by the urban scale. In the city that is openly hostile to the presence of the immigrant, the attempted reconciliation described by Prida is both external and internal: coming to know the alien city that reminds the immigrant, daily, of his or her non-place, and struggling to know oneself in a city that actively denies or decries the immigrant's presence. Certainly not easy, this "reality of contemporary immigration" has been defined by Chaudhuri in *Staging Place* as "the radical insecurity and contingency of urban existence. The contemporary immigrant is between Scylla and Charybdis, or as Americans would say, between a rock and a hard place."[8] But in *Imaginary Homelands*, Salman Rushdie extends Prida's discussion of the immigrant quandary toward surprising possibility. Always subject to the "triple dislocation" of language, place, and history, the immigrant initially becomes caught up in the widening gyre of indeterminacy and individuation.[9] But because the immigrant finds him or herself *between* here and there, then and now, he or she becomes "obliged to find new ways of describing himself."[10] And, I would add, new ways of knowing the city within which this process of reconciliation and individuation unfolds.

This chapter considers plays that dramatize the antagonism between immigrant and the city of Los Angeles as well as the immigrants' determined, and frequently disillusioning, efforts toward reconciling this antagonism: David Henry Hwang's *FOB* and Cherrie Moraga's *Giving up the Ghost*. Neither play is the most well known for these dramatists, possibility because they represent early works in the careers of Hwang and Moraga, or because they highlight antagonism surrounding urbanism, citizenship, and identity that perhaps make the broad audiences necessary for major productions uncomfortable. This antagonism begins with the ways immigrants and their communities have been historically marginalized: pushed to the periphery and condemned through public discourse—that defines immigrant enclaves as alien, threatening, or criminal[11]—all of which serve as ways of holding multiculturalism in check. But Hwang's and Moraga's plays are surprisingly nonconfrontational; that is, they do not function as polemics. Instead, *FOB* and *Giving up the Ghost* stress the internal crisis that follows from the geographical conflicts in Los Angeles: the existential (false) dilemma in which immigrants, children of immigrants, and members of ethnic groups associated with immigration, find themselves having to choose between ethnic heritage and U.S. citizenship. More daunting perhaps, Hwang's and Moraga's dramas interrogate the dilemma confronting immigrants who have turned to enclaves like Chinatown or barrios as refuges against antagonism. There, many immigrants feel safe, feel like they belong. On the other hand, more and more immigrants and children of immigrants feel that such enclaves do more to delimit than to define them by locking them away. This dilemma leaves many immigrants frustrated and uncertain in the process of self-definition. Not endorsing one view or the other, *FOB* and *Giving up the Ghost* are parables about the dangers inherent in any identity borne of dichotomy, in this case, that of immigrant and city.

Obviously complex, this internalized conflict emerges from the general antagonism of the metropolis toward the immigrant, but this antagonism plays out and is reconciled differently for these immigrant groups. It is not my intention to generalize the experiences of Chinese and Mexican immigrants but, instead, to contrast them toward a more complex and revealing reading of the metropolis. Beginning with Hwang's *FOB*, then, means considering the history of Chinatown. On the one hand, Chinatown provides newcomers to the United States with a sense of comfort and belonging through shared history, culture, language, and beliefs. As Loo notes, "Eight out of ten residents reported that it was 'somewhat important' (44%) or 'very important' (34%) for them to live among other Chinese Americans."[12] Why such "ethnic homogeneity" is attractive to Chinese immigrants is clear enough: it provides stability in the face of discontinuity, a sense of place in the metropolis that—historically if not today—excludes Chinese immigrants. Ideally, then, the "community [of Chinatown] forms a nearly self-sufficient urban village containing a network of residence, employment and children's schooling."[13] All this was the case up until World War II, but after the war class became a mediating factor for how and where immigrants settled. "Those with better incomes moved into adjoining, outlying neighborhoods" in part because "living outside the ghetto connoted higher socioeconomic status."[14] More recently, immigrants of higher socioeconomic status have been leaving Chinatowns because of what it represents. In interviews gathered by Loo, we find these admissions: "I see Chinatown as a barrier, an obstruction. If I move out of Chinatown, it's a chance for me to progress."[15] Others interviewed "considered Chinatown a ghetto and a slum."[16] Chinatown, then, sits at the center of conflicting forces about history and culture, socioeconomics and opportunity, self-definition and ethnic identity. Recognizing this, Hwang foregrounds the internalized dilemma in immigrants from China and children of those immigrants, struggling with Chinatown as locus of ethnic identity, and Chinatown as marginalization. In many ways, the conflicts of *FOB* play out in and about the city, with the ambition being to bring audiences closer to this internal struggle.

Though starting from the similar dilemma, Cherríe Moraga's *Giving up the Ghost* begins from a distinctly different relationship among ethnicity, location, and history that speaks to the lives of Mexican immigrants in L.A. In *Latino Metropolis,* Valle and Torres detail how Hispanic populations of Los Angeles had roughly become the majority ethnic group at the time the study was published (in 2000), but they had nonetheless been rendered "*invisible* politically and economically" (original emphasis).[17] Instead of having any voice in L.A., they had become the city's "unspoken army of labor," "keeping unskilled wages . . . in check."[18] In *Dead Cities and Other Tales,* Davis describes the living conditions associated with this condition when discussing Bell Gardens, which "has become a 'rent plantation,' controlled by absentee landlords, where Mexican immigrants . . . are forced to squeeze as many as fifteen people into a unit to afford housing."[19] Cudahy, another town in this feudal class structure, had former bungalows converted into " 'six-pack' stucco tenements . . . barracks housing as many as 125 people on a formerly single-family site."[20] Herded into such ghettos, Mexican immigrants and their children were faced with a hostile landscape, in which they confronted both privation and dismissal. For the Mexican immigrant, then, the urban landscape of Los Angeles was more actively contested with hegemonic authority and less so internally. In fact, Valle and Torres contend that "the implosion [of the 1992 riots] can be understood . . . as the bitter and pained insistence on visibility."[21] Moraga's *Giving up the Ghost* anticipates this frustration with the discrepancy of living conditions in L.A., more than a decade before the rioting. More to the point, Moraga's play draws upon traditions of Chicano *teatro* that stress activism as part of theater's ambition. As Jorge Huerta notes, "Metaphorically, at least, [Chicana/o artists] wanted to light fires of social justice where there were Mexican and Chicana/os being oppressed."[22] Since Chicano theater was based on "social action," Moraga's play directly engages with the hegemonic authority denying Mexican immigrants or Mexican Americans access to the city.

Without minimizing these lived, felt, and internalized differences between Chinese and Mexican immigrants in Los Angeles, the following chapter examines Hwang's and Moraga's plays as complementary pursuits of common ends. Specifically, the plays confront the dichotomy of immigrant and city that defined much of the 1980s. In the plays, conflicts emerge and unfold from this dichotomy, which, in the case of *FOB,* has been internalized by some of the characters and is resisted by others; in the case of *Giving up the Ghost,* the conflict is more actively contested in and about the urban landscape. Beyond sharing this common ambition, the plays illustrate similar strategies for making the sociospatial concerns evident. One involves the ways that Hwang and Moraga imagine their characters, many of whom are divided into two characters, thus literalizing the existential dilemma confronting the immigrant. For Moraga, the central character is Marisa in the present and Corky in the past, and more than just showing different stages on the life of the character, they occasionally interact with each other on stage. For Hwang, two of his three characters are frequently inhabited by historical or mythical figures from Chinese legends, with the characters even shifting from English to Chinese and back again. This strategy speaks to the immigrant experience of being between two worlds, languages, and identities. Demonstrating much about how Hwang and Moraga envision audiences, this strategy reflects the experiences and perspectives of immigrants attending the plays but, more notably, presents certain challenges to white, middle-class audiences who enjoy any number of privileges in the metropolis. Instead of the comfortable relationship among actor, character, and audience attendant with realism, these plays invite more active engagement from audiences to follow the story, and most significantly, to recognize how the city influences conflicts in that story. In this way, *FOB* and *Giving up the Ghost* extend some of the reconciliation described by Prida, toward future audiences.

Another strategy central to the dramaturgy of Hwang and Moraga is the historicization of contemporary Los Angeles. Working in two ways, this strategy involves, initially, showing the history of boundary and annexation, exploitation and exclusion, propaganda and violence tied to ethnic enclaves like Chinatown or the barrio. Hwang, for instance, represents today's L.A. as informed by the history of anti-coolie gangs and violence against the Chinese during the late nineteenth century as the genesis[23] of Chinatown, and how Chinatown still implicitly serves as negation of the city. The conceptual limits of the city, in many ways, correspond with the geographical boundary of the enclave. Similarly, Moraga's play puts noticeable emphasis on themes of "excavation" and annexation, reminding us that California was originally part of Mexico, and that the struggle for self-definition and citizenship are imbricated with venerable associations with place and landscape and nation. But this historicizing of L.A. does more than merely provide context for the immigrant characters; it also challenges assumptions regarding normality and naturalness about the divisions of city/Chinatown or city/barrio. The ambition is not just to distance us from the present through reference to the past but further to show that the present is constructed according to specific "laws" of politics, culture, history—all of which are subject to change. Historicizing the metropolis means illustrating both that identity is being contested within urban space and that urban space itself is being contested around specific notions of identity. What the plays advocate is how to move beyond loggerheads in the dichotomy of metropolis/immigrant and begin to reimagine the possibility of an urban environment celebrating multicultural difference rather than condemning it.

Westwood and Beyond

David Henry Hwang's *FOB* originated from an unlikely collision (collusion?) of urban geography and Chinese American mythology. "The play began when a sketch I was writing about a limousine trip through Westwood, California," Hwang says in the Playwright's Note, "was invaded by . . . Fa Mu Lan, the girl who takes her father's place in battle, from Maxine Hong Kingston's *The Woman Warrior,* and Gwan Gung, the god of fighters and writers, from Frank Chin's *Gee, Pop!*"[24] Despite this mythic beginning, the play revolves around the often humorous sparring between Dale, a second-generation Chinese American striving toward assimilation, and Steve, the recent arrival from Hong Kong and the "FOB" or "fresh-off-the-boat" of the title, in a Chinese restaurant in Torrance, California. Ostensibly the object of their sparring is Grace, another Chinese immigrant living in Los Angeles. But what really provokes animosity between Dale and Steve is the existential (false) dilemma confronting Chinese immigrants and children of immigrants, a dilemma that involves defining oneself against Chinese myths and history if they are to be welcomed as citizens. Interviewed by Jay Mathews in 1994, Hwang describes this dilemma in his dramaturgy: "I have the experience of people assuming I'm foreign . . . and that leaves you questioning the division between the inner and outer self, feeling slightly uncomfortable in the skin I'm living in."[25] Much of the criticism[26] linking this dilemma to *FOB* suggests autobiography as key to Hwang's concern with tensions between immigrants (like Hwang's father) and U.S. citizens (like Hwang), though his biography does not support this.[27] Not just writing of himself, Hwang writes about the tensions confronting immigrants during the 1980s and, more importantly, and how those tensions exist in the urban landscape of Los Angeles. Throughout *FOB,* the three characters continually reference competing spaces of L.A.—Hollywood, Westwood, Chinatown—in ways that make evident the tensions intensely felt by these immigrants or children of immigrants who are struggling with antagonisms between ethnic enclaves and the rest of Los Angeles.

The stage history of *FOB* traces a remarkable journey of its own, this one culminating with Hwang's arrival in American theater. In the 1970s while an undergraduate at Stanford University, Hwang started going to San Francisco's Magic Theater where Sam Shepard was producing his family plays.[28] Perhaps inspired by this experience, Hwang attended the first Padua Hills Playwrights Festival in Claremont, California in 1978, a workshop where he worked with Shepard, Maria Irene Fornes, and others on writing.[29] There, he began writing *FOB*, though most accounts of his early career suggest that his initial efforts at playwriting were mostly for a "lark."[30] Once finished, *FOB* was staged in his dorm room during his senior year, a production attended by Hwang's family. He continued to revise the script during the following years, first at the Yale School of Drama and "in the summer 1979, at the O'Neill Playwright's Conference."[31] In 1980, the play debuted at Joe Papp's New York Shakespeare Festival where it won the Obie Award for the best play 1980–1981. Well before meeting Hwang, Papp had been on the lookout for drama by or about Asian Americans since they were few such plays being performed in New York. Liking Hwang almost immediately, Papp describes going to Los Angeles to meet Hwang's parents and having dinner at a French restaurant picked by his father, a telling incident that recurs in *FOB* among the three younger characters.[32] Never as successful as *M. Butterfly*, the play that won national attention, *FOB* has nonetheless had revivals, most notably the 1990 production as part of the Pan Asian Repertory Theater in New York City. Though Hwang's play was at the forefront of the sociospatial drama emerging during the 1980s, reviews of this 1990 production foreground the concerns that firmly locate Hwang's dramaturgy with this study: "the playwright entreats theatergoers to leave all preconceptions behind and to open their minds to the warring subdivisions in what would appear to be a homogeneous community."[33]

Naturally, questions follow from Gussow's review, which frame the concerns of *FOB*. What accounts for the "warring subdivisions" dramatized by Hwang? How can Hwang's play invite audiences to leave "preconceptions," about immigrants and the city, behind? To answer the first, I have leaned heavily upon Karen Shimakawa's *National Abjection*. When considering Frank Chin's *The Year of the Dragon*, which debuted in 1974, Shimakawa contends that "a quintessential site of abjection is Chinatown."[34] The term "abjection" derives from Julia Kristeva, who uses it to define "the condition/position of that which is deemed loathsome" and simultaneously "the process by which that appraisal is made."[35] More specifically, "It is, for [Kristeva], the means by which the subject/'I' is produced: by establishing perceptual and conceptual borders around the self and 'jettison[ing]' that which is deemed objectionable, the subject comes into (and maintains) self-consciousness."[36] Defining what one is, then, depends upon making explicit what one is not, in this case by exploiting difference as the boundary of definition. Shimakawa adapts this theory toward the national project of defining what it means to be American by arguing that American identity has been determined "by abjecting Asian Americanness, by making it foreign, abnormal, *not-American*" (original emphasis).[37] Asian Americans are not just excluded from being American but simultaneously a part of this definition through negation. How do many define being American? By being less Asian. Importantly, abjection plays out in the urban landscape through defining distinct geographical or ideological boundaries around Chinatowns, marking the limits of who are included in the United States. Historically, this process was overt, with Chinatowns denounced as "a disgrace to the city, the State, the nation, and to civilization."[38] Today, this abjection persists according to Zhou's *Chinatown: The Socioeconomic Potential of an Urban Enclave*, which finds the belief among recent immigrants "that in order to be fully 'Americanized' . . . they have to stay away from . . . Chinatown."[39]

Like Chin, Hwang dramatizes Chinatown within this national (and distinctly urban) project of abjection, a place that determines the limits of who or what is part of the city. In fact, Chinatown is frequently described as the antipode of Los Angeles, in *FOB*, even though the geographical locale is contained within L.A. Thus Chinatown becomes source and subject of a double bind confronting immigrants and the children of immigrants, in ways strikingly similar to Chin's play.[40] Living in Chinatown, on the one hand, makes the Engs from *The Year of the Dragon* and Dale and Grace from *FOB* feel like "less than people—they are stigmatized as 'Chinamen,' largely invisible in U.S. American culture."[41] No doubt for this reason, Hwang's Dale describes Chinatown as a "cage" and wants to leave behind everything that makes him Chinese, including association with recent immigrants like Steve. On the other hand, leaving Chinatown means taking on the risk of becoming "even less visible because 'just be[ing] people' is to risk losing whatever level of cultural comprehensibility, agency, or ability to speak they may have had."[42] Knowledge of this double bind confronting for the Chinese American community begins to answer the first of the questions posed: Hwang's *FOB* highlights how the boundaries between Los Angeles and Chinatown, perceived or real, are always informing/inhibiting the self-definition of Chinese immigrants and their children. Beset by this problem, they fight with others they define as being "more" Chinese and themselves about how they will be defined. Consequently, Hwang's play foregrounds the difficulty implicit in what ethnographers have documented about immigrants: becoming American is directly correlated with literal as well as metaphorical distance from Chinatown.[43] Additionally, knowledge of how this abjection plays out in cities like L.A. begins to address the second question posed above: how can plays challenge audiences' assumptions about Chinatown (that immigrants always want to cluster there), and about the metropolis (that immigrants are not really a part of it). Notably, both of these concerns are highlighted in the prologue of *FOB*.

Getting Around in Los Angeles

Defining the tensions surrounding the abjection of Chineseness in *FOB* is Dale, a second generation American of Chinese descent in his early twenties. Dressed in "preppie clothes" that signal his efforts toward assimilation, Dale crosses the stage after the lights come up to stand before a swiveling blackboard and "lectures like a professor."[44] "What words can you think of that characterize the FOB?" he asks rhetorically after defining the acronym as "fresh-off-the-boat." After a brief pause, perhaps, he answers himself with stereotypes about Chinese immigrants: "Clumsy, ugly, greasy FOB. Loud, stupid, four-eyed FOB. Big feet. Horny. Like Lenny in *Of Mice and Men*."[45] Then he defines the FOB through negation: "Someone you wouldn't want your sister to marry. If you are a sister, someone you wouldn't want to marry." Noteworthy is how Dale's lecture provides evidence of the intra-ethnic animosity among immigrants in the Chinese community about questions of identity, belonging, and assimilation prior to the plot of *FOB* (where he encounters and argues with Steve, the FOB). Little inference is necessary to understand this animosity given Dale's candor: "They are the sworn enemies of all ABC—oh, that's 'American-Born Chinese'—of all ABC girls."[46] Working through negation, Dale defines what it means to be ABC, if not American, by illustrating the limits of that definition: though he, may look Chinese, Dale is American because he has rejected association with recent immigrants from China, all of whom (at least according to Dale's lecture) are recognizable by their aberrations in appearance and behavior. Interesting, too, is how Hwang signals the pedagogical, if not rhetorical, ambition of *FOB* through the semiotics of a classroom during the prologue (the blackboard, lecturing), thus drawing attention to audiences and including them, at least metaphorically, through this trope in the play's exploration of the "warring subdivisions" made evident through the distinction insisted upon between ABC and FOB by Dale.

Importantly, Dale locates these conflicts in the urban landscape of Los Angeles. After defining differences between ABC and FOB, he reveals how significant this distinction is with the following: "Before an ABC girl will be seen with a boy FOB in Westwood, she would rather burn her face off."[47] The geographical reference "in Westwood" no doubt sounds parenthetical to the self-inflicted violence; but, in fact, the play will suggest that this mutilation of self for American-Born Chinese in certain urban locales is indelibly linked to tensions within the interplay of ethnic identity and urban geography. Implicitly in the prologue and explicitly in the play, Westwood is defined as a distinctly "American" space, a space where only those who are most comfortable with, most assimilated into American culture can confidently go. There is a correlation between the ability to negotiate spaces linguistically and culturally and the access to those spaces taken for granted in much of what Dale believes about ABC and FOB, probably because Westwood is bordered by communities like Bel-Air and Beverley Hills with their high-rise apartments and luxury, all of which contrasts markedly with those living conditions of Chinatown.[48] The self-inflicted violence described by Dale speaks to profound anxiety about belonging and assimilation: the injury done to ethnic identity in order to move freely throughout parts of L.A. where the ethnic umbilical of recent immigrants only marks one as aberrant, if not abject. Suggested here is how deeply imbricated the antagonisms toward immigrants in the metropolis are for those like Dale. After defining Westwood as an American space, Dale swivels the blackboard to reveal notes that further outline spatialized antagonisms against immigrants. Since FOBs are not allowed access to certain places, "there are some locations where they cluster in particularly large swarms. Community colleges, Chinese club discos, Asian sororities, Asian fraternities, Oriental churches, shopping malls."[49] Left out, of course, is Chinatown, probably because it is not part of the city to Dale. But the underlying point is clear: to Dale, the city is divided into particular places associated with being Chinese and being American.

These antagonisms in the urban landscape become evident during the initial encounter between Dale and Steve at Grace's family's restaurant in Torrance. Already having agreed that the three will have dinner together, Dale starts an argument with Steve over the question of where they will go. When Grace mentions that Steve has picked the restaurant, Dale makes no effort to hide his condescension: "That limits the possibilities. Guess we're going to Chinatown or something, right?"[50] When Steve explains that they are going to a French restaurant in downtown Los Angeles, Dale is first surprised ("Oh, we're going to a Western place?") and then skeptical (To Grace: "Are you sure he made the reservations?").[51] Based on Steve's Chinese accent and appearance, he had grouped him with the FOB, but his assumptions are continually challenged during this encounter, leaving him increasingly unsure and therefore combative. When it is clear that Grace trusts Steve's decision, Dale turns to mode of transportation: "Look—why don't you let me drive? You've got enough to do without worrying about—you know—how to get around in L.A., read the stop signs, all that," he says, again condescendingly.[52] But Steve again surprises Dale by explaining that he has ordered a limousine to drive them, though this revelation does little to assuage Dale's frustration. In fact, once it becomes clear that the limo is the best option (Dale's car only seats two), Dale begins arguing with Grace about how the scene on their arrival would look: "Getting out of a limo in the middle of Westwood? People staring, thinking we're from SC? Wouldn't you feel like dirt?"[53] Even though the link is not made explicitly, the connection is to the prologue's argument about an ABC being seen in Westwood—defined as a distinctly American locale—and inflicting damage to oneself. The subtext of his argument with Grace gestures toward the danger of association with Chineseness that Dale finds troubling. Eventually the three decide to avoid public space altogether and have dinner in Grace's family's restaurant, where the play takes place.

During this encounter two concerns that prove central to the sociospatial ambitions of *FOB* come to the fore. The first involves Dale's internalized dichotomy between American and Chinese, which manifests itself in the tension between himself and Steve, who he recognizes—and shortly after they decide to remain at the family restaurant, names him—as the FOB of the title. Closely linked with this concern is the second: the frustrating limits of this dichotomy for the immigrant (Steve) or children of immigrants (Dale). However clumsily, Dale attempts to embarrass Steven through the quarrel about where and how to go to dinner. Presuming Steve's unfamiliarity with Los Angeles and consequently invoking ethnic divisions encoded within the landscape of greater L.A., Dale suggests that Steve's interests in dining or his ability to negotiate the city are limited to Chinatown, the enclave where new immigrants like Dale's and Grace's parents, years before, lived because the city is defined against immigrants from China. Dale takes for granted that immigrants would be contained within the dichotomy of immigrant/city or Chinatown/Los Angeles. When Steve eludes this easy categorization, Dale attempts to relocate him, conceptually, within the limits of this dichotomy by highlighting the difficulty of getting around in L.A., which is compounded by the linguistic challenges of street signs in English. Although this effort fails as well, the fundamental assumptions guiding Dale's behavior originate from this dichotomy. Perhaps subconsciously at first but then increasingly deliberately, Dale intends to reinforce the distance between himself and the FOB by defining each of them through urban spaces: Steve through Chinatown, and Dale with Los Angeles itself. Put in terms of Shimakawa's argument on abjection, Dale is trying to demonstrate himself as "more" American and therefore less, like Steve, Chinese. Made evident by the prologue, this concern with how Dale defines himself in and through the urban landscape proves integral to the play's conflicts that play out among the three characters and within the three characters.

When Dale recognizes that he cannot abject Steve through the urban geography of Los Angeles alone, he changes his spatial locations but continues the same strategy. "You feel like you're an American?" Dale asks after Grace goes to the kitchen to prepare dinner; and without waiting for any response, he begins mocking Steve's family as responsible for a kind of reverse-colonialism. "Like those little cameras with the slides inside? I bought one at Disneyland once and it ended up having pictures of Hong Kong in it. You know how shitty it is to expect the Magic Kingdom and wind up with the skyline of Kowloon?"[54] Only peripherally about Chinese exportation of toys to the United States, Dale's antagonism is part of his definition of the limits of "American" through invoking ethnically encoded spaces of definition. If he cannot limit Steve to the stereotype of the FOB through Los Angeles, he can attempt to do so metonymically, by choosing locales within the regions of L.A. and Hong Kong that stand for the cities and cultures therein. Subconsciously, Dale is trying to draw unquestionable boundaries between being Chinese and being American, boundaries distinctly located within urban geography. He is trying to trap Steve in the existential dilemma, which Dale has thoroughly internalized and that provides a foundation for abjection. Unfortunately in picking Disneyland, with its geography of borne of simulacra,[55] as his quintessential American space, Dale mediates his self-definition with the ontological confusions of original versus copy. Though this detail may not be evident during production, the struggles that Dale goes through in trying to trap Steve in the dichotomy of immigrant/city or Chinatown/Los Angeles or Kowloon/Disneyland demonstrate the limits of this dichotomy in two ways. First, this struggle suggests that what emerges from this dichotomy is as self-destructive as the image of an ABC girl burning her face off. Second, it demonstrates how limited the dichotomy is in trying to contain the diversity in the Chinese American community living in Los Angeles and elsewhere. Working dialectically with the prologue, this encounter and others like it suggest that Dale epitomizes the problems of self-definition, assimilation, and ethnic community confronting immigrants living in Los Angeles as much as describes it.

Cage of Chineseness

The more frustrated Dale becomes with Steve during act one, the more *FOB* foregrounds the magnitude of dichotomy—geographically and psychologically—to immigrants living in Los Angeles. The opening of act two onto Dale's monologue, delivered in spotlight on an otherwise darkened stage, metaphorically shifts the focus toward psychology of immigrant self-definition and further explicates Dale's antagonism toward Steve. Like the landscape described by the characters, Dale's definition of himself is divided across distinct spatial boundaries evident through the contrast made between friends and family. His friend, never named, enjoys privilege and freedom in Los Angeles that Dale envies: driving a "Porsche Carreras" and, more notably, having "a house up in the Hollywood Hills where I can stand and look down on the lights of L.A."[56] Metonymically, this house represents open space and even authorization toward the city below, in part obviously due to the cost of such a home but further through the panoramic perspective attendant with living in this space where the entire city unfolds before one's eyes. Connotations of privilege, power, authority, and freedom all attend this house in the Hollywood Hills. Never introduced in the play, this friend is likely Dale's wish fulfillment for himself, particularly when he acknowledges that "I guess I haven't really been there yet. But I could easily go."[57] Nonetheless, this place in and perspective of Los Angeles reveals much about how Dale and other immigrants like him[58] defines himself, through fantasies, about the city. Looking up toward the Hollywood Hills, he envisions himself sharing in—if not having for himself—the freedom and advantage of his "friend." He imagines the city opening up before him because of the geographical and metaphorical distance from Chinatown, where his family lived and presumably still lives. In fact, Dale makes the contrast through language that stresses, at least to him, distinctly American activities in American places: "My parents—they don't know nothing about the world, about watching Benson at the Roxy, about ordering hors d'oeuvres at Scandia's, downshifting onto the Ventura Freeway at midnight."[59]

Contrasted with this freedom in the city is Chinatown, though Dale never names this enclave during the monologue probably because he has worked so hard to psychologically erase connections to this place that functions as the antipode of Los Angeles. When he does think about Chinatown, it is in direct contrast—literally in the monologue—with the freedoms associated with the Hollywood Hills. He describes his parents as "yellow ghosts," suggesting that they are linked and, to him, limited to a past or place that is distinctly Chinese and not, by extension, American.[60] Worse, his parents "tried to cage me up with the Chineseness when all the time we were in America." Noteworthy is how Dale, like many interviewed in ethnographies of Chinatown, conceptualizes this enclave as circumscribing him and his future in contrast to the freedom in the fantasy about Hollywood Hills. Not surprisingly, he considers his heritage, embodied in Chinatown, as something that he must escape to have the possibility of his friend's house in the Hollywood Hills. Like many immigrants, he believes that admission of connection to his Chinese heritage means the loss of places like Westwood, Hollywood Hills, or Los Angeles. Making this point, Dale says about leaving behind Chinatown: "I've had to work real hard—real hard—to be myself. To not be a Chinese, a yellow, a slant, a gook. To be just a human being, like everyone else."[61] Evident here is the abjection of Chineseness at work in the urban landscape, a city where children of immigrants so thoroughly internalize the dichotomy of immigrant/city or Chinatown/Los Angeles they can believe that being Chinese or living in Chinatown means becoming less than human. So naturally, Dale does whatever he can—including insult and attack Steve—to distance himself from any vestiges of Chineseness. Noteworthy, too, is that *FOB* never depicts the formation of this dichotomy but presents it as already sedimented. If anything, Dale blames his parents for not adapting to this dichotomy, which he believes to be normal—though Hwang's play works against this normativity.

Demonstrating that the problem is not merely psychological, that is, not limited simply to Dale's perceptions of Los Angeles, *FOB* extends this dichotomy of immigrant/city towards Grace, Dale's cousin. At the end of act one, while Dale and Steve are "frozen" on stage in the middle of further contestation (of bravado, as they are eating Chinese food covered with hot sauce), Grace describes how "tough [it was] trying to live in Chinatown" via monologue.[62] She immigrated with her parents when she was ten and lived in this ethic enclave during her school years. Though living in Chinatown no doubt provided the necessary transition to L.A. for Grace, who had limited English at the time, it still limited her interactions with others in—and perhaps with—America in ways that she understood even as a child. "There were a few Chinese girls in the fourth grade, but they were American-born, so they wouldn't even talk to me," Grace explains.[63] Considering the concerns of *FOB*, this distance between American-born Chinese girls and the immigrant Grace most likely derived from the dichotomy outlined above. These girls, like Dale, internalized the idea that it was necessary to renounce not just their family's heritage (speaking English, not associating with immigrants, buying American clothes) but further with anyone embodying this ethnic umbilical to China: specifically those like Grace because of her poor English and her home in Chinatown. They were defining themselves, however unconsciously, through the distance from Chinatown through their taunting of those like Grace for their accents or through the middle-class mobility of their parents that allowed them to afford the clothing that identifies them as American and, perhaps more importantly, not Chinese. Delivered through monologue during the encounter of Dale and Steve, this memory from Grace's childhood historicizes the antagonism playing out during *FOB's* storyline as a product of the long-standing hostility toward the immigrant in the city.

Confronted with this dichotomy during her childhood, Grace began rebelling against her Chinese heritage because she, at least initially, saw that heritage as limiting her freedoms and opportunities in Los Angeles. She bleached her hair, sat with the white children at school, and started "hanging out at the beach"—many little rebellions that functioned simultaneously as renunciations of her heritage and performance of her Americanness.[64] Like Dale, then, she internalized the abjection defining the landscape of Los Angeles and tried to adapt herself to the dichotomy implicit therein: if being Chinese was the limit of being American, she would do what she could to erase the vestiges of her ethnicity. More significantly, her transgressions grew more rebellious and more closely related to the city itself. When older, "one night I took Dad's car and drove on Hollywood Boulevard, all the way from downtown to Beverly Hills, then back to Sunset."[65] Anticipating the contrast of Hollywood Hills and Chinatown in Dale's monologue, Grace's driving suggests how abjection is imbricated in the landscape. Her transgression was twofold: the borrowing of her dad's car, probably without his permission, and the putting distance between herself and the "cage" of Chineseness. Grace highlights this second aspect when remembering driving in Los Angeles: "I was looking around and listening—all the time with the window down, just so I'd feel like I was part of the city."[66] During the drive, she brings herself closer to the city itself, to the sounds and sights that were so different than Chinatown. What is implicit here is revealing about how the city abjects Chinatown, which Grace defines almost as an absence from the city: only when she escapes the enclave in her father's car does she become "part of the city." Unlike Dale, however, Grace recognizes some of the dangers attendant with defining herself within this dichotomy, most obviously when she remember saying to herself during the drive, "I'm lonely. And I don't know it. I don't like being alone," suggesting the consequence of rejecting her ethnicity.[67] And in her acknowledgment, at the beginning of her monologue that, like Chinatown, "it's tough trying to live in Torrance, too."[68]

Beyond Abjection

Hwang's *FOB*, then, highlights the existential (false) dilemma confronting immigrants and children of immigrants from China living in Los Angeles by demonstrating how abjection of Chineseness inhibits self-definition for Dale, Grace, and the young girls from Grace's school. Not focusing on the formation or enforcement of the dichotomy, Hwang locates this abjection primarily in the urban geography with the city's implicit boundaries around Chinatown—and secondly in the perceptions of immigrants or children of immigrants. Living in this city, Dale and Grace become conditioned by the spaces they move through in much the same way theorized by Cresswell: that spaces themselves endorse a set of assumptions of what is "out of place" or aberrant.[69] Silently acknowledged by many in the play, though loudly announced by Dale during the prologue, the tensions toward immigrants in the city are triggered by the arrival of Steve, the "FOB" of the play. Recently come from Hong Kong, where Grace says, "people are dressing really well now—and the whole place has become really stylish... they're really kinda classy."[70] Perhaps because of this western education and background, which corresponds with trends in Hong Kong families documented by ethnographers, Steve refuses to be trapped in either half of the dichotomy of city/immigrant or America/Chinese.[71] Unlike Dale, Steve speaks Chinese, knows and enjoys Chinese foods (a common signifier for cultural identity in Chinese literature), and shares stories from Chinese mythology, especially that of Gwan Gung, "god of warriors, writers, and prostitutes" (more below). Unlike the immigrants defined by Dale during the prologue, Steve is not intimidated by Los Angeles nor made to "cluster" in enclaves like Chinatown. Not only does Steve make reservations at a French restaurant, just as Hwang's father did when meeting with Joe Papp, but further, when Dale talks about going dancing after dinner, Steve brings up a disco called Dillons in Westwood. Through Steve's confidence with L.A., Hwang shows how the ideological boundaries that deny Chinese immigrants a place in the city and even the status of people can be contested, transgressed, and perhaps overcome.

Beyond triggering the tensions toward Chinese immigrants in 1980s Los Angeles, Steve brings with him, at least figuratively, the history of Chinese immigration. Several times during the play, Steve steps out of the dramatic world and speaks with the voice of Chinese sojourners from different points in U.S. history, a gesture that simultaneously interrupts and comments on the story unfolding in *FOB*. The first of these monologues comes just before Steve meets Dale in Grace's family's restaurant, when Grace and Dale "freeze" onstage except for Dale's arm, which strokes Grace's hair in a gesture of possessiveness or protection and Steve turns to the audience and demands the following in the broken English of the Chinese sojourner: "Why will you not let me enter in America?"[72] This anonymous immigrant reveals the deep frustration born of the promise of America contrasted with the reality: "Five times, I first come here, you say to me I am illegal, you return me on boat to fathers and uncles with no gold, no treasure, no fortune, no rice."[73] Describing America as the "Mountain of Gold," this sojourner surely like many others believed in the opportunity that America promised but was confronted with anti-Chinese immigration laws. Forced to pay bribes but still denied the chance to pursue a future, this immigrant declares the following:

"I hate Mountain and I hate American and I hate you!"[74] In act two, Hwang repeats this monologic intrusion onto the storyline while Dale attempts to make Steve clean the table after their meal. Once again, Dale and Grace freeze save for the stroking of her hair, and Steve speaks to audiences, this time having gone further back in history to sojourners who are tempted by the promise of America. "The white ghosts came into the harbor today. They promised that... in America we would never want for anything."[75] Lavished with stories of the wealth awaiting them in America, the sojourner intriguingly describes this opportunity in terms combining utopia and urbanism: "One white ghost told how the streets are paved with diamonds, how the land is so rich that pieces of gold lie on the road, and the worker-devils consider them too insignificant to bend down for."[76] Most exciting for this particular sojourner, "the white ghosts are providing free passage both ways."

Importantly, Steve's monologues contrast directly with arguments proceeding from or about abjection put forth within the play and thereby become ways of historicizing the present. The first precedes the debate between Dale and Steve about where and how they will go out to dinner already discussed. Dale's determination to prove himself as more American by proving Steve to be more Chinese (than Dale) and consequently less American, then, corresponds with and maybe emerges from the exclusionary practices and legislature (anti-Chinese immigration laws, for instance) that kept the sojourner out of America in 1914. Nearly 70 years later in Los Angeles, this exclusionary ethos has become sedimented into the urban landscape with its demarcations of space, society, and citizenship. Delivered to "the audience as if it were a panel of judges," according to Hwang's stage directions, this first monologue proves confrontational: it demands that audiences consider what follows—in particular, Dale's attempts to abject Steve through references to the urban landscape of Los Angeles—through the antagonism toward the Chinese in U.S. history. Much the same point emerges from the second monologue, which follows shortly after Dale's monologue about Hollywood Hills and Chinatown that begins the second act. During Dale's fantasy of going to (live in) Hollywood Hills and thereby escape the "cage of Chineseness," audiences are invited to recognize how the city puts him and others like him in an existential dilemma of choosing between being human or being Chinese. When Dale's monologue is contrasted with Steve's, the problem becomes increasingly historicized so that the dichotomy that Dale infers from the landscape corresponds with the hostility toward Chinese immigrants, who were brought to the United States only for labor and then sent back or denied access when that labor was no longer necessary. What is suggested in these contrasts is that the very organization of the city along demarcations against ethnic difference is simultaneously a product and extension of the historical antagonism toward immigrants. Noteworthy, however, is that the second monologue is delivered to "the audience as if speaking with his family."[77] In this way, Hwang invites audiences toward the play's sociospatial ambition of rethinking the ways that the city is organized rather than holding them accountable for inequity therein.

Implicit in this denaturalizing the abjection in Los Angeles is the possibility or necessity of change. Specifically, changing how immigrants are defined or define themselves in the city and how this new identity can begin to redefine the city itself. Evident from the opening of the play, this reimagining of the terms of self-definition, like the aforementioned historicization, is linked with Steve. During the first scene of *FOB*, while Grace and Steve playfully banter about who is he and why he is there, Steve calls himself "Gwan Gung! God of warriors, writers, and prostitutes!"[78] To this declaration of himself as mythical figure from Chinese legend, Grace with responds with due skepticism: "Bullshit!" Shortly thereafter and playing along, she explains that legends of Gwan Gung, like other markers of Chineseness, have been devalued by immigrants in the United States: "You died way back . . . hell, no one event noticed when you died—that's how bad your PR was. You died and no one even missed a burp."[79] After returning from the kitchen, where none of the staff recognize the name Gwan Gung, Steve demands to know what has happened to Chinese identity in noteworthy terms: "What city is this now?"[80] "Los Angeles," Grace answers, making it explicit that identity here is defined through abjection. Despite this skepticism about his mythical identity, Steve not only continues defining himself, as Gwan Gung, but further, he becomes the embodiment of the legendary figure through the "living memory" that he recites during the play, more fantastic intrusions into the storyline of *FOB*. In Hwang's play, if not the city represented in this play, Steve shifts easily between different identities. During this monologue and elsewhere in act two, Steve defies the ontological binary of either/or and becomes, during moments of theatrical monologue, and/also. He becomes the modern immigrant from Hong Kong who enjoyed a western education and is undaunted by Los Angeles *and* the legendary figure from Chinese mythology, bringing together the mythic and the mundane as Hwang notes was the beginning of the play. Furthermore, this ontological instability of acting, performance, and theater informs the question of self-definition for immigrants in L.A.

Characters in Hwang's play generally feel confined within the dichotomy of abjection, which draws distinct boundaries between one identity and another; indeed, the central premise of abjection is that one identity supplies the limit of another, whether expressed psychologically or geographically. But Steve endorses a new mode of self-definition for immigrants that comes close to Edward Soja's "thirding" or the introduction into binary of a "third term that disrupts, disorders, and begins to reconstitute" that binary.[81] Instead of allowing himself to be defined as American-Born Chinese or Fresh-Off-the-Boat, as does Dale, Steve becomes both or neither or, in truth, something that defies the limits of dichotomy. And it is not just Steve who does this. Grace, too, becomes Fa Mu Lan, "the Woman Warrior" from Chinese legend, another thirding of the binary. This collapsing of dichotomy becomes clearest during "The Group Story" told by all three characters near the conclusion. This story, beginning with Dale, becomes a story of reverse-immigration, the story of a bear that swims from the United States to China, suffering injury and trauma along the way. More important than the details are how it is told. Each of the three characters contribute to the story so that it grows out of fragments of their experiences, their perspectives, their opinions—implicitly about immigration and identity—a trend that becomes increasingly literalized when Steve and Grace take on mythic identities. With Dale as the narrator, Steve (Gwan Gung) and Grace (Fa Mu Lan) confront one another in the Torrance restaurant *and* on an imagined, mythic plane, where Gwan Gung is forced to recognize his sins in killing Fa Mu Lan's father. As the story continues, though, Steve's role continually morphs from the immigrant from Hong Kong, to Gwan Gung, to an embodiment of immigrants during history that becomes apparent during a scene when Dale and Grace force Steve, the immigrant, to leave for America to support the family. During this scene, the very landscape imagined by the characters changes from the L.A. restaurant to the shores of China to a mythical landscape. Metaphorically, the Group Story suggests the agency of any community in terms of self-definition from different voices, perspectives, places, or stories. Concretely, this definition for immigrants begins with imbuing the landscape with history, myth, and legend.

Most noteworthy for Hwang's sociospatial concerns in *FOB* is what follows this Group Story. Holding hands, Steve and Grace leave the restaurant to go dancing, presumably at the disco described by Steve earlier, Dillon's in Westwood. They go not to erase their Chineseness but instead to celebrate it, to celebrate their hands, their foods, and their culture—all of which were highlighted at the end of the Group Story. They have, seemingly, moved beyond abjection and have found ways of seeing themselves as "part of the city" without having to sacrifice anything of their ethnic identity. Endorsed here is what Patti Hartigan of *The Boston Globe* notes during a review of Hwang's play: "What's happening in this country is fascinating. We're attempting to create a culture that is based on all these different cultures . . . The incredible challenge is to find a common identity but also let all these people maintain their individual cultures."[82] But Hwang fully recognizes that the changes in and to the landscape of abjection is not necessarily so easily accomplished. Contrasted with Steve and Grace is Dale, who stays in the backroom of the restaurant, literally and metaphorically marginalized against the geography of Los Angeles. More notably, the play's epilogue deliberately echoes the prologue, with Dale repeating many of the racist pronouncements that began the play: "Clumsy, ugly, greasy FOB. Loud, stupid, four-eyed FOB."[83] Much depends upon the actor's body language and intonation here, but it seems likely that Dale's lecture is delivered with considerably less enthusiasm even as he still clings to the dichotomy that he believes to be natural. In any event, the play itself illustrates that this landscape of abjection can—but need not—constrain the self-definition of immigrants or children of immigrants from China, a conclusion made clear by Dale left alone, still trying to find a way to believe that he is "part of the city." Clearly the play has argued that what Dale insists on during the prologue and epilogue—the either/or—can or should become both/also when it comes to Chinese identity in Los Angeles and elsewhere. Audiences, in other words, most likely hear the last words ironically, having witnessed the consequences and, to some degree the causes, of the abjection that Dale continues to describe and perhaps believe.

A Milestone in Chicana Dramaturgy

Cherríe Moraga's *Giving up the Ghost* is described as "a milestone in the history of and evolution of a Chicana/o dramaturgy" in Jorge Huerta's *Chicano Drama: Performance, Society and Myth*.[84] Huerta's argument begins from the premise that Moraga's play "exposed (and exposes) its audiences to a topic they might never have encountered in public space otherwise."[85] The topic was lesbian desire, and Huerta maintains that *Giving up the Ghost* was the first play about this taboo subject, especially during the overwhelmingly conservative 1980s, written by a lesbian to be produced and published. Originally conceived of as a set of monologues by and about women, which Catalina Cariaga called a series of poems "emerging from Moraga's collective unconscious,"[86] *Giving up the Ghost* eventually was revised around three characters derived from these monologues. One is Amalia, an older immigrant from Mexico living in Los Angeles while still longing for the Mexican landscape that she left behind. The others are two halves of a Mexican American woman named Marisa (as an adult) and Corky (as a teenager), who struggles with sexual and ethnic identity while Amalia's lover. In this incarnation *Giving up the Ghost* debuted as a staged reading at the Foot of the Mountain Theatre in Minneapolis in 1984. After further revision the play was produced at San Francisco's Theatre Rhinoceros in 1989, with this version ultimately published as part of Moraga's trilogy *Heroes and Saints and Other*

Plays in 1994. Noteworthy, here, are the dates that precede Kushner's *Angels in America* by nearly a decade. *Giving up the Ghost* anticipates many of the themes of *Angels in America*, including the assumption that urban geography serves a central role in the battle for identity politics for gay/lesbian rights in the 1980s. In terms of Huerta's praise for Moraga's play, then, the following pages consider how *Giving up the Ghost* brings the topic of lesbian desire into "public space" and how "public space" informs the negotiation of layers of self-definition undertaken by the women: gender, sexuality, ethnicity in 1980s Los Angeles.

Huerta's highlighting the play's representation of homosexuality is not surprising given the stage history following the early, monologue versions. In many ways, Theatre Rhinoceros was the perfect venue for *Giving up the Ghost's* world premiere in 1989. Founded in 1977 by Allan B. Estes Jr., Theatre Rhinoceros staged its earliest productions (like *The West Street Gang* by Doric Wilson) in the gay and lesbian community—literally in a "leather bar" called The Black and Blue.[87] After moving to the Goodman Building on Geary Boulevard, the theater's first home, it actively promoted the work of a number of lesbian writers including Pat Bond, Jane Chambers, and Adele Prandini. Currently located in the Mission District's Redstone Building, the theater has continued its mandate, established by Estes, of producing theater for and about gays and lesbians, including investigating the impact of AIDS on the gay community during the 1980s and early 1990s. No doubt benefiting from the theater's mandate, *Giving up the Ghost*, debuted to enthusiasm[88] even though—unlike other Moraga plays—it has enjoyed few revivals. One revival occurred at Diversionary Theatre in San Diego in 1998. Divisionary Theatre was founded in 1986 with the ambition of fostering and maintaining "quality theatre for the lesbian, gay, bisexual and transgender community." Like Theatre Rhinoceros, Divisionary Theatre intends to produce plays that explore gay and lesbian themes but, more importantly perhaps, dramatize the complexity or diversity within the gay and lesbian communities. Recent productions include *Cloud 9, Gross Indecency: The 3 Trials of Oscar Wilde,* and *Looking for Normal.* Implicit in the theater's mandate, of course, is the challenging of stereotypes about gays and lesbians, which Moraga's play certainly attempts. But much about *Giving up the Ghost* is confrontational—especially its emphasis on transgression of social, cultural, and geographical norms—and I wonder to what extent the sociospatial ambitions of Moraga's play might have, inadvertently, been hindered by having the play performed before receptive audiences and in theaters that can easily be bracketed by those who would benefit most from the play's intent of staging the tensions among identity politics, social justice, and urban geography in L.A.

My intention in the following pages is not to disagree with Huerta's conclusions about Moraga's play but rather to augment them with consideration of how the play's conflicts unfold in and about Los Angeles. *Giving up the Ghost* is fundamentally about place and placelessness: figuratively of lesbians trying to find their place in a society defined by heterosexual normalcy and literally of Mexican immigrants and Mexican Americans trying to find their place in a city defined through segregative boundaries. About the latter: living in East Los Angeles, Marisa struggles with the psychological, existential and, in some cases, physical scars accumulated during her childhood in a Chicano barrio. So traumatic was this childhood that she was left divided within and against herself, an existential condition made plain through the divided-character of Marisa/Corky. Likewise Amalia, the immigrant from Mexico living in another barrio in the city, continually tries to reconcile the feeling of between in between the Mexico of her past with the Los Angeles of her present. This geographical tension between place and placelessness highlights antagonisms among Mexican immigrants, Chicano barrios, and Los Angeles playing out in the landscape of Southern California. About the figurative tensions of place and placelessness, the play follows two women struggling to fulfill their lesbian desires within two societies—Mexican and American—defined through heterosexuality and patriarchy. Victimized metaphorically through the presumptions about what is "normal" and what is "aberrant" as well as physically by rape, these women seek a place where they can live their desires. In the dramatic world represented by *Giving up the Ghost,* the characters have been determined to be "out of place" in urban culture and landscape. Doubly disenfranchised, as lesbians and Chicanas, Marisa/Corky and Amalia perceive the city from the interstices, from outside the borders and boundaries inscribed in Los Angeles, which consign them to anonymity while these demarcations remain invisible or "natural." In revisiting the question of who has access to and authority over urban geography, *Giving up the Ghost* intends to make such demarcations visible and debatable for those enjoying the privilege of being "in place."

Unlike Hwang's *FOB,* which invokes Los Angeles almost exclusively through reference made by characters and not, notably, through the staging itself, Moraga's *Giving up the Ghost* is continually highlighting the negotiation of space theatrically. Highly simple, the scenography described by the stage directions includes little more than a raised platform, a table and chairs, and a portrait of a Mexican landscape hung on the upstage wall. During much of the play, this portrait is unseen, but it is illuminated during "scenes evoking indigenous Mexico," suggesting an expressionism in the staging.[89] Not fixed or stable, the stage of *Giving up the Ghost* reacts to and reflects the psychology of the characters, in particular Amalia, illustrating indelible links of place and identity. Similar is how the play evokes the urban landscape of Los Angeles that is the setting: through sounds of traffic, children playing, street repairs and music that introduces what Moraga describes as the " 'streetwise *ritmo*' [rhythm or tempo] of the urban life of these Chicanos"—music that swells loudly during significant scenes and, again expressionistically, locates incidents or admissions of the characters against the urban environment.[90] Most noteworthy about the way Moraga imagines the interplay of identity politics, social justice, and urban geography in *Giving up the Ghost* is how references to the city are always conspicuously incomplete: not representing the landscape directly as much as quoting it in the tradition of Brecht.[91] There is just enough for audiences to imagine, but not enough see directly. In effect, Moraga implicitly highlights the presence and responsibility of audiences toward the completion of the stage by having them fill in the semiotic gaps within such staging: to imagine streets and neighborhoods when the characters speak of them or the music swells or the portrait of Mexico is illuminated like the reception envisioned by Shakespeare's *Henry V.*[92] With this fragmentary staging, *Giving up the Ghost* underscores the negotiation of place and perspective both in the play and in watching the play. Put in an epistemological corollary to the characters' existential condition, audiences are always trying to comprehend where they are in the metropolis.

Neither Here, Nor There

In the initial stage directions, Moraga defines (the importance of) the play's geography: "This is the urban Southwest, a Chicano barrio within the sprawling Los Angeles basin."[93] Interesting, though, is how she reveals this environment. At first, this occurs semiotically: Corky, Marisa's teenage self, comes strutting across the stage wearing "khaki pants with razor-sharp creases, pressed white undershirt"—what Moraga calls "Cholo style."[94] With hair "cut short and slicked back," she carries herself with self-conscious bravado, performing toughness through exaggerated rolling of the shoulders or long, loping strides,[95] toward the upstage wall where she begins spray painting graffiti. Encoded in the clothing and gestures, then, are a number of key signifiers for the Chicano barrio: the gang-style attire, the way she moves, and the defacement of property. Drawing on cultural (and criminal) gestures of ethnicity, Moraga begins her explication of place with audiences' complicity. Meant to recognize and draw conclusions from this pantomimic portion of the prologue, which takes place with the "street sounds" playing in the background, many in the audiences beyond the venues that have produced *Giving up the Ghost* might feel anxious about what, to borrow from Huerta, is brought into public space. Much later in the play, during the third act,

Moraga complements this semiotic opening with more conventional exposition through Marisa/Corky describing the barrio of her childhood. Spoken
against "Chicano urban sounds," Marisa describes her neighborhood as "a
war zone" for many reasons: the "muggers, mexicanos sucking their damn
lips at you, gringo stupidity, drunks like old garbage sacks thrown around the
street" that she would encounter daily.[96] Evident in this description are the
poverty, crime, and hopelessness pervading the childhood that Marisa had in
the barrio, a place where men were seen as predatory and women vulnerable
to crime and violence—a point made plain in Marisa's admission that she
"got raped once."[97]

Worth considering closely is how this exposition during scene ten occurs.
Like much of the play, the scene works almost dialectically: with Marisa functioning as narrator to the events depicted and Corky reenacting—in this case,
verbally—the incidents. Beginning from Marisa's admission of the rape, her
narration moves toward details about the barrio that, like the music playing
out in the background, further explicates what occurred. The urban environment of the Chicano barrio and the violence against women happening there
are connected in Moraga's play through synecdoches for poverty ("drunks like
old garbage sacks"), for crime ("muggers"), and implicitly through discrimination in Los Angeles ("gringo stupidity"). At the same time, Marisa turns
to description because she has a difficult time confronting the memory itself:
"I guess I never wanted to believe I was raped."[98] Description, here, serves
denial: a way of avoiding the incident by foregrounding the circumstances of
the incident. But Corky enters during the monologue and begins describing
what happened that day when she was twelve and going to Catholic school.
While walking past a classroom, "this man a mexicano motions to me to
come inside."[99] Assuming that he was one of the Mexicans often hired by the
school, Corky agrees, but then finds herself thrown to the floor and sexually
assaulted, an experience that she relates partially through description of the
events and partially through emotional associations. "He made me a hole!"
she laments at the end of the story, and Marisa wraps a *rebozo* [a woman's
scarf or shawl] around her in a comforting gesture.[100] The doubling of characters during this scene and throughout the play for that matter, no doubt
owe much to the beginnings of *Giving up the Ghost* as a series of monologues.
But this doubling in the final version demonstrates the trauma endured by
Marisa when she was twelve, the violence *of place* that made necessary the psychological or existential creation of Corky, the personality that would allow
her to walk down the streets of the barrio, which become what Mary Patricia
Brady calls a "geography of fear" in her study of Chicano literature—after the
rape.[101] Likewise, Moraga illustrates how traumatically self-definition for the
Chicana can be mediated by urban geography.

Necessary for understanding this last point, though, is discussion of how the Chicano barrio is represented in relation to Los Angeles in *Giving up the Ghost*. This information comes from Amalia, the Mexican immigrant who initially becomes Marisa's artistic mentor and then her lover in a tumultuous and short-lived romance. Long before Marisa's admission of being raped come Amalia's first words in the play: "I am a failure."[102] Immediately following this admission, as if functioning as an appositive, Amalia remarks, "I observe the Americans. Their security. Their houses. Their dogs. Their children are happy. They are not *un*...happy."[103] Described through synecdoche here is the American Dream enjoyed by the privileged groups imagined—but never represented—in Moraga's play, probably the middle-class living in the suburbanism considered in Chapter 3. Implicit in Amalia's description is the distance, literally and figuratively, of these Americans from the barrio where she lives: in her eyes, lives defined in contrast to the deprivations and dangers of the Chicano barrio. Instead of muggers they have security and houses; instead of drunks they have children and dogs. Notably, it is Amalia, the Mexican immigrant, who introduces this contrast and distance between American and immigrant in Los Angeles into the play, suggesting how this informs self-definition. Even when acknowledging that Americans "have their struggles, their *problemas*," she nevertheless reaches a telling conclusion: "but...it's a life. I always say this, it's a life."[104] Underlying this observation is the corollary: that immigrants or even Mexican Americans like Marisa living in the barrio do not have a life or possibly not a life worth having: that they are defined through rejection or, like in Hwang's *FOB*, through abjection. In Amalia's language is evidence of this when she uses the double-negative "not *un*...happy," and suggests that if Americans are happy, those living in the barrio are *un*: *un*-American, *un*-citizens, and even *un*-people. *Giving up the Ghost* locates the internal and external struggles of Chicanas in the increasingly polarized demography of inner-city and edge-city in Los Angeles.[105]

Defined through dichotomy, the landscape of Los Angeles leaves those like Amalia in much the existential dilemma considered in the previous section. If Mexican immigrants are included in discussions of the city at all, and often they are not,[106] they become the limits of being an American citizen—an ideological argument about geography and boundary that has played a prominent role in U.S. politics. This is probably what Amalia means when she tells Marisa, at the beginning of the second act, "I have always felt like an outsider."[107] In L.A., the feeling derives from living in the interstices while remaining cognizant of privileged lifestyles that always remains out of reach. Metaphorically, this feeling is linked to Amalia's health problems that she ascribes to living in America and consoles herself with the belief that those problems were "nothing that Mexico couldn't cure."[108] Here emerges the fundamental dilemma confronting the immigrant in the United States in the 1980s: she is emotionally and culturally connected to a place geographically distant, and geographically located in a place that feels emotionally and culturally distant. But *Giving up the Ghost* does not confront one dichotomy with another—and thereby corroborate the notion of dichotomy—by deploying an idealized Mexico against a discriminatory Los Angeles. However nostalgic they become, Amalia's memories of Mexico and Alejandro, the lover she had while living there, are always tempered by the knowledge that staying in Mexico would have meant subordinating her lesbian desires. "Not that I would have been any happier staying there," she admits during a monologue, "How *could* I have stayed there, been some man's wife ... after so many years in this country, so many years on my own?" (original emphasis).[109] Moraga complicates the ethnic dichotomy in the contrast of Mexico and L.A. with the sexual dichotomy of these same places, not that L.A. is particularly welcoming to lesbian desires but instead that her anonymity provides freedom. In the end, Amalia is plagued by discontinuity that works on several levels, leaving her feeling *ni de aqui, ni de alla*—neither here nor there—and instead caught in a daunting liminality.[110]

Interestingly, Amalia sees the same liminality in Marisa even though Marisa was born in and has lived her entire life in L.A. During the last scene of act one, Amalia comments, "when I closed my eyes to search for her, it was in the Mexican desert that I found her."[111] Adding, "Her nostalgia for the land she had never seen was everywhere. In her face, her drawings, her love of the hottest sand by the sea." Such remarks may be more informative about Amalia's investment in Mexican identity that ultimately pulls her away from Marisa. But they additionally suggest much about the way that Los Angeles is represented in *Giving up the Ghost*. In her perspective, the animosity toward Mexican immigrants evident in crowding them into barrios where crime and poverty and violence against women are rampant is so powerful that it extends toward those of Mexican descent. The national or ideological boundary between Mexican and American becomes inscribed onto the geography of Los Angeles so that even those who have never seen Mexico, like Marisa, become marginalized in favor of middle-class Americans. The story told by Corky about throwing another child's bike into the street and then being forced to apologize to the child's family mainly because her own family was on the margins of society is telling: they are singled out as a troublesome family by their behavior, linked stereotypically to their Mexican ancestry. Moreover, the division of Marisa/Corky doubles the condition of Amalia being between worlds and thus illustrates what Lou Rosenberg has described how "difficult and painful" it becomes when forced to choose between different subject positions.[112] In this case, choosing between being victimized as a woman and becoming the victimizer through the gang-attire, and between being defined, in terms of ethnicity, as "un," and denying ethnicity. But the Marisa/Corky division is distinctly different than Amalia's liminality because it serves as a form of rebellion against dichotomy underscored in Marisa's response to Amalia's nostalgia: "This *is* Mexico! . . . It was those gringos that put up those fences between us!" (original emphasis).[113]

Love of/in Disorder

Suggested in Marisa's defiance is how the sociospatial ambitions of *Giving up the Ghost* go beyond *FOB*. Beyond just demonstrating the interplay of identity politics, social justice, and urban geography, Moraga's play intends to reimagine the very nature of that interplay. In fact, *Giving up the Ghost* signals this ambition from the opening. As previously discussed, the play's prologue reveals Corky dressed in gang clothing and walking toward the upstage wall. There, she "writes in large, Chicano graffiti-style letters" the following words: "Don't know where this woman/and I will find each other again,/but I am grateful to her to something/that feels like a blessing// that I am, in fact, not trapped // which brings me to the question of prisons/politics/sex" (extra spacing in original).[114] While Corky spray paints the wall, Marisa, sitting center stage on a wooden crate writes—presumably the same words—in her sketchbook, a conclusion endorsed by Corky tossing the spray can to Marisa when finished. Several things are notable about this prologue, the most important of which may be that Moraga transforms the stage into the city. The upstage wall becomes, metonymically, the wall of a building or the side of an overpass or a billboard or any of the many spaces in Los Angeles that become subjected to graffiti, a connection that audiences of *Giving up the Ghost* no doubt intuitively make during the production. From the beginning, then, Moraga establishes the central questions of the play, questions "of prisons/politics/sex"—all of which speak to the geographical dichotomy and existential liminality discussed during the previous section—as unfolding against, within, and about the urban environment. Additionally, the doubling of the writing by Corky and Marisa during this prologue suggests the conflation of public transgression (defacing the urban space) and private self-definition (as Mexican American, as lesbian), both of which unfold against and offer resistance to Cresswell's theory of ideological boundaries determining what is "right, just, and appropriate" in particular spaces.[115] *Giving up the Ghost's* prologue functions like two Brechtian techniques, considered below, for revealing the invisible—and unquestionable—laws of that society. The words written function like a title; the writing itself like *gestus*.

Beginning with the second of these two, the act of writing graffiti concretely establishes the contestation about politics and prisons underway in *Giving up the Ghost*. For the Americans described by Amalia living the American Dream of home, wealth, and family, graffiti typically makes them feel uneasy or threatened because of what Cresswell argues in *In Place/Out of Place*. "Graffiti flagrantly disturbs notions of order. It represents a disregard for order and, it seems to those who see it, a love of disorder—of anarchy, of things out of place."[116] For *Giving up the Ghost's* Los Angeles, graffiti left on walls and buildings represents transgression against the ideological "order" in the landscape divided between the privileged neighborhoods of the "Americans" and the prison-barrios of Mexican immigrants or Mexican Americans: that is, the naturalized distance between American and Mexican. Generally speaking, graffiti is linked with minorities or immigrants which is considered "rebellious and irrational" from a middle-class perspective.[117] No doubt for this reason, many neighborhoods in Los Angeles even today fight aesthetic, legal, and communal battles with "taggers" as means of controlling and defining space. It is not just the graffiti that is unwelcome but those (ethnicities or nationalities) who write graffiti who are unwelcome because they violate the "order" of the city. By beginning with this act of transgression, Moraga introduces the spatialized conflict playing out in the play's representation of L.A., a conflict that emerges from the politics of exclusion that locks those like Corky or Amalia away from Americans and within "prisons" in the worst corners of the metropolis. In effect, the sociospatial relations between Moraga's characters and the society that denies them any meaningful place is materialized through the opening gesture—though the significance of the graffiti-*gestus* might only become evident during the play. Still, the prologue highlights the fundamental question that began this study of sociospatial drama: who has *authority over* and *access to* urban space.

Beyond introducing such concerns, the graffiti begins to undermine the imbrication of ideology and geography necessary for locking away immigrants or children of immigrants in prisons of poverty. Corky does not just write *on* the urban landscape (metonymically of course) but further writes *over* the ideology in that landscape, suggesting both the presence and agency of Chicanas like herself within Los Angeles. Her very presence, particularly in her gang attire, demands recognition and interrogates the politics of the distance hiding immigrants or children of immigrants from "Americans." Her presence visually corroborates the double meaning of her announcement, "I am, in fact, not trapped": the truth that the metropolis traps those like her and Amalia geographically and ideologically and the possibility that, through transgression, she can escape the liminality that Amalia cannot. As discussed in Chapter 1, transgression in space is particularly powerful because it allows the questioning of what was believed natural. Much the same thing occurs in *Giving up the Ghost,* beginning with the graffiti which Cresswell defines as "the ideal crime for a marginalized culture."[118] Reasoning that the "criminality" of graffiti is deeply rooted in political protest, graffiti represents a "refusal to comply with its context: it does not respect the laws of place that tell us what is and what is not appropriate."[119] This very premise goes to the heart of what *Giving up the Ghost* suggests about Chicanas in L.A. Confronted with an "order" that denies them any place other than *un* or Other, they have the choice of Amalia and acquiescence to this "order"; or the choice of Corky and transgression against that "order." Toward that second end, graffiti "subverts the authority of urban space and asserts the triumph (however fleeting) of the individual over the monuments of authority, 'the name over the nameless.'"[120] Others who have considered *Giving up the Ghost,* such as Tiffany Ann Lopez, argue that the early, monologue version was more "confrontational."[121] But the prologue's gesture retains this confrontational attitude. Left on the wall, "I am, in fact, not trapped," speaks loudly to the ways that identity is aggressively contesting the landscape.

But *Giving up the Ghost* is concerned with questions of "prisons" "politics" *and* "sex," as Corky underscores while writing the graffiti against the upstage wall. In other words, Moraga's play is concerned not merely with the contestation of space around Chicanas in Los Angeles but simultaneously with bringing lesbian desire, as Huerta argues, into "public space."[122] Never directly identified during the prologue or elsewhere the play, the woman mentioned in Corky's graffiti could be Amalia or Corky's cousin who introduced her to sex, or perhaps even Marisa—who sitting nearby onstage, Corky's future self. Regardless of this woman's identity, it is worth stressing that the graffiti begins with reference to the question of identity formation through the interplay of gender and sexuality, something reaffirmed at the beginning of act three when, once again, Corky writes graffiti against the upstage wall. The text reads as follows: "I have this rock in my hand/it is my memory/the weight is solid/in my palm it cannot fly away// because I still remember/that woman/not my savior, but an angel/with wings/ that did once lift me/ to another/self" (extra spacing in original).[123] Evident in this graffiti are tensions between the potential for rebellion (the rock in her hand), again this woman (not named), and self-definition in terms of sexuality ("that did once lift me/to another/self"). Transgression, then, extends toward the strictures prohibiting lesbian desire in the world imagined by the play, where heterosexuality precedes the play's opening as the ideological norm. Under this definition of normal, lesbian desire is more than not allowed; it is not acknowledged; it is, like Amalia feels about herself when thinking of Americans, *un*. These strictures enter the play mostly through Amalia and her desire for Alejandro, which embodied heternormativity for Catholic Mexico. Yet, the transgressions regarding lesbian desire are less confrontational, at least in regards to audiences. Most of the transgressions come in confessions of their desire for women by Amalia, Marisa, Corky, which are intended to create what Cresswell describes as a "heretical reading" of space that opens up possibility where there was only denial.

This premise becomes clear when representation of lesbian desire in *Giving up the Ghost* is contrasted with the apprehension about violating taboos felt by Amalia. Toward the end of the play, just before she disappears from the play's world, Amalia tells Marisa about her dream that they were *"indias."* "In our village some terrible taboo had been broken," she says, looking into the distance and with the portrait of Mexico illuminated on stage, "There was thunder and lightning. I am crouched down in terror, unable to move when I realize it is *you* who has gone against the code of our people" (original emphasis).[124] Not named, this code is clearly related to homosexuality by the rest of Amalia's dream. Though she insists that she was "not afraid of being punished," Amalia feared the very possibility "that the taboo *could* be broken. And if this law nearly transcribed in blood could go, then what else?" (original emphasis).[125] Thoroughly inculcated with assumptions of the morality of heterosexual normalcy, despite years of living as a lesbian in Los Angeles, Amalia cannot fully free herself from the ideology that defines what is "right, just, and appropriate." Without condemning Amalia, the play uses her to demonstrate how damaging prohibitions against lesbian desire can be to not just couples like her and Marisa but to Amalia's psyche. Like Joe from *Angels in America,* Amalia has internalized the ideological demarcation outlawing homosexual desire, demarcations that originate and persist, for her, through the geography of Mexico. While she knows she cannot be happy in Mexico, she is still drawn to it and apparently returns there during the conclusion because she has been compelled to choose between defining herself culturally in Mexico and sexually in Los Angeles, a choice that leaves her feeling "neither here nor there." Clearly, *Giving up the Ghost* challenges and hopes to change this attitude, not in Amalia, but rather in the world represented in the play and the audiences that become part of the play. Transgression, staged within *Giving up the Ghost,* intends to make possible the pronouncement and pursuit of lesbian desire by changing the terms of self-definition in space *and* those spaces of self-definition.

Making Familia from Scratch

The value of transgression in *Giving up the Ghost* is, thematically and epistemologically, twofold. On the one hand, the transgressions undertaken by Moraga's characters—the writing of graffiti, the trespass of the ethnic Other, the highlighting of lesbian desire into public space—is personally empowering for Marisa/Corky. Breaking the taboos inscribed in the landscape of Los Angeles provides Marisa/Corky outlets for her frustration and confusion regarding how to define herself; more importantly, they supply agency in that she finds ways of defining herself, at least momentarily, beyond dichotomy. Though *Giving up the Ghost* has little plot, it still has a clear trajectory in the imagery and incidents that suggest the possibility of growth, most clearly, the movement from the "prisons" that Corky invokes about "politics" and "sex" during the first graffiti writing to the image of flight expressed in the second instance: "an angel/with wings/ that did once lift me/to another/self."[126] More noteworthy for the sociospatial ambitions of Moraga's play, which are much more rhetorical than Hwang's *FOB*, is what transgression tends to produce in those witnessing Marisa/Corky's heretical readings of Los Angeles. According to Cresswell, transgression initially calls into question assumptions of normalcy by demonstrating how what was believed perfectly natural—in this case, the privilege enjoyed by white, middle-class Americans; the amalgamation of heterosexuality and patriarchy—is constructed toward endorsing and preserving particular perspectives. If this transgression continues long enough, and "if enough people follow suit," remarks Cresswell, "a whole new conception of 'normality' may arise."[127] This theory is particularly valuable for *Giving up the Ghost* illustrated, again through movement of image or incident, in the contrast of the opening gesture of the play and the central event of the third act. Moving from the violation of space by a woman (Corky's writing graffiti on the upstage wall) to the violation of a woman within space (Corky's rape), the play attempts to redefine how and what audiences value within the urban landscape. Specifically, the effort is to wrench audiences from the assumption of immigrants or children of immigrants as threat and replace that with knowledge of the threat experienced by women in the barrio, by immigrants without a place, by lesbians denied their desires—all in this city.

Toward this rhetorical end, Moraga attempts to conscript audiences as part of the play's sociospatial criticism. In the stage directions, she includes "The People," or "those viewing the performance or reading the play" among the characters of *Giving up the Ghost.*[128] Undoubtedly a remnant of the monologue version of Moraga's play, this gesture importantly locates audiences within—instead of beyond—the play's dramatization of borders and boundaries that need to be trespassed and torn down: from the fence that Marisa says was put up by whites to keep them from Mexico to the taboos about homosexuality that plague Amalia. The play tries to separate audiences from middle-class privilege that looks upon anything "diferrnt"[129] as a threat to their way of life and instead begin to see this privilege as a problem. To accomplish this, Moraga has her characters deliver their admissions about (the violations of) the borders and boundaries directly. In act one, for instance, Marisa's confession "I'm queer I am," the language of which directly links self-definition with sexuality, is delivered to "The People."[130] Likewise in act two, Amalia's admission that she feels "neither here nor there" with her nostalgia for Mexico while living in L.A. is delivered to "The People" thereby including them in this moment of uncertainty.[131] Most importantly, Marisa's admission that she was raped, along with the conditions of the barrio that made her vulnerable to violence is delivered to "The People."[132] Throughout, these instances of direct address involve either transgressions (Marisa's admission, in public, of lesbian desire) or the need for transgression (the exclusion of Mexicans from what it means to be American); consequently, audiences are drawn into their perspective, through sympathy if nothing else, and simultaneously distanced from what might have been considered normalcy in the urban environment. In effect, *Giving up the Ghost* itself does not just *stage* heretical readings of urban space but *becomes* such a reading, and in the process attempts to draw in audiences so that they begin to reconsider what it means to have a place of belonging and, more significantly, what it means to be denied that place.

During the closing monologue, Marisa thematizes the sociospatial ambitions of *Giving up the Ghost*. Left alone on the stage, after Amalia has left presumably for Mexico, Marisa comes downstage toward audiences and delivers the following lines about her future: "It's like making *familia* from scratch/each time all over again.../with strangers, if I must./If I must, I will."[133] Important here is the contrast of *familia* and stranger, the known and the unknown. Considering the threat posed by the immigrant to narratives constructed around/about space, Madan Soup maintains that "the stranger blurs a boundary line. The stranger is an anomaly, standing between the inside and the outside, order and chaos, friend and enemy."[134] In highlighting the ambiguous existentiality of the stranger, immigrant or lesbian, Soup captures something of the threat posed those like Amalia, Marisa, and Corky to the privileged world of Americans dramatized in Moraga's play. But *Giving up the Ghost* suggests in Marisa's closing monologue that within this ambiguity is the possibility of transformation by undermining the rigid boundaries in narratives of space evident throughout the landscape of

Los Angeles. Just before Marisa talks about strangers becoming *familia*, she recalls making love with Amalia in terms that reference narratives of space. She describes "that crazy *espiritu* [spirit] of hers" that would "come inside, through the door" and fill the bed with longing against the surroundings of the "fucking dreary season. This cement city."[135] In the language here is the contrast of public and private spheres, of course; but through the description of the intimacy, Marisa's memory becomes public. In effect, her story about their sexual encounter collapses this boundary by bringing the private (lesbian desire) into the "public" (of the play and the city). Most important, is how the play invites audiences—presumably strangers—toward becoming *familia* in telling stories like this, stories about lesbian desire, about immigrants and Chicanas, about the barrio, throughout the play. Played before audiences at Theatre Rhinoceros and Divisionary Theatre, two theaters known for producing gay and lesbian plays, this goal was probably met with enthusiasm. But the truly revolutionary potential of *Giving up the Ghost* may not be fully realized except during productions before white, middle-class, heterosexual audiences.

Ultimately, *Giving up the Ghost* intends to reimagine not only the layers of self-definition confronting Amalia, Marisa, and Corky but further, the constitution of community necessary for the freedoms sought by those considered "difernt" in the urban environment. This effort begins with audiences or "The People" who become surrogates for community beyond the theater, and extends toward the necessity for social justice. The play's investment in metaphorically lighting "fires of social justice" in audiences locates *Giving up the Ghost* in the tradition of Chicano drama of the 1970s and 1980s, plays which Huerta contends were fundamentally concerned with—and often produced wherever—"Mexicans and Chicana/os [were] being oppressed."[136] Implicit in the play's chronicling of the problems endured by Amalia, Marisa, and Corky is the demand for changes in the social ordering of the urban landscape that will resolve the problems: changes to the living conditions of the barrio that leave women vulnerable to violence and rape; changes to the geography of L.A. that divides economically into privileged and impoverished regions; changes to the taboos against lesbian desire. Such changes anticipate what Olalquiaga, Gomez-Pena, Valle and Torres (among others) argued about the city in the 1980s and early 1990s: that was undergoing a beneficial cultural and geographical transformation away from homogeneity or dichotomy, and toward multiculturalism or hybridity. In fact, *Giving up the Ghost's* rejection of fences and walls, borders and boundaries speak to the notion described by Valle and Torres in *Latino Metropolis* as "*mestizaje*" or "the . . . unfinished business of racial and cultural hybridization."[137] But Moraga knew full well how difficult this ambition would be to fulfill, considering how naturalized demarcations of difference had become in the urban environment, as is suggested by Marisa's admission that making *familia* from strangers would happen "each time all over again..."[138] Nevertheless, Moraga believes the effort well worth making since her play calls for a vision of a metropolis rather similar to that described by Belize in *Angels in America*: a metropolis where binaries have collapsed into joyful confusions of sexuality, ethnicity, and gender. Or, using the imagery of *Giving up the Ghost,* the change represents the shift from prisons of politics and sex to the possibilities of flight.

Notes

Introduction

1. Marvin Carlson, *Places of Performance: The Semiotics of Theatre Architecture* (Ithaca, NY and London: Cornell UP, 1989). Carlson's book was at the beginning of the spatial turn of drama and theater studies. Beyond being among the first such studies, it was the most comprehensive: considering how urbanism has provided a foundation for theater and vice versa.
2. See Mathew R. Martin, *Between Theater and Philosophy: Skepticism in the Major City Comedies of Ben Jonson and Thomas Middleton* (2001), Anthony Covatta, *Thomas Middleton's City Comedies* (1973), and Gamini Salgado, *Four Jacobean City Comedies* (1975).
3. Hooks's argument involves appropriating the "marginalized" spaces normally allowed the minority voice within the dichotomy of center/margin or insider/outsider as a way of critiquing both the center or the insider and the dichotomy itself. See *Feminist Theory: From Margin to Center* (2000).
4. This is, of course, a key point that I consider further in appropriate chapters. In Chapter 3, for instance, this involves discussion of INTAR, in New York City, with its mandate of cultivating and performing works about a Latino perspective.
5. Of course, the replication of the image does not necessarily translate to the accuracy of the image, as John Berger has famously argued. My point here is not about the distinction between the "aura" of the original and of the copy but rather the recognizability of the landscape. See Berger's *Ways of Seeing* for more details.
6. Edward Soja, *Thirdspace: Journeys to Los Angeles and Other Real-And-Imagined Places* (Cambridge, MA: Blackwell Publishers, 1996), 1.
7. Ibid., 2.
8. Ibid.
9. Henri Lefebvre, *The Production of Space,* translated by Donald Nicholson-Smith (Malden, MA: Blackwell, 1984), 27–28.
10. Ibid., 27–28.
11. Ibid.
12. David Harvey, *Social Justice and the City* (London: Edward Arnold, 1973), 11.
13. Ibid., 23.
14. Ibid., 24.
15. Ibid., 27.

16. W. B. Worthen, *Modern Drama and the Rhetoric of Theater* (Berkeley & Los Angeles: U of California P, 1992), 5.

17. Worthen discusses three "rhetorics" of theater: realistic, poetic, and political. All three begin from the premise that the formal elements of the dramatic text establish, to some degree, the blueprint for the production and reception of the work, with each one demanding more and more from audiences.

18. I am sensitive here to the counterargument made by Performance Studies: that the text of theater is never complete until the production and that this text is necessarily unstable as each production redefines the nature of the text. I am not trying to suggest that the text will produce any particular production or that this production will produce any specific reception. Instead, I am considering how the playwrights imagine the activity of the audience as part of the sociospatial concerns in the dramaturgy.

19. Originally developed to describe Goethe's *Wilhelm's Meister's Apprenticeship*, the *Bildungsroman* classically followed a pattern of discovery, maturation, and integration into society. Modernist revisions to the genre often substituted disillusionment and exile for integration. See Kenneth Millard, *Coming of Age in Contemporary American Fiction*, 2007; Breon Mitchell, "A Portrait and the Bildungsroman Tradition," *Approaches to Joyce's Portrait: Ten Essays*, 1976; and Elizabeth Abel, Marianne Hirsch, and Elizabeth Langland, *The Voyage In: Fictions of Female Development*, 1983.

20. This voyeuristic interplay of realism and reception has been thoroughly discussed by many works. See Worthen's *Modern Drama and the Rhetoric of Theatre* and Chaudhuri's *Staging Place*.

21. Benjamin Genocchio provides a good summary of this overuse of Foucault's theory. See "Discourse, Discontinuity, Difference: The Question of 'Other' Spaces" in *Postmodern Cities and Spaces*, 1995.

22. Michel Foucault, "Of Other Spaces," *Diacritics* 16, no. 1 (1986): 24.

23. Una Chaudhuri, *Staging Place: The Geography of Modern Drama* (Ann Arbor: U of Michigan P, 1995), xi.

24. Una Chaudhuri and Elinor Fuchs, introduction to *Land/Scape/Theater*, edited by Elinor Fuchs and Una Chaudhuri (Ann Arbor: U of Michigan P, 2002), 3.

25. Elinor Fuchs, "Reading for Landscape: The Case of American Drama," in *Land/Scape/Theater*, edited by Elinor Fuchs and Una Chaudhuri (Ann Arbor: U of Michigan P, 2002), 30.

26. Chaudhuri and Fuchs, introduction, 3.

27. Ibid., 3.

28. Ibid.

29. Ibid.

30. John Brinckerhoff Jackson, "The Order of a Landscape: Reason and Religion in Newtonian America," in *The Interpretation of Ordinary Landscapes: Geographical Essays,* edited by D. W. Meinig (Oxford: Oxford UP, 1979), 153.

31. Peirce Lewis, "Axioms for Reading the Landscape: Some Guides to the American Scene," in *The Interpretation of Ordinary Landscapes: Geographical Essays,* edited by D. W. Meinig (New York & Oxford: Oxford UP, 1979), 12.

32. This is the premise behind Meinig's contribution to the anthology, "The Beholding Eye: Ten Versions of the Same Scene." Take any ten people out to the same place and ask them to describe the same landscape, Meinig suggests, and you will get ten different answers based in part on what sorts of epistemological "frames" they use to interpret what they see.

33. Chaudhuri and Fuchs, introduction, 3.

34. Carlson, 2.

Chapter 1

1. This enormous rise in the numbers of the homeless has been attributed, nationally, to the Reagan administration's cuts to federal programs: HUD losing 80 percent of its budget, support for low-income families being slashed. See Arline Mathieu's "The Medicalization of Homelessness and the Theater of Repression" in *Medical Anthropology Quarterly*.

2. Benedict Giamo talks about the homeless populations of the Bowery in the late 1970s and 1980s and the dangers they faced, which included being assaulted and perhaps set on fire. See *On the Bowery: Confronting Homelessness in American Society*, 1989.

3. Tim Cresswell, *In Place/Out of Place: Geography, Ideology, and Transgression* (Minneapolis, MN and London: U of Minnesota P, 1996), 4.

4. Ibid., 8.

5. Ibid., 4.

6. Adrienne E. Christiansen and Jeremy J. Hanson, "Comedy as Cure for Tragedy: ACT UP and the Rhetoric of Aids," *Quarterly Journal of Speech* 82 (1996): 157.

7. Ibid., 157.

8. Ibid.

9. President George H. W. Bush called ACT UP "outrageous" and Mayor Koch referred to them as "fascists." For more details on the protest and the reactions to it, see Christiansen and Hanson, 157–170.

10. Cresswell, 8.

11. During the Victorian period, one kind of poverty—pauperism—was defined as some sort of inherent degeneracy of the poor themselves, something that seemed to reemerge during the 1980s around welfare and homelessness. This not only put paupers beyond the reach of philanthropy; it defined them as threats to middle-class society. See the following for more details: Gavin Jones, *American Hungers: The Problem of Poverty in U.S. Literature, 1840–1945*, 2008; David Ward, *Poverty, Ethnicity, and the American City, 1840–1925: Changing Conceptions of the Slum and Ghetto*, 1989.

12. José Rivera, Interview by Lynn Jacobson, *Studies in American Drama, 1945-Present* 6, no.1 (1991): 54.

13. See the following interviews for Kushner's anger about Reagan, homosexuality, and AIDS: "AIDS, Angels, Activism, and Sex in the Nineties," By Patrick R. Pacheco; "I Always Go Back to Brecht," By Carl Weber; "The Theater and

the Barricades," By Craig Kinzer, Sandra Richards, Frank Galati, and Lawrence Bommer; "Tony Kushner at the Royal National Theatre of Britain," By Adam Mars-Jones—all in *Tony Kushner in Conversation*, 1998.

14. Tony Kushner, Interview by Craig Kinzer, Sandra Richards, Frank Galati, and Lawrence Bommer, "The Theater and the Barricades," in *Tony Kushner in Conversation*, edited by Robert Vorlicky (Ann Arbor, MI: U of Michigan P, 1998), 192.

15. I am using this term in much the same way Fuchs and Chaudhuri intend in their discussion of landscape theory. The concerns with space and spatial contestation for Rivera and Kushner are evident not just in the content of the play but also the structure of the play. In other words, the dramaturgy itself is frequently informed by awareness of and anxiety about the ways urban spaces are continually contested.

16. See "Notes on *Angels in America* as American Epic Theater," *Approaching the Millennium: Essays on Angels in America*, 1997.

17. Arnold Aronson provides a good gloss on this point: "The simultaneous stage of the Middle Ages, the split scenes and vision scenes of melodrama, the flashback (credited to playwright Elmer Rice), and Sergei Eisenstein's idea of montage all predate in practice" what Kushner does in *Angels in America*, though I agree that "Kushner pushes it further" (223). See "Design for *Angels in America*: Envisioning the Millennium" in *Approaching the Millennium: Essays on Angels in America*, 1997.

18. Mel Gussow, "Critic's Notebook: About Death, Bad Dreams and D. Boone Debunked," *The New York Times* March 26, 1992, http://www.Lexisnexis.com (accessed Feb. 24, 2007).

19. Ibid.

20. Frank Rich, "The Angel of No Hope Visits New York," *New York Times* May 21, 1993, http://www.Lexisnexis.com (accessed Jan. 22, 2006).

21. Rich was referring to David Dinkins, who was facing reelection (which he subsequently lost to Rudy Giuliani), while Rivera's play was inspired by Ed Koch.

22. Interview by Jacobson, 55.

23. José Rivera quoted in Jon Rossini, "Marisol, Angels, and Apocalyptic Migrations," *American Drama* 10, no.2 (2001): 9.

24. Rivera never directly mentions Hobbes or the social contract, but his interviews consistently suggest that the values and themes of his plays can be traced, directly or indirectly, to this philosophy. See interviews with Norma Jenckes and Lynn Jacobson.

25. Interview by Jacobson, 54.

26. See Rossini's "Marisol, Angels, and Apocalyptic Migrations" in *American Drama* for discussion.

27. Michel de Certeau, *The Practice of Everyday Life*, Translated by Steven Rendall (Berkeley: U of California P, 1988), 93.

28. José Rivera, *Marisol, Marisol and Other Plays* (New York: Theatre Communications Group, 1997), 6.

29. Ibid., 7.
30. Ibid.
31. Ibid.
32. Ibid.
33. Ibid., 20.
34. Ibid., 42.
35. This term has certainly been overused in discussion of drama since Bertolt Brecht, but it seems particularly appropriate here, in part because Rivera has acknowledged a debt to Brecht.
36. Rivera, 47.
37. Ibid., 46.
38. Ibid., 51.
39. The stage directions call for the same actor to play Man with Golf Club as Scar Tissue (as well as Man with Ice Cream), a point which underscores this juxtaposition. But this may not be evident in production since Scar Tissue requires considerable makeup, which may obfuscate the double roles.
40. Rivera, 56.
41. Ibid.
42. Ibid., 61.
43. Ibid., 25.
44. Ibid., 14.
45. Ibid., 63.
46. Reading the Nazi's diatribe alongside Koch's speech to the American Institute of Architects proves instructive. See Cresswell's *In Place/Out of Place* for Koch's language.
47. Rivera, 63.
48. See Bonnie Marranca, Gerald Rabkin, and Johannes Birringer, "The Politics of Reception" in *Conversations on Art and Performance*.
49. Rivera, 63.
50. Rivera uses this term when talking about a teleplay he was writing, *The Maldonado Miracle*, but I have argued elsewhere that "magnify" is a good term to describe Rivera's dramaturgy.
51. Rivera, 55.
52. See "Marisol, Angels, and Apocalyptic Migrations," *American Drama* 10, no.2 (2001): 6.
53. Rossini, 6.
54. See Mathieu for more details here.
55. Rivera, 46.
56. Ibid., 48.
57. Ibid.
58. The stage directions call for the lights to come up on the back wall and then a pause before lights reveal Marisol sitting on the subway. Because of this, audiences have enough time to read the graffiti on the wall and begin to consider its implications, so that in a way, the wall functions almost as a prologue or a title in Brechtian theater.

59. Rivera, 5.

60. Ibid.

61. Susan Bennett, *Theatre Audiences: A Theory of Production and Reception* (London and New York: Routledge, 1990), 150.

62. Cresswell offers excellent semiotic and cultural analysis of graffiti, ideology, and public space. See *In Place/Out of Place*.

63. Rivera, 24.

64. This was the case for the university production mentioned above. The effect was twofold: the action slowly explicated the imagery of the poem; and the poem acted as a constant reminder of the tidy world that the play was interrogating.

65. Rivera, 47.

66. Ibid., 55.

67. Ibid., 15.

68. Ibid., 17.

69. Ibid., 20.

70. Ibid., 65.

71. Ibid., 66.

72. Ibid., 67.

73. Ibid., 68.

74. Ibid.

75. Ibid.

76. Tony Kushner, Interview by Adam Mars-Jones, "Tony Kushner at the Royal National Theatre of Britain," in *Tony Kushner in Conversation,* edited by Robert Vorlicky (Ann Arbor, MI: U of Michigan P, 1998), 19.

77. Kushner was still making revisions to *Perestroika* during the San Francisco and Los Angeles productions, in part because it was simply too long (double the length of the version published).

78. Greg Evans thought *Millennium Approaches* fabulous but *Perestroika* much weaker, even dragging down the overall accomplishment of the two-part play at the Mark Taper Forum. See "Angels in America: A Gay Fantasia on National Themes."

79. *Millennium Approaches* had the lion's share of awards, including the 1992 London Drama Critics Circle Award for Best New Play, 1993 Drama Desk Award for Best Play, 1993 New York Drama Critic's Circle Award for Best Play, and 1993 Pulitzer Prize for Drama.

80. See Steven Winn, " 'Angels' Is Born Again: ACT puts its own stamp on Kushner play"; Mike Steele, "Thrilling, provocative 'Angels' sheds light on large issues"; Frank Rich, "Perestroika: Following an Angel For a Healing Vision Of Heaven on Earth" and others.

81. Interview by Mars-Jones, 19.

82. Ibid.

83. Steven Winn, "Playwright Tony Kushner: 'I wrote the Play for San Francisco and it was Important to Me that it Play,' " *The San Francisco Chronicle* Sept. 25, 1994, http://www.Lexisnexis.com (accessed Nov. 27, 2007).

84. See "The Theater and the Barricades," a roundtable discussion with by Craig Kinzer, Sandra Richards, Frank Galati, and Lawrence Bommer and Kushner in *Tony Kushner in Conversation*.

85. Interview by Mars-Jones, 22.

86. The play includes concerns about minorities (Belize), anti-Semitism (Louis), and even the homeless (during a short scene near the end of *Millennium Approaches*).

87. See Edward Soja and Barbara Hooper, "The Spaces that Difference Makes: Some Notes on the Geographical Margins of the New Cultural Politics" in *Place and the Politics of Identity* for details.

88. Tony Kushner, *Angels in America: Part One: Millennium Approaches* (New York: Theatre Communications Group, 1993), 81.

89. Ibid., 81.

90. See Kevin Kelly, "Kushner's landmark epic kicks off with a brilliant, searing look at homophobia" for details of this production's staging.

91. See Savran, "Ambivalence, Utopia, and a Queer Sort of Materialism: How *Angels in America* Reconstructs the Nation" and Austin "Theology for the Approaching Millennium: *Angels in America*, Activism, and the American Religion."

92. David Savran, "Ambivalence, Utopia, and a Queer Sort of Materialism: How *Angels in America* Reconstructs the Nation," in *Approaching the Millennium: Essays on Angels in America*, edited by Deborah R. Geis and Steven F. Kruger (Ann Arbor, MI: U of Michigan P, 1997), 25.

93. Miriam Kahn, "Your Place and Mine: Sharing Emotional Landscapes in Wamira, Papua New Guinea," in *Senses of Place*, edited by Steven Feld and Keith H. Basso (Santa Fe, NM: School of American Research P, 1996), 168.

94. The Seagull Monument is Salt Lake Assembly Hall on Temple Square, in Salt Lake City, and commemorates the "Miracle of the Gulls," when seagulls prevented insects from destroying Mormon crops in 1848; the Mormon Pioneer Monument is located near downtown Salt Lake City and commemorates the 6,000 Mormon pioneers who died on the journey to Salt Lake; the Eagle Gate Monument is located north of the intersection at Main and South Temple Streets and honors Brigham Young, the Mormon leader who lead Mormons to Salt Lake City.

95. Kushner, *Millennium*, 83.

96. Kahn, 178.

97. See Savran, "Ambivalence, Utopia, and a Queer Sort of Materialism: How *Angels in America* Reconstructs the Nation" for discussion of this utopianism.

98. Kushner, *Millennium*, 83.

99. Ibid., 82.

100. Ibid., 83.

101. Edward S. Casey, "How to Get from Space to Place in a Fairly Short Stretch of Time," in *Senses of Place*, edited by Steven Feld and Keith H. Basso (Santa Fe, NM: School of American Research P, 1996), 23.

102. Kushner, *Millennium*, 82.

103. Cresswell, 14.

104. Here, a qualifier seems necessary, since Kushner's feelings about Mormon utopianism are complicated. Certainly, *Angels in America* suggests that this utopianism underlies the conservative ordering of identity evident in the scenes discussed in this chapter. But in interviews, Kushner is fascinated with early Mormonism as a contrast to capitalism, particularly with the organization of community, geography, and capital. See "The Theater and the Barricades."

105. Toward the end of *Millennium Approaches,* when he begins his short-lived affair with Louis, he defines it in terms of theological transgression: "I'm going to hell for doing this" (116).

106. Cresswell, 18–19.

107. Kushner, *Millennium,* 40.

108. Ibid., 82.

109. Stephen J. Bottoms, "Re-Staging Roy: Citizen Cohn and the Search for Xanadu," *Theatre Journal* 48, no.2 (1996):161.

110. Arnold Aronson, "Design for *Angels in America*: Envisioning the Millennium," in *Approaching the Millennium: Essays on Angels in America,* edited by Deborah R. Geis and Steven F. Kruger (Ann Arbor, MI: U of Michigan P, 1997), 213.

111. Kushner, *Millennium,* 110.

112. Like his attitude toward Mormonism, Kushner's feelings about Cohn are complex. Although Cohn functions as the voice of Reaganite conservatism in the play, he transgresses against the law (his efforts to have the Rosenbergs executed) and against heteronormativity (his indulgence in sex with men)—but he must publically uphold conservative values.

113. Cresswell, 26.

114. Ibid., 26.

115. Kushner, *Millennium,* 54.

116. See http://www.centralparkhistory.com/timeline/timeline_postww2_gays.html for this history of Central Park.

117. Kushner, *Millennium,* 40.

118. Ibid., 75.

119. Cresswell, 165.

120. Ibid.

121. Kushner, *Millennium,* 75.

122. Tony Kushner, *Angels in America: Part Two: Perestroika* (New York: Theatre Communications Group, 1993), 70.

123. Ibid., 70.

124. Louis begins the argument that leads to the breakup by invoking Joseph McCarthy, clearly an echo of the Reagan administration as it is represented in the play.

125. Kushner, *Millennium,* 37.

126. Ibid., 76.

127. Ibid.

128. Cresswell, 26.

129. See "The Theater and the Barricades."
130. Janelle Reinelt, "Notes on *Angels in America* as American Epic Theater," in *Approaching the Millennium: Essays on Angels in America*, edited by Deborah R. Geis and Steven F. Kruger (Ann Arbor, MI: U of Michigan P, 1997), 239.
131. Kushner, *Perestroika*, 126.
132. Interview by Mars-Jones, 19.
133. Kushner makes the contrast himself in the Mars-Jones interview.
134. Kushner, *Perestroika*, 75.
135. Ibid., 76.
136. Ibid.
137. Ibid., 142.

Chapter 2

1. Kevin Lynch, *The Image of the City* (Cambridge, MA and London: The MIT P, 1960), 2–3.
2. Lynch offers definitions of a number of elements of the urban environment, including paths: "Paths are the channels along which the observer customarily, occasionally, or potentially moves. They may be streets, walkways, transit lines, canals, railroads" (47); edges: "Edges are the linear elements not used or considered as paths by the observer. They are the boundaries between two phases, linear breaks in continuity: shores, railroad cuts, edges of development, walls. They are lateral references rather than coordinate axes" (47); districts: "Districts are the medium-to-large sections of the city, conceived of as having two-dimensional extent, which the observer mentally enters 'inside-of,' and which are recognizable as having some common, identifying character. Always identifiable from the inside, they are also used for exterior reference if visible from the outside" (47); nodes: "Nodes are points, the strategic spots in a city into which an observer can enter, and which are the intensive foci to and from which he is traveling. They may be primarily junctions, places of a break in transportation, a crossing or convergence of paths, moments of shift from one structure to another. Or the nodes may be simply concentrations, which gain their importance from being the condensation of some use or physical character, as a street-corner hangout or an enclosed square" (47).
3. Chaudhuri discusses this thoroughly; see her essay, "Land/Scape/Theory," 11–29.
4. Lynch, 4–5.
5. Ibid., 4.
6. Fredric Jameson, *Postmodernism, or the Cultural Logic of Late Capitalism* (Durham, NC: Duke UP, 1991), 38–39.
7. Ibid., 39–40.
8. David Harvey, *The Condition of Postmodernity: An Enquiry into the Origins of Cultural Change* (Cambridge, MA: Basil Blackwell, 1990), 66.
9. Jameson, 44.
10. Rivera, 43.

11. The ecological catastrophes and environmental confusion are directly linked to the senility of God, and become particularly acute after the angels begin their siege of heaven.

12. See Jesse McKinley, "Broadway Debut for Julia Roberts," *The New York Times,* July 29, 2005; and J. Kelly Nestruck, "Pretty Woman? Nah!: Critics Heap Scorn on Julia Roberts' Broadway Debut," *National Post* (Canada), April 21, 2006 for details.

13. Richard Greenberg, *Three Days of Rain. Three Days of Rain and Other Plays* (New York: Grove, 1999), 5.

14. Ibid., 6.

15. Jayne M. Blanchard, "Trying to Reclaim Life with Father; Children Now Grown Struggle to Capture Past in 'Three Days of Rain,' " *The Washington Times,* Feb. 5, 2000, http://www.Lexisnexis.com (accessed Oct. 7, 2006).

16. Greenberg, 6–7.

17. Ibid., 16.

18. In *Visions of the Modern City: Essays in History, Art, and Literature,* Sharpe and Wallock describe the crisis attendant with the contemporary "decentered" city as similar to that faced by the "observers of early industrial Manchester and later by the modernist investigators of Paris, London, and New York" (1). The point is that the changes have not, yet, been fully theorized within urban studies.

19. Greenberg, 16.

20. Ibid., 16–17.

21. Ibid., 17.

22. Jameson, 12.

23. Greenberg, 43.

24. Celeste Olalquiaga, *Megalopolis: Contemporary Cultural Sensibilities* (Minneapolis, MN and Oxford: U of Minnesota P, 1992), 2.

25. Ibid., 2.

26. Ibid.

27. Though only narrated, Lina's frantic run down the stairs compounds elements of Mary Tyrone from *Long Day's Journey into Night*: first the story of Mary running down to the docks, while delusional from morphine, to drown herself, and second, her slow descent down the stairs that concludes the play.

28. Peter Marks, "Parent's Secret Cry Out, But Children Don't Hear," *The New York Times,* Nov. 12, 1997, http://www.Lexisnexis.com (accessed Oct. 7, 2006).

29. Greenberg, 21.

30. Ibid.

31. Steven Winn, "Chance of 'Rain' Glimmers, Fades; Play's Potential Never Fulfilled," *The San Francisco Chronicle,* Nov. 2, 1998, http://www.Lexisnexis.com (accessed Oct. 7, 2006).

32. Greenberg, 41.

33. Ibid., 6.

34. John Lechte, "(Not) Belonging in Postmodern Space," in *Postmodern Cities and Spaces,* edited by Sophie Watson and Katherine Gibson (Oxford and Cambridge, MA: Blackwell, 1995), 106.

35. Greenberg, 6.
36. Ibid., 15.
37. Ibid., 14.
38. Ibid.
39. Ibid., 15.
40. Ibid., 44.
41. Ibid., 80.
42. Ibid., 81.
43. Ibid., 71.
44. Ibid., 72.
45. Ibid.
46. Lynch, 10.
47. Greenberg, 73.
48. Lynch talks about how the English language encodes some relationship between geographical and epistemological uncertainty in the word "lost"—something that clearly informs Greenberg's dramaturgy and the play's concern with urbanism.
49. Greenberg, 72.
50. Ibid., 72.
51. Steven Marcuse, "Reading the Illegible: Some Modern Representations of Urban Experience," in *Visions of the Modern City: Essays in History, Art, and Literature,* edited by William Sharpe and Leonard Wallock (Baltimore and London: The Johns Hopkins UP, 1987), 240.
52. Lechte, 103.
53. Perhaps the only overt element of the play that is not realistic are the frequent direct addresses of the audience, which break the frame of realism and invite audiences to become aware of themselves.
54. Greenberg, 74.
55. Ibid., 18.
56. Ibid.
57. Ibid., 21.
58. Ibid.
59. See the theater's website (http://www.passemuraille.on.ca/) for its history and mandate. See Denis Johnston's *Up the Mainstream: The Rise of Toronto's Alternative Theatres, 1968–1975,* 1991, for discussion of this history, with emphasis on cultural identity by Canadian theaters.
60. See the theater's website (http://www.touchstonetheatre.com/).
61. Jameson's point is that changes of postmodernity were (and perhaps still are) outstripping our evolved perceptual or cognitive capacity to comprehend the urban environment; we cannot make sense of the new organizations of space because they violate so completely our epistemological assumptions. See chapter 1 of *Postmodernism or, The Cultural Logic of Late Capitalism* for further discussion.
62. This phrase defines one of the major shifts of postmodernity from Jameson's perspective. Instead of buildings defining themselves through relationality to the surrounding environment, the buildings of postmodernity separate themselves

visually and structurally from that environment and attempt to replace it. This phenomenon is particularly appropriate for the shopping mall, which simultaneously cuts off connects to the outside world and replicates them. The shift can be described as the move from metaphor to metonymy. See chapter 1 of *Postmodernism or, The Cultural Logic of Late Capitalism* for further discussion. Eaton Centre is certainly not the only mall in Canada to attempt this. See Margaret Crawford's discussion of the West Edmonton Mall, "The World in a Shopping Mall," in *Variations on a Theme Park: The New American City and the End of Public Space.*

63. Toronto was undergoing significant topographical and cultural changes during the late 1970s and early 1980s with the rise of malls and condominiums, all of which were radically changing the downtown core. See Jon Caulfield's *City Form and Everyday Life: Toronto's Gentrification and Critical Social Practice,* 1994.

64. Sally Clark, *Lost Souls and Missing Persons* (Burnaby, British Columbia: Talonbooks, 1998), 5.

65. These references include Ned's discussion of the *flâneur* figure as well as the implicit address of those like Walter Benjamin, who has theorized the activity and significance of this figure. Also cited are works like *Hedda Gabler* and others.

66. The term "perspective" here corresponds with definitions from art history as well as urban planning. See H. W. Janson's *History of Art: A Survey of the Major Visual Arts from the Dawn of History to the Present Day,* 1969.

67. Clark, 9.

68. Ibid., 46.

69. Ibid., 28.

70. Ibid., 40.

71. Ibid.

72. Ibid.

73. Ibid., 20.

74. Ibid., 119.

75. Stein famously took landscape as a structuring principle for her plays, specifically, the cubist landscape that breaks up coherence in favor of fragmentation. See Jane Palatini Bowers's "The Composition That All the World Can See: Gertrude Stein's Theater Landscapes," in *Land/Scape/Theater.*

76. Clark, 115.

77. Olalquiaga, 1–2.

78. Ibid., xviii.

79. Ibid., 4.

80. Ibid.

81. Clark, 83.

82. Harvey, 289.

83. See Paul Goldberger's "Architecture; A Huge Architecture Show in Times Square," *The New York Times,* Sept. 9, 1990.

84. Harvey, 289–290.

85. Clark, 28.

86. Ibid., 9.
87. Ibid.
88. Ibid., 62.
89. Olalquiaga, 2.
90. Clark even suggests competing ways of costuming Hannah during the "Zombie" scenes: "This play can be done with Hannah dressed as Zombie throughout. All the flashbacks are then perceived as Zombie's memories. Or, you can use a Zombie overdress suit and blouse sewn together" (5). The decision made here would change how audiences interpret the chronology and no doubt the significance of Hannah, but this could be different during each production, suggesting further uncertainty.
91. Clark, 88.
92. Ibid.
93. Ibid.
94. Ibid., 110.
95. Ibid.
96. Lynch, 92 and 119.
97. Clark, 115.
98. Ibid.

Chapter 3

1. James Howard Kunstler, *The Geography of Nowhere: The Rise and Decline of America's Man-Made Landscape* (New York: Simon & Schuster, 1993), 10.
2. Ibid.
3. Kunstler provides a summary of this history of urban development. See chapter five of *The Geography of Nowhere*. David Harvey, too, discusses the impulses by modernist urban planning in chapter three of *The Condition of Postmodernism: An Enquiry into the Origins of Cultural Change*.
4. Kunstler, 219.
5. Ibid., 186.
6. Ibid., 15.
7. See "Utopia Achieved" in *America* for Baudrillard's discussion of utopianism in U.S. culture.
8. James S. Duncan and David R. Lambert, "Landscape, Aesthetics, and Power," in *American Space/American Place: Geographies of the Contemporary United States*, edited by John A. Agnew and Jonathan M. Smith (Edinburgh: Edinburgh UP, 2002), 282–283.
9. Kunstler, 50.
10. Duncan and Lambert, 284.
11. Ibid., 282–283.
12. Ibid., 274.
13. Ibid., 279.
14. Ibid., 281.

15. Ibid., 287.
16. See Doris Auerbach's *Sam Shepard, Arthur Kopit, and the Off Broadway Theater,* 1982; or Bonnie Marranca's *American Dreams: The Imagination of Sam Shepard,* 1981.
17. Sam Shepard, *True West,* in *Seven Plays* (Toronto, ON: Bantam, 1984), 39.
18. Worthen considers three rhetorics of drama: "The rhetoric of realism frames dramatic meaning as a function of the integrated stage *scene*; poetic theater uses the poet's text, the *word,* to determine the contours of the spectacle and the experience of the audience; and contemporary political theater works to dramatize the theatrical subjection of the *spectator* as a part of its political action" (5).
19. Turner's definition of the frontier was that it had promised the opportunity for regeneration, both individual and cultural, for the United States during much of the nineteenth century. But the purpose of Turner's writing about the frontier was to mark its closing. See Harold P. Simonson's *The Closed Frontier: Studies in American Literary Tragedy,* 1970.
20. Bonnie Marranca, Introduction to *American Dreams: The Imagination of Sam Shepard,* edited by Bonnie Marranca (New York: Performing Arts Journal P, 1981), 17.
21. Marranca, 18.
22. Marc Robinson, *The Other American Drama* (Cambridge: Cambridge UP, 1994), 68.
23. John M. Findlay, *Magic Lands: Western Cityscapes and American Culture After 1940* (Berkeley, CA: U of California P, 1992), 2.
24. Ibid., 2.
25. John Beaufort, "Return of the Sprightly 1901, Comedy that made a Star of Ethel Barrymore; *True West* Play by Sam Shepard," *Christian Science Monitor,* Dec. 31, 1980.
26. Alvin Klein, "Theater; George St. Offering Play by Shepard," *The New York Times,* May 5, 1985, http://www.Lexisnexis.com (accessed Oct. 1, 2007).
27. William Kleb, "Worse Than Being Homeless: *True West* and The Divided Self," in *American Dreams: The Imagination of Sam Shepard,* edited by Bonnie Marranca (New York: Performing Arts Journal P, 1981), 118 and 122.
28. Peter Vaughn, "Forceful Acting Powers Cricket's Revisited 'True West,'" *Star Tribune,* Sept. 10, 1994.
29. Shepard, 7.
30. This is based on the direction and distance in the stage directions: 40 miles east of L.A.
31. Shepard, 7.
32. Ibid., 31.
33. Ibid., 12.
34. Ibid.
35. Ibid., 39.
36. Ibid., 10.
37. Duncan and Lambert, 281.

38. These different strategies characterized the approaches of different suburban communities near Los Angeles, including Hidden Hills, San Marino, and Bel Air. See Duncan and Lambert in *American Space/American Place: Geographies of the Contemporary United States* for further discussion.

39. Ibid., 281.

40. Shepard, 8.

41. Ibid., 37.

42. Mike Davis, "Fortress Los Angeles: The Militarization of Urban Space," in *Variations on a Theme Park: The New American City and the End of Public Space*, edited by Michael Sorkin (New York: Hill and Wang, 1992), 155.

43. Austin denounces Lee's cliché western by arguing, loudly, that the American West is a dead issue. This is certainly something that contributes to the play and the characterization of Austin and Lee. Despite the West being cliché and dead, it still holds some promise for Shepard's male characters. See Mark Busby, "Sam Shepard and Frontier Gothic" in *Frontier Gothic: Terror and Wonder at the Frontier in American Literature*; John M. Clum, "The Classic Western and Sam Shepard's Family Sagas" in *The Cambridge Companion to Sam Shepard*.

44. Shepard, 38.

45. See Yungduk Kim's "Shepard's *True West*: Demythisizing American Manhood"; Tsu-Chung Su's "The Double in Sam Shepard's *Buried Child* and *True West*," and Juan Tarancon's "Visions of the True West: Sam Shepard, Identity, and Myth" for examples.

46. Shepard, 37.

47. Shepard's dramaturgy demonstrates less of the concerns with rationalism and argument than Brecht's, or with those who were directly informed by Brecht, like Caryl Churchill or Tony Kushner. Of course, Shepard has linked his dramaturgy more with Samuel Beckett than anyone else with the story of reading *Waiting for Godot* as a teenager.

48. Bertolt Brecht, *Brecht on Theatre: The Development of an Aesthetic*, edited and translated by John Willett (New York: Hill and Wang, 1992), 86.

49. Lewis, 12.

50. Duncan and Lambert, 287.

51. Shepard, 3.

52. Reviews frequently highlighted words like "accessible" as Shepard moved into this stage of his writing career. See Leah D. Frank's "Shepard's 'West': A Tale Well Told"; Charles Isherwood, "True West" among others.

53. Chaudhuri, *Staging Place*, 29.

54. Ibid., 29.

55. Much of this debate derives from feminist criticism of theater. See Catherine Wiley's "The Matter with Manners: The New Woman and the Problem Play" in *Women in Theatre* for an example.

56. Shepard, 50.

57. Ibid., 49.

58. Austin agrees to help Lee write his screenplay if Lee takes him out on the desert.

59. Shepard, 49.
60. Ibid., 49.
61. Jean Baudrillard, *Simulacra and Simulation*, translated by Sheila Faria Glaser (Ann Arbor: U of Michigan P, 1994), 3.
62. Shepard, 56.
63. Jean Baudrillard, *America*, translated by Chris Turner (London: Verso, 1988), 98.
64. Duncan and Lambert, 274. In addition, see the works of Mike Davis works cited here, see Susan Anderson's "A City Called Heaven: Black Enchantment and Despair in Los Angeles" or Raymond A. Rocco's "Latino Los Angeles: Reframing Boundaries/Borders" both in *The City: Los Angeles and Urban Theory at the End of the Twentieth Century*, edited by Allen J. Scott and Edward W. Soja (Berkeley: U of California P, 1996).
65. See INTAR's website (http://www.intartheatre.org/) for details about the theater's history and mandate. See also Liesl Schillinger, "The Playwright Rewriting Latino Theater" and Christine Dolen's "Hispanic playwrights are finding acceptance, but not smooth sailing" for discussion of Machado's work with INTAR.
66. See Dolen's "Hispanic playwrights are finding acceptance, but not smooth sailing" for an overview of Machado's biography.
67. See Schillinger, "The Playwright Rewriting Latino Theater," *The New York Times*, Dec. 12, 2004 for discussion of Machado's early work with INTAR and Fornes.
68. Ibid.
69. One of the actors on this tour, Ms. Martinez-Casado, was reunited with brothers she had not seen in nearly decades and spent her off hours rediscovering places in Cuba. But her return to Cuba on the tour came with financial costs when she returned to the United States, including losing an advertising contract. See Navarro's "Building a Bridge, a Theater Troupe From the U.S. Is Embraced by Havana," *The New York Times*, Sept. 29, 1998, http://www.Lexisnexis.com (accessed Oct. 10, 2007).
70. Eduardo Machado, *Broken Eggs* in *The Floating Island Plays* (New York: Theatre Communications Group, 1991), 172.
71. These data come from a number of sources including the Woodland Hills-Tarzana Chamber of Commerce website (http://www.woodlandhillscc.net/Scripts/openExtra.asp?extra=5) and the city's entry on Wikipedia (http://en.wikipedia.org/wiki/Woodland_Hills,_California#Demographics).
72. Mike Davis, "Who Killed LA? A Political Autopsy," in *Dead Cities and Other Tales* (New York: The New P, 2002), 255.
73. See Davis's *Dead Cities and Other Tales* for discussion about the Watts Riots and the subsequent white flight that redefined the landscape of Los Angeles.
74. Davis, 255.
75. In making the Rifkins, a Jewish family, the "insiders" to this community, Machado complicates the notion of insider, of course. There is a long history of anti-Semitism in much of Los Angeles, which goes unacknowledged in *Broken Eggs*.
76. Machado, 210.

77. Ibid., 210.
78. In Cuba, before Castro, Sonia's family owned a bussing company and enjoyed considerable privilege as evidenced by their real estate and staff, all of which makes their new lives in Los Angeles even more disorienting. Notably, though, there seems little awareness of the class barriers evident in Cuba itself, even after the family has lived in the United States and reversed positions on the economic ladder.
79. Machado, 177.
80. Ibid., 180.
81. Ibid., 177.
82. Ibid., 181.
83. Oscar is gay, though he has remained closeted in regard to his family. Nevertheless, he taunts his father by making suggestions about his father's homosexual tendencies, an insult not just to Catholic beliefs but to the machismo of Cuban manhood.
84. Machado, 172.
85. Worthen is talking about the fallen woman play, where this woman is under scrutiny while other characters in the drama are anonymous and empowered to judge her, something suggested through keeping them offstage. They are never subject to the same scrutiny as the fallen woman. Much the same premise applies to discussion of suburbanism in Machado's play.
86. The story is simple: Osvaldo trying to go shopping in Canoga Park but not knowing how to buy produce. More significant is how he feels helpless in public, in part because of the class privilege he enjoyed when living in Cuba but also because of ethnic difference, with its cultural and linguistic barriers dividing the immigrant or exile from everyday life.
87. Cresswell, 154.
88. Machado, 200.
89. This goes back to Lizette's "No Cuba today," a plea that suggests her awareness of how ethnic difference and vice (drugs, crime, aberrance) become conflated in efforts to define cultural Others.
90. Worthen, 146.
91. Machado, 196.
92. Ibid.
93. Ibid., 218.
94. Ibid.
95. Ibid., 195.
96. This must have been particularly powerful during the debut of the play, in 1984, the middle years of Reagan's presidency and during the Cold War with Russia. Anything communist was defined as something "bad" in the cultural imagination of Americans during this time, and Siberia was the worst of these. This certainly complicated the portrait of Small Town America advocated by conservatism.
97. Machado, 208.

Chapter 4

1. Neil Smith, "New City, New Frontier: The Lower East Side as Wild, Wild West," in *Variations on a Theme Park: The New American City and the End of Public Place,* edited by Michael Sorkin (New York: Noonday P, 1992), 61.
2. The melee apparently raged back and forth for hours, leading to a short term "victory" for protestors which was ultimately undone by gentrification efforts in the long term.
3. Ibid., 61.
4. Anna Deavere Smith, Introduction to *Fires in the Mirror: Crown Heights, Brooklyn, and Other Identities* (New York: Anchor, 1993), xliii.
5. Carl Weber, "Brecht's 'Street Scene'—On Broadway, of all Places? A Conversation with Anna Deavere Smith," *The Brecht Yearbook* 20 (1995): 51–52.
6. Jim Masselos, "Postmodern Bombay: Fractured Discourses," in *Postmodern Cities and Spaces,* edited by Sophie Watson and Katherine Gibson (Oxford and Cambridge, MA: Blackwell, 1995), 204.
7. Lorraine Hansberry, *A Raisin in the Sun* (New York: Vintage, 1994), 93.
8. This involved Federal Housing Administration refusing to "guarantee loans or homes that were not in racially homogenous areas," a policy that was explicit until 1962 and, after being altered in that year, remained implicit as a way of discouraging racial integration (225). See M. Patricia Fernandez Kelly's "Slums, Ghettos, and Other Conundrums in the Anthropology of Lower Income Urban Enclaves" in *The Anthropology of Lower Income Urban Enclaves: The Case of East Harlem.*
9. M. Patricia Kelly, "Slums, Ghettos, and Other Conundrums in the Anthropology of Lower Income Urban Enclaves," in *The Anthropology of Lower Income Urban Enclaves: The Case of East Harlem,* edited by Judith Freidenberg (New York: New York Academy of Sciences, 1995), 226.
10. The revival was nominated for four Tony Awards, including Best Revival, Best Performance by a Leading Actress (which Phylicia Rashad won), Best Performance by a Featured Actress twice (Audra McDonald won in this category). Other awards included the Drama Desk Award (Rashad and McDonald), Outer Critics Circle Award (McDonald), Theater World Award (Sanaa Lathan).
11. Anna Deavere Smith, *Twilight Los Angeles, 1992* (New York: Anchor, 1994), 115.
12. Davis makes this argument directly in *Dead Cities and Other Tales.*
13. Djanet Sears, *Harlem Duet* (Winnipeg, MB: J. Gordon Shillingford, 2002), 21.
14. See Gerry Mooney in *Unruly Cities?: Order/Disorder* for discussions of the potential benefits of creating ethnic enclaves, including some regions that would overlap, denotatively, with ghettos.
15. Brecht, *Brecht on Theatre,* 86.
16. For discussion of this history, consider the following sources: Jervis Anderson's *This Was Harlem: A Cultural Portrait, 1900–1950*; Davis, *Dead Cities and Other Tales*; Susan Anderson's "A City Called Heaven: Black Enchantment and Despair in Los Angeles" in *The City: Los Angeles and Urban Theory at the End*

of the Twentieth Century; Davis's "Fortress Los Angeles: The Militarization of Urban Space" in *Variations on a Theme Park: The New American City and the End of Public Space.*

17. Benjamin Forest, "A New Geography of Identity? Race, Ethnicity, and American Citizenship," in *American Space/American Place: Geographies of the Contemporary United States,* edited by John A. Agnew and Jonathan M. Smith (Edinburgh: Edinburgh UP, 2002), 234.

18. Richard Ouzounian, "Staging of Harlem Duet Overcomes Casting Crisis: Toronto's Sears has 'Something to be Proud of,' " *Toronto Star,* Nov. 24, 2002, http://www.Lexisnexis.com (accessed Sept. 7, 2007).

19. The problems were apparently with Sears's directing. See Kamal al-Solaylee's "Baring the Burden of Race."

20. See Malcolm Kelly's "One Playwright in Search of Herself: Djanet Sears Says Her New Play, Like All Her Work, is about Her Black Experience."

21. Kamal al-Solaylee, "Stratford Finally Changes its Tune," *The Globe and Mail,* June 16, 2006, http://www.Lexisnexis.com (accessed Sept. 7, 2007).

22. Ouzounian.

23. Ibid.

24. This was part of Brecht's theory of *Vrefremdungseffeckt,* particularly that for the actor. Instead of becoming the character portrayed, Brecht worked on strategies for the actor to stay outside the character—delivering lines in the third person rather than the first—in ways that were like quoting dialogue. The goal was to encourage critical distance in actors and audiences. See *Brecht on Theatre.*

25. al Solaylee.

26. Sears, 21.

27. Donna Bailey Nurse, "An Othello Built for the Nineties IN PERSON: Djanet Sears Mixes Shakespeare and the Blues to Tackle Current Taboos in Harlem Duets," *The Globe and Mail,* Nov. 18, 1997, http://www.Lexisnexis.com (accessed Sept. 7, 2007).

28. See Anderson, *This Was Harlem* for this history.

29. Sears, 106.

30. Billie's remarks come, notably, toward the end of the play: after the breakup of Billie and Othello and many of the scenes about the history of racism that persists in Harlem. Naturally, then, audiences view such comments through a skeptical framing during this scene.

31. Lynch, *The Image of the City,* 26.

32. Ibid., 26.

33. Jervis Anderson, *This Was Harlem: A Cultural Portrait 1900–1950* (New York: Noonday, 1982), 238.

34. Sears, 66.

35. Ibid., 25.

36. Forest, 248–249.

37. Sears, 106.

38. Ibid., 79.

39. Peter Marcuse, "Not Chaos, but Walls: Postmodernism and the Partitioned City," in *Postmodern Cities and Spaces,* edited by Sophie Watson and Katherine Gibson (Oxford and Cambridge, MA: Blackwell, 1995), 244.
40. Ibid., 248.
41. Sears, 53.
42. Ibid., 57.
43. al-Solaylee.
44. Sears, 66.
45. Ibid., 53.
46. Ibid., 75.
47. Ibid., 101.
48. Ibid., 63.
49. Ibid., 103.
50. The purpose of titles for Brecht was twofold: to locate the incidents about to occur in a historical, cultural, and political context so that the incidents were framed by and framing that context. And, to undermine the realist emphasis on suspense: if audiences already know what is going to happen, then are less likely to be emotionally swept up in the scenes. *Harlem Duet* comes closer to the first part.
51. Sears, 24.
52. See Freidenberg's "Lower Income Urban Enclaves: Introduction" in *The Anthropology of Lower Income Urban Enclaves: The Case of East Harlem.*
53. Sears, 33.
54. Ibid., 34.
55. Ibid., 47.
56. Ibid., 51.
57. Ibid., 92.
58. Foucault, "Of Other Spaces," 25.
59. See Benjamin Genocchio's "Discourse, Discontinuity, Difference: The Question of 'Other' Spaces" in *Postmodern Cities and Spaces* for just a hint of the bandwagon appeal of heterotopia.
60. Martin Luther King Jr., "I have a Dream," August 28, 1963.
61. Sears, 54.
62. Ibid., 116.
63. Smith, Introduction to *Twilight Los Angeles, 1992,* xvii.
64. Patti Hartigan, "Anna Deavere Smith's Triumphant 'Twilight,'" *The Boston Globe,* June 19, 1996, http://www.Lexisnexis.com (accessed July 4, 2007).
65. Struck by Smith's performance in *Twilight Los Angeles, 1992,* a number of reviewers repeated this error. The history of documentary theater is, actually, quite long and well documented. See Gary Fisher Dawson's *Documentary Theatre in the United States: An Historical Survey and Analysis of Its Content, Form, and Stagecraft,* 1999.
66. Bernard Weinraub, "Condensing a Riot's Cacophony into the Voice of One Woman," *The New York Times,* June 16, 1993, http://www.Lexisnexis.com (accessed July 4, 2007).

67. Christopher Meeks, "*Twilight Los Angeles, 1992,*" *The Daily Variety,* June 15, 1993, http://www.Lexisnexis.com (accessed July 4, 2007).

68. Meeks's concern is specifically with Smith's imitation of "Stanley K. Sheinbaum's New York accent," but it suggests a larger concern that has been echoed about Smith's performance of the characters. In adopting their mannerisms and vocal inflections, there is always the danger that Smith reduces the individuals—and the communities they represent—to ethnic types.

69. J. Chris Westgate, "'This Electrifying Moment': An Interview with Anna Deavere Smith," *Writing on the Edge: On Writing and Teaching Writing* 15, no.1 (2004): 105.

70. Michael Kuchwara, "'*Twilight: Los Angeles, 1992*' by Anna Deavere Smith Opens Off-Broadway," *The Associated Press,* March 23, 1994, http://www.Lexisnexis.com (accessed Oct. 10, 2007).

71. David Patrick Stearns, "Broadway's Glare Hides 'Twilight,'" *USA Today,* June 10, 1994, http://www.Lexisnexis.com (accessed July 4, 2007).

72. Her becoming this conduit is certainly not without controversy. Obviously, having the voices of Koreans or Latinos or other immigrant groups filtered through the body/voice of an African American woman has a number of consequences about representation and agency that could actually reinforce some of the distance between ethnic groups in Los Angeles or elsewhere.

73. See *Dead Cities and Other Tales.*

74. Hartigan.

75. Brecht would frequently relocate concerns of his day in the past, with the assumption that this relocation would both alienate audiences from the events (allowing them to be more critical about the event itself) and demonstrate how the events were products of historical forces. Smith does much the same in the local geography of Los Angeles.

76. Brecht, 122.

77. Ibid., 122.

78. Smith is a little uncomfortable with the term "mimicry," perhaps because of the implications of caricaturing. Nevertheless, this term is one frequently invoked when describing her performances. See Lloyd Rose, "A Singular Talent For Multiple Parts"; Dennis Harvey, "Twilight Los Angeles" and others.

79. Smith, 14.

80. Ibid., 15.

81. Part of the criticism of *Twilight Los Angeles* as a response to the rioting is that it takes on too much without making judgments about responsibility or significance. Complaints suggest that there is a certain sentimentalism about Smith's approach, though this overstates the issue. Others disagree and suggest that there is something valuable in having many voices heard, even if without filtering.

82. Smith, 15.

83. Ibid., 16.

84. Ibid., 17.

85. Ibid., 33.

86. Ibid.
87. Ibid., 38.
88. Ibid., 100.
89. Ibid., 101.
90. Ibid.
91. Ibid., 161.
92. Ibid., 160.
93. Ibid., 159.
94. Ibid., 160.
95. Ibid., 161.
96. Ibid., 101.
97. This was an organization dedicated to the defense of the four African Americans who pulled Reginald Denny from his truck and assaulted in on the street.
98. Smith, 175.
99. Delmos Jones, "The Anthropology of Lower Income Urban Enclaves," in *The Anthropology of Lower Income Urban Enclaves: The Case of East Harlem,* edited by Judith Freidenberg (New York: New York Academy of Sciences, 1995), 195.
100. When interviewed during the writing of this book, she emphasized distance, literal and experiential, from one another as central to the nature of Los Angeles. See "This Electrifying Moment."
101. Smith, 162.
102. Ibid., 251–252.
103. Victor M. Valle and Rodolfo D. Torres, *Latino Metropolis* (Minneapolis, MN and London: U of Minnesota P, 2000), 51–52.
104. Ibid., 47.
105. Mike Davis, "Burning All Illusions," in *Dead Cities: And Other Tales* (New York: The New P, 2002), 232.
106. Harlins was shot, theoretically, in self-defense as she was trying to rob the grocery, but the African American community became outraged with not just the incident but the LAPD's handling of the case. See *Dead Cities and Other Tales* for more details.
107. Smith, 3.
108. Ibid., 2.
109. Ibid., 245.
110. Ibid., 107.
111. Denny had no memory of being rescued by the four Samaritans, as he was suffering from a concussion and other injuries.
112. Smith, 108.
113. Ibid., 110.
114. Ibid., 111.
115. Ibid., 172.
116. Ibid., 177.
117. Ibid., 178.
118. Hartigan.

119. Smith, 102.
120. Ibid., 169.
121. Ibid., 187.
122. Enough emphasis falls on this juxtaposing that it becomes evident in production, as demonstrated by Hartigan's review of the 1996 revival in Boston, where she makes note of the same contrast of Denny and Parker outlined here. See "Anna Deavere Smith's triumphant 'Twilight.' "
123. Brecht, 144.
124. This, too, comes from Brecht. At the heart of epic theater, at least as theorized by Brecht, was the notion that the theater can function pedagogically, that is, it can develop our critical faculties for examining the world. See *Brecht on Theatre.*
125. Smith, Interview by Westgate, 108.
126. Worthen, *Modern Drama and the Rhetoric of Theater,* 146.
127. Smith, 232.
128. Ibid., 233.
129. This terminology comes from Janelle Reinelt's discussion of *Angels in America,* which posits a number of necessary conditions for the production to become a successful epic play. See "Notes on Angels in America as American Epic Theater."
130. Robin Bernstein, "Rodney King, Shifting Modes of Vision, and Anna Deavere Smith's *Twilight Los Angeles, 1992,*" *Journal of Dramatic Theory and Criticism* 14, no.2 (2000): 132.
131. Ibid., 132.
132. Smith, 67.
133. These quarters range from privileged regions to tenements and abandoned portions of the city. See Marcuse, "Not Chaos, but Walls: Postmodernism and the Partitioned City."
134. Smith, 200.
135. Ibid., 256.
136. Ibid., 254–255.
137. Ibid., 255.
138. Ibid.
139. Ibid., 167.

Chapter 5

1. Chalsa M. Loo, *Chinatown: Most Time, Hard Time* (New York: Praeger, 1991), 6.
2. Olalquiaga, *Megalopolis,* 80–81.
3. Ibid., 76.
4. Guillermo Gomez-Pena, *Warrior for Gringostroika: Essays, Performance Texts, and Poetry* (Saint Paul, MN: Graywolf P, 1993), 39.
5. Loo's *Chinatown* begins with a summary of some of the violence against immigrants, particularly Asian immigrants during the 1980s, including intimidation, assault, and killings.

6. Though I do not attend to them in the following discussion, the differences between immigrant, exile, and refugee have been thoroughly theorized and add another layer of complexity to the conflicts of newcomer self-definition and urbanism. See Irit Rogoff, *Terra Infirma: Geography's Visual Culture*, 2000; *Travellers' Tales: Narratives of Home and Displacement*, 1994; Arjun Appadurai, *Modernity at Large: Cultural Dimensions of Globalization*, 2000.

7. Dolores Prida, "The Show Must Go On," in *Breaking Boundaries: Latina Writing and Critical Readings*, edited by Asuncion Horno-Delgado et. al. (Amherst: U of Massachusetts P, 1989), 182.

8. Chaudhuri, *Staging Place*, 202.

9. Salman Rushdie, *Imaginary Homelands: Essays and Criticism 1981–1991* (London: Granta, 1991), 278.

10. Ibid.

11. There is a long history of this conflation in U.S. conception of immigration. See Chalsa M. Loo, *Chinatown: Most Time, Hard Time*; Valle, Victor M. and Rodolfo D. Torres, *Latino Metropolis*.

12. Loo, 63.

13. Ibid., 62.

14. Ibid.

15. Ibid., 66.

16. Ibid., 67–68.

17. Valle and Torres, *Latino Metropolis*, 9.

18. Ibid., 9.

19. Mike Davis, "The New Industrial Peonage," in *Dead Cities: And Other Tales* (New York: The New P, 2002), 197.

20. Ibid.

21. Valle and Torres, 9.

22. Jorge Huerta, *Chicano Drama: Performance, Society and Myth* (Cambridge: Cambridge UP, 2000), 3.

23. See Loo; see also Min Zhou, *Chinatown: The Socioeconomic Potential of an Urban Enclave*.

24. David Henry Hwang, Introduction to *FOB* in *Trying to Find Chinatown: The Selected Plays* (New York: Theatre Communications Group, 2000), 6.

25. Jay Mathews, " 'Golden Gates': David Henry Hwang: Burning Bridges," *The Washington Post*, Jan. 30, 1994, http://www.Lexisnexis.com (accessed March 12, 2007).

26. This discussion is largely limited to reviews of the plays and articles about Hwang, as *FOB* has garnered little scholarship. See Jeremy Green's "David Hwang Riding on the Hyphen," Patti Hartigan's "Hwang's Political Stage: Writer Wonders How Much to Stir the Melting Pot," and Jay Matthews's " 'Golden Gates': David Henry Hwang: Burning Bridges" for examples of autobiographical readings.

27. Hwang's background was not limited by growing up in Chinatown and had planned to become a businessman or banker before going to Stanford University. See Kevin Kelly's "Hwang Looks Beyond 'Face Value.' "

28. These include *Curse of the Starving Class* (1978), *Buried Child* (1979), and *True West* (1980).
29. Jeremy Gerard, "David Hwang: Riding the Hyphen," *The New York Times,* May 13, 1988, http://www.Lexisnexis.com (accessed March 12, 2007).
30. Ibid.
31. Kevin Kelly, "M. Butterfly, Miss Saigon, and Mr. Hwang," *The Boston Globe,* Sept. 9, 1990, http://www.Lexisnexis.com (accessed March 12, 2007).
32. See Gerard.
33. Mel Gussow, "Culture Shock in Hwang's 'F.O.B.,'" *The New York Times,* May 20, 1990, http://www.Lexisnexis.com (accessed Jan. 13, 2008).
34. Karen Shimakawa, *National Abjection: The Asian American Body Onstage* (Durham, NC and London: Duke UP, 2002), 86–87.
35. Ibid., 3.
36. Ibid.
37. Ibid., 17.
38. Loo, 16.
39. Min Zhou, *Chinatown: The Socioeconomic Potential of an Urban Enclave* (Philadelphia, PA: Temple UP, 1992), 83.
40. This commonality, of course, speaks not just the possibilities of influence but further to how powerful this double bind is felt in Asian American communities, which is documented by sociologists.
41. Shimakawa, 89.
42. Ibid.
43. See Loo, *Chinatown: Most Time, Hard Time* and Zhou, *Chinatown: The Socioeconomic Potential of an Urban Enclave.*
44. David Henry Hwang, *FOB* in *Trying to Find Chinatown: The Selected Plays* (New York: Theatre Communications Group, 2000), 7.
45. Ibid.
46. Ibid.
47. Ibid.
48. Loo offers a telling description of these living conditions, which include overcrowding and poor social services among other problems, both historically and today.
49. Hwang, 7.
50. Ibid., 22.
51. Ibid.
52. Ibid., 23.
53. Ibid., 25.
54. Ibid., 26.
55. See Sorkin, *Variations on a Theme Park: The New American City and the End of Public Place,* Baudrillard, *America,* and Findlay, *Magic Lands: Western Cityscapes and American Culture After 1940* among others, for discussion here.
56. Hwang, 33.
57. Ibid.
58. See the sociological interviews conducted by Loo and Zhou.

59. Hwang, 33.
60. Ibid.
61. Ibid.
62. Ibid., 30.
63. Ibid., 31.
64. Ibid.
65. Ibid.
66. Ibid.
67. Ibid.
68. Ibid., 30.
69. As with Rivera's New York City in *Marisol,* these boundaries are distinctly racialized in Hwang's Los Angeles in *FOB.* See Chapter 1 for details.
70. Hwang, 39.
71. See chapter four of Zhou's *Chinatown: The Socioeconomic Potential of an Urban Enclave* for discussion of immigrants from Hong Kong.
72. Hwang, 21.
73. Ibid., 22.
74. Ibid.
75. Ibid., 37.
76. Ibid.
77. Ibid.
78. Ibid., 11.
79. Ibid., 14.
80. Ibid., 16.
81. Edward Soja, *Thirdspace,* 31.
82. Patti Hartigan, "Hwang's Political Stage: Writer Wonders How Much to Stir the Melting Pot," *The Boston Globe,* April 15, 1994, http://www.Lexisnexis.com (accessed March 12, 2007).
83. Hwang, 51.
84. Huerta, 166.
85. Ibid., 166.
86. This review, "The Poetics of Chisme," was published *Poetry Flash* and cited in Huerta (161).
87. See Theatre Rhinoceros's website (http://www.therhino.org/) for its history.
88. See Huerta, 161–162.
89. Cherrie Moraga, *Giving Up the Ghost Heroes and Saints and Other Plays* (Albuquerque, NM: West End P, 1994), 5.
90. Ibid., 5.
91. The fundamental premise behind Brecht's theater was that it was not mimetically representational and it would invoke its environment through metonymy: that is, through key signifiers that would suggest that environment without ever distracting audiences from being in a theater.
92. The Prologue of *Henry V* begins with an acknowledgement of the limitations of Elizabethan theater, which cannot "cram/Within this wooden O the

very casques/That did affright the air at Agincourt." Therefore, the Prologue invites audiences to put "your imaginary forces [to] work" and "Piece out our imperfections with your thoughts." Moraga's staging of the barrio falls in this premise.

93. Moraga, 6.
94. Ibid., 6.
95. Performance here includes the connotations not just of theater but identity: that Corky performs a particular subject-position in her barrio-world. See Lou Rosenberg's "The House of Difference: Gender, Culture, and the Subject-in-Process on the American Stage" for details.
96. Moraga, 25.
97. Ibid.
98. Ibid.
99. Ibid., 26.
100. Ibid., 29.
101. Brady's argument is that Chicano literature is particularly concerned with the interplay of geography and female vulnerability. See chapters 3 and 4th of *Extinct Lands, Scarred Bodies: Chicana Literature and the Reinvention of Space* for more discussion.
102. Moraga, 8.
103. Ibid., 9.
104. Ibid.
105. See Mike Davis in *Dead Tales and Other Cities* and "Fortress Los Angeles: The Militarization of Urban Space" in *Variations on a Theme Park* for discussion of this polarized demography.
106. Victor M. Valle and Rodolfo D. Torres have documented that, politically, Hispanics in Los Angeles were almost invisible during the 1980s and 1990s. See *Latino Metropolis.*
107. Moraga, 19.
108. Ibid., 24.
109. Ibid., 19.
110. Ibid.
111. Ibid., 17.
112. Lou Rosenberg, "The House of Difference: Gender, Culture, and the Subject-in-Process on the American Stage," in *Critical Essays: Gay and Lesbian Writers of Color,* edited by Emmanuel S. Nelson (New York and London: Haworth P, 1993), 100.
113. Moraga, 17.
114. Ibid., 6.
115. Cresswell, *In Place/Out of Place,* 8.
116. Ibid., 42.
117. Ibid., 45.
118. Ibid., 47.
119. Ibid.

120. Ibid.
121. See Huerta, 25.
122. Huerta, 166.
123. Moraga, 23.
124. Ibid., 33.
125. Ibid.
126. Ibid., 23.
127. Cresswell, 165.
128. Moraga, 5.
129. This alternative spelling is used in Moraga's play, though it would probably only be evident to readers of the play.
130. Ibid., 14.
131. Ibid., 19.
132. Ibid., 25.
133. Ibid., 35.
134. Madan Soup, "Home and Identity," in *Travellers' Tales: Narratives of Home and Displacement,* edited by George Robertson et al. (London and New York: Routledge, 1994), 101–102.
135. Moraga, 35.
136. Huerta, 3.
137. Valle and Torres, 56.
138. Moraga, 35.

Bibliography

Adorno, T. W. "Culture Industry Reconsidered." In *The Audience Studies Reader*, edited by Will Brooker and Deborah Jermyn, 55–60. London: Routledge, 2003.

Agnew, John A. Introduction to *American Space/American Place: Geographies of the Contemporary United States*, edited by John A. Agnew and Jonathan M. Smith. Edinburgh: Edinburgh UP, 2002.

al-Solaylee, Kamal. "Baring the Burden of Race." *The Globe and Mail*, July 3, 2006, http://www.Lexisnexis.com (accessed Sept. 7, 2007).

———. "Stratford Finally Changes Its Tune." *The Globe and Mail*, June 16, 2006, http://www.Lexisnexis.com (accessed Sept. 7, 2007).

Alter, Robert. *Imagined Cities: Urban Experience and the Language of the Novel*. New Haven and London: Yale UP, 2005.

Anderson, Jervis. *This Was Harlem: A Cultural Portrait 1900–1950*. New York: Noonday, 1982.

Anderson, Susan. "A City Called Heaven: Black Enchantment and Despair in Los Angeles." In *The City: Los Angeles and Urban Theory at the End of the Twentieth Century*, edited by Allen J. Scott and Edward W. Soja, 336–364. Berkeley: U of California P, 1996.

Appadurai, Arjun. *Modernity at Large: Cultural Dimensions of Globalization*. Minneapolis and London: U of Minnesota P, 2000.

Arnonson, Arnold. *American Set Design*. New York: Theatre Communications Group, 1985.

———. "Design for *Angels in America*: Envisioning the Millennium." In *Approaching the Millennium: Essays on Angels in America*, edited by Deborah R. Geis and Steven F. Kruger, 213–226. Ann Arbor: U of Michigan P, 1997.

Auerbach, Doris. *Sam Shepard, Arthur Kopit, and the Off Broadway Theater*. Boston: Twayne P, 1982.

Austin, Michael. "Theology for the Approaching Millennium: *Angels in America*, Activism, and the American Religion." *Dialogue: A Journal of Mormon Thought* 30, no. 1 (1997): 25–44.

Basso, Keith H. "Wisdom Sits in Places: Notes on a Western Apache Landscape." In *Senses of Place*, edited by Steven Feld and Keith H. Basso, 53–90. Santa Fe: School of American Research P, 1996.

Baudrillard, Jean. *America*. Translated by Chris Turner. London: Verso, 1988.

———. *Simulacra and Simulation*. Translated by Sheila Faria Glaser. Ann Arbor: U of Michigan P, 1994.

Beaufort, John. "Return of the Sprightly 1901, Comedy That Made a Star of Ethel Barrymore; *True West* Play by Sam Shepard." *Christian Science Monitor*, Dec. 31, 1980.

Bender, Thomas and William R. Taylor. "Culture and Architecture: Some Aesthetic Tensions in the Shaping of Modern New York City." In *Visions of the Modern City: Essays in History, Art, and Literature*, edited by William Sharpe and Leonard Wallock, 189–219. Baltimore and London: The Johns Hopkins UP, 1987.

Bennett, Susan. *Theatre Audiences: A Theory of Production and Reception*. London and New York: Routledge, 1990.

Bernstein, Robin. "Rodney King, Shifting Modes of Vision, and Anna Deavere Smith's *Twilight Los Angeles, 1992*." *Journal of Dramatic Theory and Criticism* 14, no.2 (2000): 121–134.

Betsky, Aaron. "Riding the Train to the Aleph: Eight Utopias for Los Angeles." In *Heterotopia: Postmodern Utopia and the Body Politic*, edited by Tobin Siebers, 96–121. Ann Arbor: U of Michigan P, 1997.

Blanchard, Jayne M. "Trying to Reclaim Life with Father; Children Now Grown Struggle to Capture Past in 'Three Days of Rain.'" *The Washington Times*, Feb. 5, 2000, http://www.Lexisnexis.com (accessed Oct. 7, 2006).

Bottoms, Stephen J. "Re-Staging Roy: Citizen Cohn and the Search for Xanadu." *Theatre Journal* 48, no.2 (1996): 157–184.

Bowers, Jane Palatini. "The Composition That All the World Can See: Gertrude Stein's Theater Landscapes." In *Land/Scape/Theater*, edited by Elinor Fuchs and Una Chaudhuri, 121–144. Ann Arbor: U of Michigan P, 2002.

Brady, Mary Patricia. *Extinct Lands, Scarred Bodies: Chicana Literature and the Reinvention of Space*. Ann Arbor: UMI, 1996.

Brecht, Bertolt. *Brecht on Theatre: The Development of an Aesthetic*, edited and translated by John Willett. New York: Hill and Wang, 1992.

Bruckner, D. J. R. "Stage: *Repertorio Espanol's 'Revoltillo.'*" *The New York Times*, Feb. 9, 1988, http://www.Lexisnexis.com (accessed Oct. 10, 2007).

Brustein, Robert. Review of *Marisol*, by José Rivera. *The New Republic* 209, no. 3–4 (1993): 29–30.

Bryant-Bertail, Sarah. *Space and Time in Epic Theater: The Brechtian Legacy*. New York: Camden House, 2000.

Busby, Mark. "Sam Shepard and Frontier Gothic." In *Frontier Gothic: Terror and Wonder at the Frontier in American Literature*, edited by David Mogen, Scott P. Sanders, and Joanne B. Karpinski, 84–93. London and Toronto: Fairleigh Dickinson UP, 1993.

Carlson, Marvin. *The Haunted Stage: The Theatre as Memory Machine*. Ann Arbor: U of Michigan P, 2001.

———. *Places of Performance: The Semiotics of Theatre Architecture*. Ithaca and London: Cornell UP, 1989.

———. *Theories of the Theatre: A Historical and Critical Survey from the Greeks to the Present*. Ithaca and London: Cornell UP, 1984.

Casey, Edward S. "How to Get from Space to Place in a Fairly Short Stretch of Time." In *Senses of Place,* edited by Steven Feld and Keith H. Basso, 13–52. Santa Fe: School of American Research P, 1996.

Catsoulis, Jeannette. "Three Days of Rain." *The New York Times,* Sept. 30, 2005, http://www.Lexisnexis.com (accessed Oct. 7, 2006).

Chapman, Geoff. "A Brittle Exploration of Race and Gender." *The Toronto Star,* Nov. 2, 1997, http://www.Lexisnexis.com (accessed Sept. 7, 2007).

Chaudhuri, Una. "Land/Scape/Theory." In *Land/Scape/Theater,* edited by Elinor Fuchs and Una Chaudhuri, 11–29. Ann Arbor: U of Michigan P, 2002.

———. *Staging Place: The Geography of Modern Drama.* Ann Arbor: U of Michigan P, 1995.

Chaudhuri, Una and Elinor Fuchs. Introduction to *Land/Scape/Theater,* edited by Elinor Fuchs and Una Chaudhuri. Ann Arbor: U of Michigan P, 2002.

Christiansen, Adrienne E. and Jeremy J. Hanson. "Comedy as Cure for Tragedy: ACT UP and the Rhetoric of Aids." *Quarterly Journal of Speech* 82 (1996): 157–170.

Clark, Sally. *Lost Souls and Missing Persons.* Burnaby, British Columbia: Talonbooks, 1998.

Clum, John M. "The Classic Western and Sam Shepard's Family Sagas." In *The Cambridge Companion to Sam Shepard,* edited by Matthew Roudané, 171–188. Cambridge: Cambridge UP, 2002.

Coulbourn, John. "Djanet's Sears' Play is 'Lyrical, Witty, Angry, and Insightful.'" *The Toronto Sun,* July 4, 2006, http://www.Lexisnexis.com (accessed Sept. 7, 2007).

Crawford, Margaret. "The World in a Shopping Mall." In *Variations on a Theme Park: The New American City and the End of Public Space,* edited by Michael Sorkin, 3–30. New York: Hill and Wang, 1992.

Cresswell, Tim. *In Place/Out of Place: Geography, Ideology, and Transgression.* Minneapolis and London: U of Minnesota P, 1996.

Davis, Mike. *City of Quartz: Excavating the Future in Los Angeles.* New York: Vintage, 1992.

———. *Dead Cities and Other Tales.* New York: The New P, 2002.

———. "Fortress Los Angeles: The Militarization of Urban Space." In *Variations on a Theme Park: The New American City and the End of Public Space,* edited by Michael Sorkin, 154–180. New York: Hill and Wang, 1992.

de Certeau, Michel. *The Practice of Everyday Life.* Translated by Steven Rendall. Berkeley: U of California P, 1988.

Dolan, Jill. "Performance, Utopia, and the 'Utopian Performative.'" *Theatre Journal* 53, no.3 (2001): 455–459.

Dolen, Christine. "Hispanic Playwrights are Finding Acceptance, But Not Smooth Sailing." *The Miami Herald,* June 5, 2003, http://www.Lexisnexis.com (accessed Oct. 17, 2006).

———. "Playwright Brings to the Stage a Portrait of Cuban Exile Experience." *The Miami Herald,* May 1, 2003, http://www.Lexisnexis.com (accessed Oct. 17, 2006).

Donahue, Anne Marie. "Accept Mystery in 'Three Days.'" *The Boston Globe,* April 21, 1999, http://www.Lexisnexis.com (accessed Oct. 7, 2006).

Duncan, James S. and David R. Lambert. "Landscape, Aesthetics, and Power." In *American Space/American Place: Geographies of the Contemporary United States,* edited by John A. Agnew and Jonathan M. Smith, 264–291. Edinburgh: Edinburgh UP, 2002.

Elam, Keir. *The Semiotics of Theatre and Drama.* 2nd ed. London and New York: Routledge, 2002.

Evans, Greg. "Angels in America: A Gay Fantasia on National Themes." *Daily Variety,* Nov. 10, 1992, http://www.Lexisnexis.com (accessed Nov. 27, 2007).

Feliciano, Wilma. " 'I Am A Hyphenated American': Interview with Dolores Prida." *Latin American Theatre Review* 29, no.1 (1995): 113–118.

Findlay, John M. *Magic Lands: Western Cityscapes and American Culture After 1940.* Berkeley: U of California P, 1992.

Fink, Joel G. "Review of *Marisol,* by José Rivera." *Theatre Journal* 48, no.1 (1996): 101–102.

Forest, Benjamin. "A New Geography of Identity? Race, Ethnicity, and American Citizenship." In *American Space/American Place: Geographies of the Contemporary United States,* edited by John A. Agnew and Jonathan M. Smith, 231–263. Edinburgh: Edinburgh UP, 2002.

Foucault, Michel. *The Order of Things: An Archaeology of the Human Sciences.* London and New York: Routledge, 2003.

———. "Of Other Spaces." *Diacritics* 16, no.1 (1986): 22–27.

Frank, Leah D. "Shepard's 'West': A Tale Well Told." *The New York Times,* April 28, 1985, http://www.Lexisnexis.com (accessed March 3, 2006).

———. "Theater: Cain and Abel in California." *The New York Times,* May 3, 1987, http://www.Lexisnexis.com (accessed March 3, 2006).

Freidenberg, Judith. Introduction to *The Anthropology of Lower Income Urban Enclaves: The Case of East Harlem,* edited by Judith Freidenberg. New York: New York Academy of Sciences, 1995.

Fricker, Karen. "Another Playwright Confronts an Angel and the Apocalypse." *New York Times,* May 16, 1993, http://www.Lexisnexis.com (accessed Jan. 22, 2006).

Fuchs, Elinor. "Reading for Landscape: The Case of American Drama." In *Land/Scape/Theater,* edited by Elinor Fuchs and Una Chaudhuri, 30–50. Ann Arbor: U of Michigan P, 2002.

Fuchs, Elinor, Bonnie Marranca, and Gerald Rabkin. "The Politics of Representation." In *Conversations on Art and Performance,* edited by Bonnie Marranca and Gautam Dasgupta, 311–328. Baltimore and London: The Johns Hopkins UP, 1999.

Garner, Stanton B. Jr. "Urban Landscapes, Theatrical Encounters: Staging the City." In *Land/Scape/Theater,* edited by Elinor Fuchs and Una Chaudhuri, 94–118. Ann Arbor: U of Michigan P, 2002.

Genocchio, Benjamin. "Discourse, Discontinuity, Difference: The Question of 'Other' Spaces." In *Postmodern Cities and Spaces,* edited by Sophie Watson and Katherine Gibson, 35–46. Oxford and Cambridge, MA: Blackwell, 1995.

Gerard, Jeremy. "David Hwang: Riding the Hyphen." *The New York Times,* May 13, 1988, http://www.Lexisnexis.com (accessed March 12, 2007).

Giamo, Benedict. *On the Bowery: Confronting Homelessness in American Society.* Iowa City: U of Iowa P, 1989.

Goldberger, Paul. "Architecture; A Huge Architecture Show in Times Square." *The New York Times,* Sept. 9, 1990, http://www.Lexisnexis.com (accessed May 7, 2007).

Gomez-Pena, Guillermo. *Warrior for Gringostroika: Essays, Performance Texts, and Poetry.* Saint Paul: Graywolf P, 1993.

Greenberg, Richard. *Three Days of Rain. Three Days of Rain and Other Plays.* New York: Grove, 1999.

Gussow, Mel. "Critic's Notebook: About Death, Bad Dreams and D. Boone Debunked." *The New York Times,* March 26, 1992, http://www.Lexisnexis.com (accessed Feb. 24, 2007).

———. "Culture Shock in Hwang's 'F.O.B.'" *The New York Times,* May 20, 1990, http://www.Lexisnexis.com (accessed Jan. 13, 2008).

Hansberry, Lorraine. *A Raisin in the Sun.* New York: Vintage, 1994.

Hartigan, Patti. "Anna Deavere Smith's Triumphant 'Twilight.'" *The Boston Globe,* June 19, 1996, http://www.Lexisnexis.com (accessed July 4, 2007).

———. "Hwang's Political Stage: Writer Wonders How Much to Stir the Melting Pot." *The Boston Globe,* April 15, 1994, http://www.Lexisnexis.com (accessed March 12, 2007).

———. "Pared-Down 'Angels' Full of Humanity." *The Boston Globe,* May 3, 1996, http://www.Lexisnexis.com (accessed Nov. 27, 2007).

———. "Smith's 'Twilight' Illuminates Racial Rift." *The Boston Globe,* June 7, 1996, http://www.Lexisnexis.com (accessed July 4, 2007).

Harvey, David. *The Condition of Postmodernity: An Enquiry into the Origins of Cultural Change.* Cambridge, MA: Basil Blackwell, 1990.

———. *Social Justice and the City.* London: Edward Arnold, 1973.

———. *Spaces of Hope.* Berkeley and Los Angeles: U of California P, 2000.

Harvey, Dennis. "Review of *Twilight Los Angeles, 1992.*" *Daily Variety,* Feb. 18, 2000, http://www.Lexisnexis.com (accessed July 4, 2007).

Henderson, Mary C. *The City and the Theatre: The History of New York Playhouses: A 250-Year Journey from Bowling Green to Times Square.* New York: Back Stage, 2004.

Howard, Pamela. *What Is Scenography?* London and New York: Routledge, 2002.

Huerta, Jorge. *Chicano Drama: Performance, Society and Myth.* Cambridge: Cambridge UP, 2000.

Hwang, David Henry. *FOB.* In *Trying to Find Chinatown: The Selected Plays.* New York: Theatre Communications Group, 2000.

———. *Trying to Find Chinatown.* In *Trying to Find Chinatown: The Selected Plays.* New York: Theatre Communications Group, 2000.

Isherwood, Charles. "True West." *Daily Variety,* March 10, 2000, http://www.Lexisnexis.com (accessed March 3, 2006).

Issacharoff, Michael. *Discourse as Performance*. Stanford: Stanford UP, 1989.

Jackson, John Brinckerhoff. "The Order of a Landscape: Reason and Religion in Newtonian America." In *The Interpretation of Ordinary Landscapes: Geographical Essays*, edited by D. W. Meinig, 153–163. Oxford: Oxford UP, 1979.

Jakle, John A. "Landscapes Redesigned for the Automobile." In *The Making of the American Landscape*, edited by Michael P. Conzen, 293–310. Boston: Unwin Hyman, 1990.

Jameson, Fredric. *Postmodernism, or the Cultural Logic of Late Capitalism*. Durham: Duke UP, 1991.

Janson, H. W. *History of Art: A Survey of the Major Visual Arts from the Dawn of History to the Present Day*. Englewood Cliffs, N.J.: Prentice-Hall, 1969.

Jefferson, Margo. "Castro: Patience Heals Economic Rift." *The New York Times*, Sept 7, 1998, http://www.Lexisnexis.com (accessed Oct. 10, 2007).

Jencks, Charles. "Hetero-Architecture and the L.A. School." In *The City: Los Angeles and Urban Theory at the End of the Twentieth Century*, edited by Allen J. Scott and Edward W. Soja, 47–75. Berkeley: U of California P, 1996.

Jones, Delmos J. "The Anthropology of Lower Income Urban Enclaves." In *The Anthropology of Lower Income Urban Enclaves: The Case of East Harlem*, edited by Judith Freidenberg, 189–203. New York: New York Academy of Sciences, 1995.

Kahn, Miriam. "Your Place and Mine: Sharing Emotional Landscapes in Wamira, Papua New Guinea." In *Senses of Place*, edited by Steven Feld and Keith H. Basso, 167–196. Santa Fe: School of American Research P, 1996.

Keith, Michael and Steve Pile. "Introduction Part I: The Politics of Place." In *Place and the Politics of Identity*, edited by Michael Keith and Steve Pile, 1–21. London and New York: Routledge, 1993.

———. "Introduction Part 2: The Place of Politics." In *Place and the Politics of Identity*, edited by Michael Keith and Steve Pile, 22–40. London and New York: Routledge, 1993.

Kelly, Kevin. "Anna Deavere Smith Tracks the Rage of LA." *The Boston Globe*, May 9, 1994, http://www.Lexisnexis.com (accessed July 4, 2007).

———. "Hwang Looks Beyond 'Face Value.'" *The Boston Globe*, Feb. 17, 1993, http://www.Lexisnexis.com (accessed March 12, 2007).

———. "Kushner's Landmark Epic Kicks Off with a Brilliant, Searing Look at Homophobia." *The Boston Globe*, May 5, 1993, http://www.Lexisnexis.com (accessed Nov. 27, 2007).

———. "M. Butterfly, Miss Saigon, and Mr. Hwang." *The Boston Globe*, Sept. 9, 1990, http://www.Lexisnexis.com (accessed March 12, 2007).

Kelly, M. Patricia Fernandez. "Slums, Ghettos, and Other Conundrums in the Anthropology of Lower Income Urban Enclaves." In *The Anthropology of Lower Income Urban Enclaves: The Case of East Harlem*, edited by Judith Freidenberg, 219–233. New York: New York Academy of Sciences, 1995.

Kelly, Malcolm. "One Playwright in Search of Herself: Djanet Sears Says Her New Play, Like All Her Work, is about Her Black Experience." *National Post*, Feb. 2, 2002, http://www.Lexisnexis.com (accessed Sept. 7, 2007).

Kim, Yungduk. "Shepard's True West: Demythisizing American Manhood." *Journal of Modern British and American Drama* 20, no.2 (2007): 5–26.

Kleb, William. "Worse Than Being Homeless: *True West* and The Divided Self." In *American Dreams: The Imagination of Sam Shepard,* edited by Bonnie Marranca, 117–125. New York: Performing Arts Journal P, 1981.

Klein, Alvin. "Theater; George St. Offering Play by Shepard." *The New York Times,* May 5, 1985, http://www.Lexisnexis.com (accessed Oct. 1, 2007).

———. "Theater; Taking 'Angels in America' to Storrs." *The New York Times,* Sept. 26, 1999, http://www.Lexisnexis.com (accessed Nov. 27, 2007).

Koh, Barbara. "Minority Matters: David Henry Hwang, the Only Chinese-American Playwright to Broadway, is Fascinated by Shifting Perceptions of Identity." *Financial Times,* Aug. 13, 2005, http://www.Lexisnexis.com (accessed March 12, 2007).

Kruger, Steven F. "Identity and Conversion in *Angels in America.*" In *Approaching the Millennium: Essays on Angels in America,* edited by Deborah R. Geis and Steven F. Kruger, 151–169. Ann Arbor: U of Michigan P, 1997.

Kuchwara, Michael. " 'Twilight: Los Angeles, 1992' by Anna Deavere Smith Opens Off-Broadway." *The Associated Press,* March 23, http://www.Lexisnexis.com (accessed Oct. 10, 2007).

Kunstler, James Howard. *The Geography of Nowhere: The Rise and Decline of America's Man-Made Landscape.* New York: Simon and Schuster, 1993.

Kushner, Tony. Interview by Patrick R. Pacheco. "AIDS, Angels, Activism, and Sex in the Nineties." In *Tony Kushner in Conversation,* edited by Robert Vorlicky, 51–61. Ann Arbor: U of Michigan P, 1998.

———. *Angels in America: Part One: Millennium Approaches.* New York: Theatre Communications Group, 1993.

———. *Angels in America: Part Two: Perestroika.* New York: Theatre Communications Group, 1993.

———. Interview by Carl Weber. "I Always Go Back to Brecht." In *Tony Kushner in Conversation,* edited by Robert Vorlicky, 105–124. Ann Arbor: U of Michigan P, 1998.

———. Interview by by Craig Kinzer, Sandra Richards, Frank Galati, and Lawrence Bommer. "The Theater and the Barricades." In *Tony Kushner in Conversation,* edited by Robert Vorlicky, 188–216. Ann Arbor: U of Michigan P, 1998.

———. Interview by Adam Mars-Jones. "Tony Kushner at the Royal National Theatre of Britain." In *Tony Kushner in Conversation,* edited by Robert Vorlicky, 18–29. Ann Arbor: U of Michigan P, 1998.

Lechte, John. "(Not) Belonging in Postmodern Space." In *Postmodern Cities and Spaces,* edited by Sophie Watson and Katherine Gibson, 99–111. Oxford and Cambridge, MA: Blackwell, 1995.

Lefebvre, Henri. *The Production of Space.* Translated by Donald Nicholson-Smith. Malden, MA: Blackwell, 1984.

Lewis, Peirce F. "Axioms for Reading the Landscape: Some Guides to the American Scene." In *The Interpretation of Ordinary Landscapes: Geographical Essays,* edited by D. W. Meinig, 11–32. New York and Oxford: Oxford UP, 1979.

Liston, William T. "Review of *the Sixteenth Annual Humana Festival of New American Plays*." *Theatre Journal* 45, no.1 (1993): 112–115.

Loo, Chalsa M. *Chinatown: Most Time, Hard Time*. New York: Praeger, 1991.

Lynch, Kevin. *The Image of the City*. Cambridge, MA and London: The MIT P, 1960.

Machado, Eduardo. *Broken Eggs. The Floating Island Plays*. New York: Theatre Communications Group, 1991.

Marcuse, Peter. "Not Chaos, but Walls: Postmodernism and the Partitioned City." In *Postmodern Cities and Spaces,* edited by Sophie Watson and Katherine Gibson, 243–253. Oxford and Cambridge, MA: Blackwell, 1995.

Marcus, Steven. "Reading the Illegible: Some Modern Representations of Urban Experience." In *Visions of the Modern City: Essays in History, Art, and Literature,* edited by William Sharpe and Leonard Wallock, 232–255. Baltimore and London: The Johns Hopkins UP, 1987.

Marks, Peter. "Parent's Secret Cry Out, But Children Don't Hear." *The New York Times,* Nov. 12, 1997, http://www.Lexisnexis.com (accessed Oct. 7, 2006).

Marranca, Bonnie. Introduction to *American Dreams: The Imagination of Sam Shepard,* edited by Bonnie Marranca. New York: Performing Arts Journal P, 1981.

Marranca, Bonnie, Gerald Rabkin, and Johannes Birringer. "The Politics of Reception." In *Conversations on Art and Performance,* edited by Bonnie Marranca and Gautam Dasgupta, 77–101. Baltimore and London: The Johns Hopkins UP, 1999.

Masselos, Jim. "Postmodern Bombay: Fractured Discourses." In *Postmodern Cities and Spaces,* edited by Sophie Watson and Katherine Gibson, 199–215. Oxford and Cambridge, MA: Blackwell, 1995.

Massey, Doreen. *Spatial Divisions of Labor: Social Structures and the Geography of Production*. 2nd ed. New York: Routledge, 1995.

Mathews, Jay. "'Golden Gates': David Henry Hwang: Burning Bridges." *The Washington Post,* Jan. 30, 1994, http://www.Lexisnexis.com (accessed March 12, 2007).

Mathieu, Arline. "The Medicalization of Homelessness and the Theater of Repression." *Medical Anthropology Quarterly* 7, no.2 (1993): 170–184.

McKinley, Jesse. "Broadway Debut for Julia Roberts." *The New York Times,* July 29, 2005, http://www.Lexisnexis.com (accessed July 20, 2008).

McKittrick, Ryan. "Stage Review: *Three Days of Rain*: A Play in Two Acts." *The Boston Globe,* Oct. 27, 2001, http://www.Lexisnexis.com (accessed Oct. 7, 2006).

———. "Stage Review: *Twilight Los Angeles, 1992*." *The Boston Globe,* Nov. 14, 2002, http://www.Lexisnexis.com (accessed July 4, 2007).

Meeks, Christopher. "*Twilight Los Angeles, 1992*." *The Daily Variety,* June 15, 1993, http://www.Lexisnexis.com (accessed July 4, 2007).

Meinig, D. W. "The Beholding Eye: Ten Versions of the Same Scene." In *The Interpretation of Ordinary Landscapes: Geographical Essays,* edited by D. W. Meinig, 33–48. New York and Oxford: Oxford UP, 1979.

———. Introduction to *The Interpretation of Ordinary Landscapes: Geographical Essays,* edited by D. W. Meinig. New York and Oxford: Oxford UP, 1979.

Moeller, Susan D. "The Cultural Construction of Urban Poverty: Images of Poverty in New York City, 1890–1917." *Journal of American Culture* 18, no.4 (1995): 1–16.

Mooney, Gerry. "Urban 'Disorders.'" In *Unruly Cities?: Order/Disorder*, edited by Steve Pile, Christopher Brook and Gerry Mooney, 53–102. London and New York: Routledge, 1999.

Moraga, Cherríe. *Circle in the Dirt: El Pueblo de East Palo Alto. Watsonville/Circle in the Dirt*. Albuquerque: West End P, 2002.

——. *Giving Up the Ghost. Heroes and Saints and Other Plays*. Albuquerque: West End P, 1994.

——. *The Hungry Woman: A Mexican Medea. The Hungry Woman*. Albuquerque: West End P, 2001.

——. *Watsonville: Some Place Not Here. Watsonville/Circle in the Dirt*. Albuquerque: West End P, 2002.

Morsberger, Katharine. "The Mark Taper Forum: LA." In *20th Century American Dramatists, Part 2*, edited by Christopher J. Wheatley, 441–447. Detroit: Gale, 2000.

Mouffe, Chantal. "For a Politics of Nomadic Identity." In *Travellers' Tales: Narratives of Home and Displacement*, edited by George Robertson et al., 105–113. London and New York: Routledge, 1994.

Navarro, Mireya. "Building a Bridge, A Theater Troupe from the U.S. is Embraced by Havana." *The New York Times*, Sept. 29, 1998, http://www.Lexisnexis.com (accessed Oct. 10, 2007).

Nestruck, J. Kelly. "Pretty Woman? Nah!: Critics Heap Scorn on Julia Roberts' Broadway Debut." *National Post* (Canada), April 21, 2006, http://www.Lexisnexis.com (accessed July 20, 2008).

Nurse, Donna Bailey. "An Othello Built for the Nineties IN PERSON: Djanet Sears Mixes Shakespeare and the Blues to Tackle Current Taboos in Harlem Duets." *The Globe and Mail*, Nov. 18, 1997, http://www.Lexisnexis.com (accessed Sept. 7, 2007).

Olalquiaga, Celeste. *Megalopolis: Contemporary Cultural Sensibilities*. Minneapolis and Oxford: U of Minnesota P, 1992.

Osborne, Robert. *The Hollywood Reporter*, Aug. 2, 2005, http://www.Lexisnexis.com (accessed Oct. 7, 2006).

Ouzounian, Richard. "Staging of Harlem Duet Overcomes Casting Crisis: Toronto's Sears has 'Something to be Proud of.'" *Toronto Star*, Nov. 24, 2002, http://www.Lexisnexis.com (accessed Sept. 7, 2007).

Patton, Paul. "Imaginary Cities: Images of Postmodernity." In *Postmodern Cities and Spaces*, edited by Sophie Watson and Katherine Gibson, 112–121. Oxford and Cambridge, MA: Blackwell, 1995.

Prida, Dolores. "The Show Must Go On." In *Breaking Boundaries: Latina Writing and Critical Readings*, edited by Asuncion Horno-Delgado et al., 181–188. Amherst: U of Massachusetts P, 1989.

Reinelt, Janelle. "Notes on *Angels in America* as American Epic Theater." In *Approaching the Millennium: Essays on Angels in America*, edited by Deborah R. Geis and Steven F. Kruger, 234–244. Ann Arbor: U of Michigan P, 1997.

Rich, Frank. "Angels in America; Millennium Approaches; Embracing All Possibilities in Art and Life." *The New York Times*, May 5, 1993, http://www.Lexisnexis.com (accessed Nov. 27 2007).

——. "The Angel of No Hope Visits New York." *The New York Times*, May 21, 1993, http://www.Lexisnexis.com (accessed Jan. 22, 2006).

——. "Perestroika; Following an Angel for a Healing Vision of Heaven on Earth." *The New York Times*, Nov. 24, 1993, http://www.Lexisnexis.com (accessed Nov. 27, 2007).

——. "Theater: 'Broken Eggs.'" *The New York Times*, Feb. 23, 1984, http://www. Lexisnexis.com (accessed Oct. 10, 2007).

——. "Theater: 'FOB' Rites of Immigrant Passage." *The New York Times*, June 10, 1980, http://www.Lexisnexis.com (accessed Jan. 13, 2008).

——. "Theater: Two Sam Shepard Pieces Open at La Mama." *The New York Times*, Sept. 20, 1983, http://www.Lexisnexis.com (accessed March 3, 2006).

Richards, David. "Another Epic, With 4 Plays in 6 Hours." *The New York Times*, Nov. 10, 1994, http://www.Lexisnexis.com (accessed Oct. 17, 2006).

Rivera, José. Interview by Lynn Jacobson. *Studies in American Drama, 1945-Present* 6, no.1 (1991): 49–58.

——. Interview by Norma Jenckes. *American Drama* 10, no.2 (2001): 21–47.

——. *Marisol. Marisol and Other Plays*. New York: Theatre Communications Group, 1997.

Robinson, Marc. *The Other American Drama*. Cambridge: Cambridge UP, 1994.

Rocco, Raymond A. "Latino Los Angeles: Reframing Boundaries/Borders." In *The City: Los Angeles and Urban Theory at the End of the Twentieth Century*, edited by Allen J. Scott and Edward W. Soja, 365–389. Berkeley: U of California P, 1996.

Rose, Lloyd. "A Singular Talent for Multiple Parts." *The Washington Post*, Feb. 3, 1997, http://www.Lexisnexis.com (accessed July 4, 2007).

Rosenberg, Lou. "The House of Difference: Gender, Culture, and the Subject-in-Process on the American Stage." In *Critical Essays: Gay and Lesbian Writers of Color*, edited by Emmanuel S. Nelson, 97–110. New York and London: Haworth P, 1993.

Roskill, Mark. *The Languages of Landscapes*. University Park, PA: The Pennsylvania State UP, 1997.

Rossini, Jon. "Marisol, Angels, and Apocalyptic Migrations." *American Drama* 10, no.2 (2001): 1–20.

Rushdie, Salman. *Imaginary Homelands: Essays and Criticism 1981–1991*. London: Granta, 1991.

Sandoval, Alberto. "Dolores Prida's *Coser y cantar*: Mapping the Dialectics of Ethnic Identity and Assimilation." In *Breaking Boundaries: Latina Writing and Critical Readings*, edited by Asuncion Horno-Delgado et al., 201–220. Amherst: U of Massachusetts P, 1989.

Savran, David. "Ambivalence, Utopia, and a Queer Sort of Materialism: How *Angels in America* Reconstructs the Nation." In *Approaching the Millennium: Essays on Angels in America*, edited by Deborah R. Geis and Steven F. Kruger, 13–39. Ann Arbor: U of Michigan P, 1997.

Schillinger, Liesl. "The Playwright Rewriting Latino Theater." *The New York Times,* Dec. 12, 2004, http://www.Lexisnexis.com (accessed Oct. 17, 2006).

Sears, Djanet. *Harlem Duet.* Winnipeg: J. Gordon Shillingford, 2002.

Sharpe, William and Leonard Wallock. "From 'Great Town' to 'Nonplace Urban Realm': Reading the Modern City." In *Visions of the Modern City: Essays in History, Art, and Literature,* edited by William Sharpe and Leonard Wallock, 1–50. Baltimore and London: The Johns Hopkins UP, 1987.

Shepard, Sam. *True West. Seven Plays.* Toronto: Bantam, 1984.

Shields, Rob. *Places on the Margin: Alternative Geographies of Modernity.* London and New York: Routledge, 1991.

Shimakawa, Karen. *National Abjection: The Asian American Body Onstage.* Durham and London: Duke UP, 2002.

Shklar, Judith N. "What is the Use of Utopia?" In *Heterotopia: Postmodern Utopia and the Body Politic,* edited by Tobin Siebers, 40–57. Ann Arbor: U of Michigan P, 1997.

Siebers, Tobin. "What Does Postmodernism Want? Utopia." In *Heterotopia: Postmodern Utopia and the Body Politic,* edited by Tobin Siebers, 1–38. Ann Arbor: U of Michigan P, 1997.

Siegel, Ed. "Anna Deavere Smith's 'Twilight' Opens Minds and Hearts." *The Boston Globe,* Nov. 14, 1996, http://www.Lexisnexis.com (accessed July 4, 2007).

——. " 'Perestroika' Caps Kushner's Tour de Force." *The Boston Globe,* March 16, 1995, http://www.Lexisnexis.com (accessed Nov. 27, 2007).

Simonson, Harold P. *The Closed Frontier: Studies in American Literary Tragedy.* New York: Holt, Rinehart and Wilson, 1970.

Smith, Anna Deavere. Interview by J. Chris Westgate. " 'This Electrifying Moment': An Interview with Anna Deavere Smith." *Writing on the Edge: On Writing and Teaching Writing* 15, no.1 (2004): 101–110.

——. *Fires in the Mirror: Crown Heights, Brooklyn, and Other Identities.* New York: Anchor, 1993.

——. *Twilight Los Angeles, 1992.* New York: Anchor, 1994.

Smith, Neil. "New City, New Frontier: The Lower East Side as Wild, Wild West." In *Variations on a Theme Park: The New American City and the End of Public Place,* edited by Michael Sorkin, 61–93. New York: Noonday P, 1992.

——. *Uneven Development: Nature, Capital, and the Production of Space.* Oxford: Basil Blackwell, 1984.

Smith, Neil and Cindi Katz. "Grounding Metaphor: Towards a Spatialized Politics." In *Place and the Politics of Identity,* edited by Michael Keith and Steve Pile, 67–83. London and New York: Routledge, 1993.

Soja, Edward W. "Heterotopologies: A Remembrance of Other Spaces in the Citadel-LA." In *Postmodern Cities and Spaces,* edited by Sophie Watson and Katherine Gibson, 13–34. Oxford and Cambridge, MA: Blackwell, 1995.

——. "Inside Exopolis: Scenes from Orange County." In *Variations on a Theme Park: The New American City and the End of Public Place,* edited by Michael Sorkin, 94–122. New York: Noonday P, 1992.

———. *Postmodern Geographies: The Reassertion of Space in Critical Social Theory.* London and New York: Verso, 1989.

———. "Postmodern Urbanization: The Six Restructurings of Los Angeles." In *Postmodern Cities and Spaces,* edited by Sophie Watson and Katherine Gibson, 125–137. Oxford and Cambridge, MA: Blackwell, 1995.

———. *Thirdspace: Journeys to Los Angeles and Other Real-And-Imagined Places.* Cambridge, MA: Blackwell Publishers, 1996.

Soja, Edward and Barbara Hooper. "The Spaces That Difference Makes: Some Notes on the Geographical Margins of the New Cultural Politics." In *Place and the Politics of Identity,* edited by Michael Keith and Steve Pile, 183–205. London and New York: Routledge, 1993.

Sorkin, Michael. Introduction to *Variations on a Theme Park: The New American City and the End of Public Place,* edited by Michael Sorkin. New York: Noonday P, 1992.

———. "See You in Disneyland." In *Variations on a Theme Park: The New American City and the End of Public Place,* edited by Michael Sorkin, 205–232. New York: Noonday P, 1992.

Soup, Madan. "Home and Identity." In *Travellers' Tales: Narratives of Home and Displacement,* edited by George Robertson et al., 93–104. London and New York: Routledge, 1994.

States, Bert O. *Great Reckonings in Little Rooms: On the Phenomenology of Theater.* Berkeley: U of California P, 1985.

Stearns, David Patrick. "Broadway's Glare Hides 'Twilight.'" *USA Today,* June 10, 1994, http://www.Lexisnexis.com (accessed July 4, 2007).

Steele, Mike. "Seven-Hour Epic 'Angels' a Superb Story Told Politically." *The Star Tribune,* July 15, 1995, http://www.Lexisnexis.com (accessed Nov. 27, 2007).

———. "Thrilling, Provocative 'Angels' Sheds Light on Large Issues." *The Star Tribune,* May 14, 1993, http://www.Lexisnexis.com (accessed Nov. 27, 2007).

Street, Douglas. *David Henry Hwang.* Boise: Boise State U, 1989.

Su, Tsu-chung. "The Double in Sam Shepard's *Buried Child* and *True West.*" *Studies in Language and Literature* 8 (1998): 65–83.

Turner, Frederick Jackson. *The Frontier in American History.* Malabar, FLA: Robert E. Krieger, 1985.

Valle, Victor M. and Rodolfo D. Torres. *Latino Metropolis.* Minneapolis and London: U of Minnesota P, 2000.

Vaughn, Peter. "Forceful Acting Powers Cricket's Revisited 'True West.'" *The Star Tribune,* Sept. 10, 1994.

Wagner, Vit. "A New Take on Gender and Race." *The Toronto Star,* Oct. 30, 1997, http://www.Lexisnexis.com (accessed Sept. 7, 2007).

Watson, Sophie and Katherine Gibson. "Postmodern Politics and Planning: A Postscript." In *Postmodern Cities and Spaces,* edited by Sophie Watson and Katherine Gibson, 254–264. Oxford and Cambridge, MA: Blackwell, 1995.

Weber, Carl. "Brecht's 'Street Scene'—On Broadway, of All Places? A Conversation with Anna Deavere Smith." *The Brecht Yearbook* 20 (1995): 50–64.

Weinraub, Bernard. "Condensing a Riot's Cacophony into the Voice of One Woman." *The New York Times,* June 16, 1993, http://www.Lexisnexis.com (accessed July 4, 2007).

Westgate, J. Chris. "Negotiating the American West in Sam Shepard's Family Plays." *Modern Drama* 48, no.4 (2005): 726–743.

Wiley, Catherine. "The Matter with Manners: The New Woman and the Problem Play." In *Women in Theatre,* edited by James Redmond, 109–127. Cambridge: Cambridge UP, 1989.

Winn, Steven. " 'Angels' Glorious Return: It All Started at S.F.'s Eureka Theatre—The Original Cast Looks Back." *The San Francisco Chronicle,* Sept. 25, 1994, http://www.Lexisnexis.com (accessed Nov. 27, 2007).

———. " 'Angels' is Born Again: ACT Puts Its Own Stamp on Kushner Play." *The San Francisco Chronicle,* Oct. 14, 1994, http://www.Lexisnexis.com (accessed Nov. 27, 2007).

———. "Chance of 'Rain' Glimmers, Fades; Play's Potential Never Fulfilled." *The San Francisco Chronicle,* Nov. 2, 1998, http://www.Lexisnexis.com (accessed Oct. 7, 2006).

———. "An Epic Drama Unfolding." *The San Francisco Chronicle,* July 4, 1991, http://www.Lexisnexis.com (accessed Nov. 27, 2007).

———. "Hwang's 'FOB' Probes Asian Assimilation." *The San Francisco Chronicle,* Sept. 18, 1992, http://www.Lexisnexis.com (accessed Jan. 13, 2008).

———. " 'Kiss Me, Kate' Brings Warmth Back to the Musical; 'True West' Revival an Acting Feat." *The San Francisco Chronicle,* April 9, 2000, http://www.Lexisnexis.com (accessed March 3, 2006).

———. "Kushner's Angelic Conclusion 'Perestroika' Completes Epic Drama." *The San Francisco Chronicle,* Nov. 24, 1993, http://www.Lexisnexis.com (accessed Nov. 27, 2007).

———. "Playwright Tony Kushner: 'I wrote the Play for San Francisco and it was Important to Me that it Play.' " *The San Francisco Chronicle,* Sept. 25, 1994, http://www.Lexisnexis.com (accessed Nov. 27, 2007).

———. " 'West' Blazes Own Trail in Familiar Territory: Revival of Shepard Drama opens the Magic's Season." *The San Francisco Chronicle,* Oct. 9, 1997, http://www.Lexisnexis.com (accessed March 3, 2006).

———. "Winning 'Angels' Born in SF." *The San Francisco Chronicle,* April 14, 1993, http://www.Lexisnexis.com (accessed Nov. 27, 2007).

Wolch, Jennifer. "From Global to Local: The Rise of Homelessness in Los Angeles during the 1980s." In *The City: Los Angeles and Urban Theory at the End of the Twentieth Century,* edited by Allen J. Scott and Edward W. Soja, 390–425. Berkeley: U of California P, 1996.

Worthen, W. B. *Modern Drama and the Rhetoric of Theater.* Berkeley and Los Angeles: U of California P, 1992.

Zhou, Min. *Chinatown: The Socioeconomic Potential of an Urban Enclave.* Philadelphia: Temple UP, 1992.

Index

Note: The letter "n" following the locators refers to notes.